Althusser and Education

Radical Politics and Education

Series editors: Derek R. Ford and Tyson E. Lewis

With movements against oppression and exploitation heightening across the globe, radical activists and researchers are increasingly turning to educational theory to understand the pedagogical aspects of struggle. The Radical Politics and Education series opens a space at this critical juncture, one that pushes past standard expositions of critical education and critical pedagogy. Recognizing the need to push political and educational formulations into new theoretical and practical terrains, the series is an opportunity for activists, political thinkers, and educational philosophers to cross disciplinary divides and meet in common. This kind of dialogue is crucially needed as political struggles are increasingly concerned with questions of how to educate themselves and others, and as educational philosophy attempts to redefine itself beyond academic norms and disciplinary values. This series serves to facilitate new conversations at and beyond these borders.

Advisory Board:
Jodi Dean *(Hobart and William Smith Colleges, USA)*
Margret Grebowicz *(University of Silesia, Poland)*
Davide Panagia *(University of California, Los Angeles, USA)*
Patti Lather *(Ohio State University, USA)*
Nathan Snaza *(University of Richmond, USA)*
Stefano Harney *(Singapore Management University, Singapore)*

Also available in the series:
Against Sex Education: Pedagogy, Sex Work, and State Violence, Caitlin Howlett
A History of Education for the Many: From Colonization and Slavery to the Decline of US Imperialism, Curry Malott
Experiments in Decolonizing the University: Towards an Ecology of Study, Hans Schildermans
Rethinking Philosophy for Children: Agamben and Education as Pure Means, Tyson E. Lewis and Igor Jasinski
Althusser and Education: Reassessing Critical Education, David I. Backer

Forthcoming in the series:
A Voice for Maria Favela: An Adventure in Creative Literacy, Antonio Leal
Rancière and Emancipatory Art Pedagogies: The Politics of Childhood Art, Hayon Park
Queers Teach This!: Queer and Trans Pleasures, Politics, and Pedagogues, Adam J. Greteman

Althusser and Education

Reassessing Critical Education

David I. Backer

BLOOMSBURY ACADEMIC
LONDON • NEW YORK • OXFORD • NEW DELHI • SYDNEY

BLOOMSBURY ACADEMIC
Bloomsbury Publishing Plc
50 Bedford Square, London, WC1B 3DP, UK
1385 Broadway, New York, NY 10018, USA
29 Earlsfort Terrace, Dublin 2, Ireland

BLOOMSBURY, BLOOMSBURY ACADEMIC and the Diana logo are trademarks of Bloomsbury Publishing Plc

First published in Great Britain 2022
Paperback edition published 2024

Copyright © David I. Backer, 2022

David I. Backer has asserted his right under the Copyright, Designs and Patents Act, 1988, to be identified as Author of this work.

For legal purposes the Acknowledgments on pp. ix–x constitute an extension of this copyright page.

Cover design: Charlotte James
Cover image © Vince Cavataio/Getty Images

This work is published open access subject to a Creative Commons Attribution-NonCommercial-NoDerivatives 3.0 licence (CC BY-NC-ND 3.0, https://creativecommons.org/licenses/by-nc-nd/3.0/). You may re-use, distribute, and reproduce this work in any medium for non-commercial purposes, provided you give attribution to the copyright holder and the publisher and provide a link to the Creative Commons licence.

Bloomsbury Publishing Plc does not have any control over, or responsibility for, any third-party websites referred to or in this book. All internet addresses given in this book were correct at the time of going to press. The author and publisher regret any inconvenience caused if addresses have changed or sites have ceased to exist, but can accept no responsibility for any such changes.

A catalogue record for this book is available from the British Library.

A catalog record for this book is available from the Library of Congress.

ISBN: HB: 978-1-3501-0148-7
PB: 978-1-3502-2684-5
ePDF: 978-1-3501-0149-4
eBook: 978-1-3501-0150-0

Series: Radical Politics and Education

Typeset by Newgen KnowledgeWorks Pvt. Ltd., Chennai, India

To find out more about our authors and books visit www.bloomsbury.com and sign up for our newsletters.

To John Elmore, for the Department

Contents

Acknowledgments ix

Introduction 1

Part I Education as an Ideological State Apparatus: Eleven Rules

1   An Attempt to Interpret the Events of May   13
2   The Rule of Keys: Social Reproduction   17
3   The Rule of Hands: Relations of Production   21
4   The Competency Rule   25
5   The Rule of Special Thirds: Base and Superstructure   33
6   The System, Toe, and Anchor Rules: ISA Basics   39
7   The Causality Rule: Grey Cows and Green Cheese   43
8   The Struggle Rule: The Necessity of Contingency   49
9   The School Rule   53
10 The Go Rule   59
11 Conclusion   67

Part II The Common Sense about Althusser: Reassessing Critical Education

12 The Three Critiques   73
13 Foundations of Critical Education: Apple and Giroux's Indecision 77
14 Roots of the Common Sense   91
15 A Frustrated Student: Rancière and the ISAs   95
16 Formalization of the Provocation: Erben and Gleesen   101
17 Against Generality: Hirst   107
18 A Trotskyite Calling Stalin: Callinicos   111
19 The Eagle's Apostasy: E. P. Thompson   113
20 Ashes and Promiscuity: Willis and Connell   121
21 Conclusion   123

Part III Structural Education: Toward an Althusserian Pedagogy

22	Developments in Structure	129
23	The Structure of Race in Education: From Hall to Leonardo	143
24	The Structure of Gender in Education: Wolpe, Barrett, Arnot, Deem, and Valli	155
25	Ideology in Struggle: Advances in Interpellation	169

Conclusion — 179
Epilogue — 187

References — 193
Index — 203

Acknowledgments

This book started when Tyson Lewis recommended I read Jameson on Althusser's structural causality for my dissertation. After that I was hooked and there have been so many people that have helped, guided, and pushed me since.

Michael Apple, Raewyn Connell, and Zeus Leonardo provided essential background interviews, comments, and encouragement. Isaac Gottesman gave me feedback and guidance on the historical aspects of the research, while Asad Haider, G. M. Goshgarian, Warren Montag, and Dave Mesing helped keep me on track on the Althusser studies side.

Derek Ford has cheered me on since we were in graduate school, along with Brad Porfilio who, with Bill Reynolds, asked me to write a short book on Althusser for their series at Brill-Sense. I'm especially thankful they were flexible when I realized I was writing two books, *The Gold and the Dross* for them and then a longer manuscript that I eventually pitched to Mark Richardson, Derek Ford, and Tyson Lewis at Bloomsbury for the Radical Politics and Education Series. Everyone involved in these series and the publishers were generous and understanding as I muddled through how to set all this down on paper. The team at Bloomsbury has been great, particularly in their decision to make the book open access and in extending my deadline several times.

Jessica Lussier did a first full edit when I completed a draft of the manuscript and also helped with research on the Marxist feminist angle of the project. Kermit O. and Ash Yezulita have been amazing student assistants helping with edits and background research at different stages. Thanks to the Transformative Education and Social Change (TESC) program at West Chester University for providing them graduate assistantships and letting them work with me, and also generally supporting and advancing critical educational research in Philadelphia. Jason Wozniak and Dana Morrison, leaders of this program, are also my foundations team and have given me a constant resource of support, feedback, and opportunities to be eloquent about this project as it was underway. They both read drafts of chapters, shorter essays I published along the way, and have assigned my writing on ideology to their students in the TESC program and other classes.

I must also thank my students at Cleveland State University who helped me work through Althusser's ideas, particularly those from China, Saudi Arabia, and Cleveland proper whose unique mixture of experiences and perspectives gave me a much deeper appreciation for the structure of education today.

John Elmore, to whom the book is dedicated, told me that I should go as far into critical education as I wanted to and not hold back due to a sense of impracticality or needing to pitch my work to a less critical audience when it came to the tenure process. His encouragement and the Department of Educational Foundations and Policy Studies that he has helped foster at West Chester were central to this project continuing (he also kindly donated his research funds to pay for the index, completed with rigor by John Beauregard).

Kate Cairns has been a great thought partner, co-author, and friend during this project. She was willing to hear me out on many issues about Althusser and social reproduction, as well as contributing to numerous socialist feminist organizing projects. Kate connected us with Sue Ferguson, who also provided helpful background and perspective on social reproduction.

I started this project in the wake of Occupy Wall Street's dissolution, but the friendships and connections I made there have lasted beyond the movement moment. Jason Wozniak, Winter Casuccio, Aleks Perisic, Jacques Laroche, Kylie Benton-Connell, Rodrigo Nunes, and Joe North have been constant comrades.

Jonathan Turcotte-Summers and Sam Rocha wrote a thoughtful and helpful review of my early work on Althusser that influenced the direction of this book. Richard Hudson-Miles wrote an equally helpful review pushing on several themes in *The Gold and the Dross* for which I have tried to account here. Wayne Ross published two pieces in *Critical Education* that were early sketches. Tony Carusi, Ken McGrew, Matthew Lampert, and Elen Kirkpatrick have helped me with their own work, comments, and thinking about Althusser and education. Pilar Goñalons Pons and Daniel Aldana Cohen have also been great friends, comrades, and dialogue partners along the way.

Finally, thanks to my partner Shelly Ronen for everything she is and does, particularly her strength, engagement, and support with this project. And thanks to Thisbe Ronen-Backer, a light in dark times, who was born while I was writing the book and whose epic cuteness aided its completion.

Introduction

A student or researcher interested in the French communist philosopher Louis Althusser's theory of education might encounter a recent entry in the *Encyclopedia of Educational Theory and Philosophy*. According to the entry, Althusser's theory of the ideological state apparatuses was an attempt to overcome economic determinism. However, the theory failed due to Althusser's structuralism, which, the entry notes, was widely criticized for its functionalism and its denial of individual and group agency. The entry concludes that, according to Althusser's theory, students and teachers and others involved in education are "mere puppets of controlling coercive and ideological structures" (Morrow 2014: 708).

The entry's author is Raymond A. Morrow, co-author of the seminal tome *Social Theory and Education: A Critique of Social and Cultural Theories of Reproduction* (1995), tracing the history of social reproduction theory and education that includes a full-fledged version of his entry's interpretation of Althusser. Morrow is not alone in this interpretation. He follows a common sense about Althusser in the critical education literature more broadly. One can find a version of Morrow's reading in early foundational texts by the field's founders Michael Apple (Apple 1982, 1985, 2012) and Henry A. Giroux (1980a, 1980b, 1984, 2001) to more contemporary references. The consensus in the field, still prevalent today, is that while Althusser's theory of ideological state apparatuses (ISAs) was an important attempt at understanding education in a capitalist society from a Marxist perspective, it ultimately failed because of its functionalism and inability to recognize the concrete agency of people in and around schools.

While this reading has an air of finality, in the same year Morrow's entry in the *Encyclopedia* was published, Althusser's book *On the Reproduction of Capitalism* (2014) appeared for the first time in English translation. The significance of this translation should not be understated. The book is the full text from which Althusser's (1970) famous essay on the ISAs was initially excerpted. That essay, called "Ideology and the Ideological State Apparatuses: Notes towards an Investigation," has for more than a generation provided the definitive account of Althusser's thinking about education; but the book from which it was excerpted was rarely mentioned in educational research literature, if ever. It was only available in French in 1993 and had not been available for English readers until sixty years after its excerpt was published.

Juxtaposing Morrow's *Encyclopedia* entry on Althusser and *On the Reproduction of Capitalism*, published in the same year, broaches the question of revisiting Althusser's theory of education. Althusser is having something of a renaissance in the humanities and social sciences (Resch 1992; Montag 2002, 2013; McInerney 2005; Diefenbach et al. 2013; Sotiris 2014; Bargu 2015; Pfeifer 2015; Barker 2016; Nesbitt 2017) with several other new translations published (Althusser 2003, 2006, 2017, 2019a, 2019b, 2020), including the first full English translation of *Reading Capital* (2016). Part of this resurgence has focused specifically on the ISAs, ideology, and reproduction (Edwards 2007; Wolf 2008, 2013; Alloggio 2012; Macherey 2012; Gallas 2017; Beetz and Schwab 2018; Kukla 2018; Montag 2018; Sakellaropoulos 2019; Kirkpatrick 2020). While some early voices hinted at such a revision (Benadé 1984), the more recent return to Althusser has yet to hit educational research. Given that we have the full text from which the original expression of Althusser's groundbreaking theory of education was excerpted, and given the new wave of interest in the theory, education scholars should be curious about the content of Althusser's theory of education, how the common sense reading of it emerged in critical education, and whether that common sense holds up.

Althusser and Education looks at these issues. Following recent examinations of critical education's presumptions and history (McGrew 2011; Gottesman 2016), this book is a clarificatory project for critical education, both regarding Althusser's theory of education specifically, how it was critiqued, and how it was advanced; and examining assumptions, frameworks, and axioms in left education thinking more generally.

The book has three main parts. In Part I, "Education as an Ideological State Apparatus: Eleven Rules," I lay out Althusser's theory of education by doing a close educational rereading of the ISAs essay as an excerpt of the book from which it was taken, *On the Reproduction of Capitalism*. The book provides much needed detail, clarification, and elaboration on the notes toward an investigation that Althusser made in the ISAs essay fifty years ago. From this educational rereading of the ISAs essay, deepened by a reading of the book from which it was originally excerpted, I derive eleven rules of thumb for understanding Althusser's theory of education in its fullness. These rules cover major themes in the theory like social reproduction, relation of production, structural causality, apparatus, and so on. Table 1 lists these rules and the theoretical terms to which they apply.

The rules are best summarized as follows. Social reproduction for Althusser is the key to the key to production, the process of maintaining the continuity of dominance for the relations of production preferred by the ruling class (distinctly Marxist as compared to earlier references to the concept, like Durkheim [2005]). These relations of production are how people have their hands on the means of production and thus define an economy. Relations of production set out positions which people occupy, or functions that they bear, but crucially for Althusser these positions exist immanently rather than transcendently. The ruling class cannot maintain their preferred relations of production solely through economic power, they need state power too. According to Marx, the state is a superstructure exerting the kind of downward-facing force needed to keep certain relations of production dominant now and over time.

In Althusser's rendering, building on a distinction from Gramsci, there are two superstructures: ideological and repressive, the former manifesting as imagined relations to real conditions while the latter works through violence. These two apparatuses are relatively autonomous from one another and from the economy, each exerting a special third of the total social force in the society. The ideological state apparatuses are themselves composed of systems of institutions. These institutions reproduce dominant ideology to the extent that people in them toe a dominant line. Toeing a line in this case means engaging in certain practices that anchor aspects of (and thereby reproduce) the dominant relations of production. Education is the number one ideological state apparatus in modern capitalist societies since it instructs so many young people in skills and submission to the dominant ideology. In schools, students learn to go all by themselves and toe the line without a cop in their heads or the immediate threat of violence. This recruitment, which occurs through what Althusser calls interpellation, does not happen because there are a group of evil priests or diabolical leaders pulling peoples' strings like puppeteers, but rather occurs largely unconsciously in the everyday experience of class struggle.

All these claims regarding school and reproduction of the relations of production rely on a particular concept of causality, since apparatuses in this theory are a means for intervening in society, exerting a force toward some group's interest. Following a Spinozist ontological turn, Althusser's concept of causality is structural rather than linear or expressive, distinctive for its emphasis on unevenness and complexity, refusing the fustian (or unclear) thought that—as Althusser cites Hegel citing Schelling (1988)—sees all cows as grey in the night. According to this structural concept of causality, ideologies do not determine institutions but rather the other way around. While class struggle impacts schools, it does so via primary ideologies external to them and secondary ideologies from within them, the latter tending to be specific to their context. In this sense, schools contribute to the larger class struggle. Insurgent classes have used ideology as a weapon and won victories against the ruling class, making the ISAs a site of struggle.

The first part of the book explains each of these rules using textual evidence and arguments Althusser sketched in the ISAs essay and detailed with many more premises and elaboration in *On the Reproduction of Capitalism*. The rules form a basic framework for Althusser's theory of education, incorporating crucial philosophical and political premises that undergird the idea that education is an ideological state apparatus. In general, I find that the theory is a dynamic and profoundly influential Marxist theory of education whose immanent structural framework emphasizes schools' complex contribution to class struggle, from the large-scale relative autonomy of schools in Althusser's conception of the base-superstructure model to the significance of small-scale everyday school gestures in his concept of interpellation.

The theory was taken up in a different way in education, however. The common sense about Althusser remains stubbornly in place. Left education literatures inherit that interpretation today in the form of the critiques mentioned at the outset, of which Morrow's entry is just one example. In Part II, "The Common Sense about Althusser: Reassessing Critical Education," I trace the provenance of this common sense. Using Morrow and Torres's (1995) history of social reproduction theory as a guide, I begin with two founders of critical education Michael Apple and Henry Giroux, looking at references to Althusser in their early publications leading up to Giroux's (2001) *Theory and Resistance in Education* and Apple's (1985) *Education and Power*. When it came to Althusser, I find a mixture of reverence and repulsion, with accompanying indecision and reversals in their readings. I call these readings the Foundations of Critical Education, since the texts which include these inconsistent readings of Althusser did so much to construct the presumptions on which critical education is founded, like the dichotomy between reproduction and resistance.

I also find that Giroux and Apple's readings relied on a number of other interpretations. Giroux went so far as to say that these interpretations were so definitive as to not require his further attention. As part of their larger project to contrast critical education from neo-Marxist education, they leaned on a line of critique against Althusser running from Jacques Rancière (2011), Michael Erben and Denis

Gleeson (1975), Alex Callinicos (1976), Paul Hirst (1976), E. P. Thompson (1978), R. W. Connell (1979), and ending with Paul Willis's reading (1981a). While Giroux writes that Althusser has already been interpreted by these authors so we do not have to, I delve into these texts to reconstruct the line of critique on which Giroux and Apple relied (but also informed other similar critiques like that by Clarke [1980]). I do some historical work to contextualize these critiques and their authors, summarize their arguments, and show how each account has limitations that Apple and Giroux (and those who followed them like Morrow and Torres) failed to consider. I use two tests for this reassessment of the texts Apple and Giroux cited. The first test is whether the text has an argument. The second test is whether that argument poses significant issues for the framework set out in Part I.

Generally, the common sense about Althusser in critical education and the line of critique on which it rests are composed of three planks: the critique from functionalism, the critique from agency, and the critique from tragedy. The first characterizes Althusser's theory as being part of a school of social theory, functionalism, which is at odds with basic premises of Marxism. This critique points to functionalism's tendency to understand social phenomena as having simple and clear purposes in maintaining equilibrium, and its rootedness in non-Marxist trends of intellectual history as a point against Althusser. Functionalism's focus on cohesion and order is ultimately bourgeois, says the critique, and thus so is Althusser's theory.

Perhaps more devastating, however, is the second plank: that Althusser's theory does not provide a proper concept of agency. According to this critique from agency, the theory is at best silent on the question of freedom and at worst antithetical to any notion of it. On this view, Althusser's theory renders social forces so strong that they determine the thoughts, actions, and group activity of individuals (such as student organizers, teachers, and the entire working class) or whole institutions (such as schools). Finally, the last critique is that from tragedy. While Althusser's theory is a worthy attempt to de-Stalinize Marxism, it ultimately fails to do so on its own terms.

I find that only one of the texts composing this line of critique passes both tests mentioned earlier, R. W. Connell's critique from promiscuity. I do not find many arguments convincing in the texts themselves that Althusser's theory of education is functionalist, lacks an account of agency, or fails on its own terms. Yet my account in Part II is not meant to be, and cannot be, exhaustive. The purpose is show that there is much to be desired in the line of critique cited by Apple and Giroux in their configuration of critical education, and that critical education researchers should accordingly reconsider presumptions in the paradigm (e.g., like the reproduction-resistance dichotomy).

The line of critique generally speaking is also vulnerable to a reductio ad absurdum argument when it comes to those scholars who applied Althusser's theory. If we assume the line of critique is true, we would expect there to be little worthy Marxist research inspired by Althusser. We might even expect to see non-Marxists, non-activists, bourgeois functionalists, and those committed to capitalist determinism taking up the claims. These claims would reduce social phenomena to their usefulness in maintaining equilibrium, leaving out notions of agency and class struggle. But this is far from the case. In Part III, I present a line of scholarship providing ample evidence to the contrary. This line of scholarship also provides resources to respond to a question that has emerged recently in Altusserian studies of education (Hudson-Miles 2021; Lewis 2017): what would an Althusserian pedagogy look like?

Paulo Freire (1970), perhaps the most famous and important figure in critical education, wrote that Althusser's theory of overdetermination "prevents us from falling into mechanistic explanations or, what is worse, mechanistic action" (216). This brief mention shows that a figure such as Freire understood Althusser's theory as non-mechanistic rather than functionalist and helpful for thinking through political action, rather than leaving out a notion of agency. The passage from Freire gestures toward a line of thinking produced by a diverse group of researchers by race, gender, and nationality that offer meaningful applications, extensions, and constructive readings of Althusser's theory of education. Focusing on advancements in structure, reproduction, race, gender, and ideology I argue that this line of advance—distinct from the line of critique—converges on a distinct paradigm for left education thinking I call structural education, which furnishes resources for a properly Althusserian pedagogy

Stuart Hall's work is an undercurrent running throughout the line of advance. His writing on the theory of articulation, race/class, and encoding/decoding, provide a theoretical underpinning for many of the line of advance's insights for education, particularly true in Zeus Leonardo's (2009) work on whiteness and education. In terms of structural thinking about education, Christian Baudelot and Roger Establet's (1973) *The Capitalist School in France* is a paradigm case of little-considered texts inspired by Althusser's theory of education. (I did not have time or space to consider carefully all such texts I found, such as Vasconi [1974], which deserves translation and careful study). Looking at data from the French school system between 1968 and 1973, the authors use a framework that understands schools as part of an ideological state apparatus that are determined by and determine class struggle in a social formation. Baudelot and Establet critique ideologies of school to show that this apparently unified system is actually an uneven, bifurcated network structured along class lines. I show how the book's argument is original research to which Althusser's theory of education gave rise.

Other examples of texts in the line of advance include Richard Johnson (2018) who, in 1979, charted an interesting synthesis between Althusserian and Thompsonian arguments when it comes to social reproduction, offering a concept of reproduction-in-struggle. Nicos Poulantzas's (1978) claims about education in the opening essay of *Classes and Contemporary Capitalism* takes up the theme of causality and pointing to the stupidity of the bourgeois education problematic that understands schools as the cause of inequality. Rather, critiquing prominent stratification theories, he asserts the opposite: an unequal structure is what causes schools to be as they are, not the other way around.

American political economist of education Martin Carnoy (1982; Carnoy and Levin 1985) clarifies this premise further in his early work on education and the state from the 1980s. Putting Althusser and Poulantzas's thinking into context with Marx and Engels, Lenin, and Gramsci, Carnoy advances a theory of mediation. This theory claims that education—as part of the state—softens contradictions and struggles in the base. This theory also includes key contradictions in schools' contribution to class struggle as a mediator: such as the problem of over-education, the symbol of democracy, grade inflation, and underemployment.

The Althusserian theory also inspired a little-studied (Lussier and Backer 2020) cohort of Marxist feminist research on gender/class and education. AnnMarie Wolpe (1978, 1995) is a great example. A liberation fighter with the African National Congress who, among other things, helped her husband (a comrade of Nelson Mandela) escape from prison, uses Althusser to build out Poulantzas's insights on structural determination to analyze girls' education. She also uses the theory of the ISAs to think through issues in South African Bantu education (Wolpe 1995).

Other examples include Michèle Barrett's (2014) well-known theory of dual systems, a uniquely historical theory of how patriarchy articulates with capitalist exploitation in educational practice. Barrett devotes an entire chapter of the landmark *Women's Oppression Today* to education spelling out this thinking, which I examine. I then look to a cohort of Marxist feminist education researchers who built on Althusser's research, providing examples of Barrett's historical approach to the articulation of patriarchy and capitalism in education. Madeleine Arnot (1982) offered a political economy of girls' education focusing on docility. Rosemary Deem (2012), in her history of gender and education in *Women and Schooling*, provides examples of gendered/classed interpellations from the history of school policy, curriculum, and practice. The American educational researcher Linda Valli (1986) put Althusser's theory to use in analyzing gender/class in a vocational education program focused on girls becoming clerical workers. Like Deem, Valli's study provides a case study of interpellations into what this cohort of Marxist feminists called the sexual division of labor.

Finally, Althusser's theory inspired advances in thinking about ideology, specifically his landmark concept of interpellation. Stuart Hall (1985) made significant advances. He famously claimed that there are no guarantees in ideology, which emerges from his reading of Althusser's concept of uneven development. Hall (2001) applied these ideas in another seminal essay on encoding/decoding messages in media, putting forward the idea that codes get negotiated in the process of their being issued as interpellations to recruit for dominant relations of production, leaving space for oppositional codes to emerge either through misunderstanding or creative rearticulation. These essays provide a clear and distinct account of contingency, freedom, and contradiction in Althusserian structuralism.

While Hall does not explicitly extend the concept of interpellation to cover oppositional and negotiated codes, Jean-Jacques Lecercle (2006) wrote of the notion of counter-interpellation to this end, naming what is perhaps implicit in Hall. Lecercle's counter-interpellation refers to the taking up and taking on of interpellations that shifts a balance of forces, insulting the insult of an interpellation of dominant ideology. The concept has important implications for critical education (Backer 2018). Yet interpellation has been taken in still other directions in educational theory. Tyson Lewis (2017), in his provocative reading of early vs. late Althusser, conceived of disinterpellation, a moment of suspension between interpellation and counter-interpellation, which Lewis claims is more educative than counter-interpellation. Consistent with Hall's findings regarding the power of creative misunderstanding, and the space of possibility between the coded message and its decoding, the literary theorist James Martel (2017) has elaborated the concept of misinterpellation, or when recruitment misfires, breaks down, or has unintended consequences. He cites the cases of Haitian revolutionaries misinterpreting the French calls for universal dignity and Third World revolutionaries responding to Woodrow Wilson's call for sovereignty, pointing to the ways interpellations are subject to the anarchy of everyday life. These developments and augmentations together form a set of resources from which theorists could construct an Althusserian pedagogy.

In the Conclusion, I draw together the findings of each part of the book to put forward one account of that pedagogy by using the structural education framework initiated by Althusser's theory of education, extended by the line of advance, and challenged by the line of critique. This framework is distinct from critical education and makes different insights possible in left educational thinking. Painting in broad strokes critical education has two main principles: (1) a critique of dehumanization that, when thoroughly followed, can lead to liberation, (2) centering human experience against systems via the agency inherent in cultural practices. The line of critique against Althusser from Rancière and Thompson to Giroux and Apple covers the second premise of the critical framework for education.

Reflecting on the eleven rules and the line of advance, I contrast critical education with structural education. Thus the reassessment of Althusser's theory, how it was advanced, and the foundations of critical education and its line of critique, at minimum, is an occasion to explore other frameworks like the structural, particularly given the new resurgence of socialism into the mainstream in the United States and elsewhere. In the Epilogue, I sketch how this framework has helped me in my own teaching, organizing, and research, a set of practices which I characterize as belonging to an Althusserian pedagogy, and invite critiques of my interpretation of Althusser set out in the text.

Two related notes. First, this book on Althusser is not intuitively Althusserian in style. I have chosen to maintain what I take to be a straightforward, academic, and semi-descriptive tone throughout the text. With this style, I hope to give Althusser's ideas a hearing with audiences beyond that of Althusserian studies (relatedly, due to space constraints, I have not been able to properly trace the philosophical influences on Althusser from Gramsci, Spinoza, Lacan, and others). There is a case to be made for this style as consistent with Althusser's project of returning to texts, listening carefully, and close interpretation, as well as engaging with the specific terrain one confronts in one's moment. But readers will notice a difference, which is intentional as a contribution to Althusser studies. I have found that authors can sometimes use a certain speculary mode of expression when writing about Althusser that teeters into the unhelpful. This style may be weighed down by obscure references or technical-poetic voicing such that it becomes inscrutable at best and at worst impractical pedagogically, intellectually, and politically. This is not a critique of any account specifically but rather a stylistic preference I developed while writing this book. Finally, while Althusser's writing certainly fits this description, as Derrida scholar Samir Haddad has pointed out, we must understand this sort of writing as inhabiting a style dominant in élite French universities, particularly in the humanities, during the time when Althusser was attending school and university. I did not have this curricular and pedagogical upbringing and see nothing essentially Althusserian about mimicking it.

Second, Althusser's personal life is and has been relevant to the project. Althusser is perhaps best known now for the psychotic break he suffered in 1980 that led him to kill his wife, Hélène Rytmann. I believe this was a terrible act committed by an individual who long suffered from mental illness. I believe the response from the French government to find Althusser unfit to stand trial was suspect and that the patriarchal forces at work in that juridical outcome still permeate legal and scholarly apparatuses. At the same time, the contributions Althusser made to left education thinking have been positive for intellectual and political struggle, including advances in Marxist feminism. They have much to teach us both about the history of left thinking in education and current struggles on the education terrain. I follow William S. Lewis (2019) in seeing both the value and danger in studying Althusser's thinking. There is value in the depth and novelty of Althusser's thought, but there is danger in lifting up an author with such a fraught life. Given the research I have completed for this book and how it has influenced my own organizing, as I discuss in the epilogue, I have decided as a scholar and organizer that the former value outweighs the latter and welcome critique along these lines.

Part I

Education as an Ideological State Apparatus: Eleven Rules

1

An Attempt to Interpret the Events of May

It started with an explosion. On March 18, 1968, a group of Parisian students identifying themselves as commandos set off bombs in the offices of American corporations, notably American Express. Sharing a "global imagination" antagonistic to imperialism (Cleaver and Katsiaficas 2018: 8), they suspected these companies of complicity in the US invasion of Vietnam ("May 68" 2018). On March 20, police arrested suspects for the bombing. The Nanterre campus of Paris University (a "concrete nightmare in a nightmarish landscape" according to Schnapp and Vidal-Naquet 1971: 95) was a site of related tensions between left student groups and the administration. Some of the student groups identified as Les Enragés, or the angry ones. One of the students suspected in the March 18 action was studying at Nanterre. On March 22, a coalition group of anarchists, Trotskyites, and Maoists in Les Enragés, along with a group called the Vietnam Solidarity Committee, occupied an administrative office at the Nanterre campus to demand the suspected student's release.

The student actions at Nanterre did not come out of nowhere. There had already been tensions in Nanterre and other campuses as part of a yearslong struggle by student unions against the French university system's dysfunctional "Fouchet Plan" (Schnapp and Vidal-Naquet 1971: 95). The Fouchet Plan both increased student enrollments and implemented restrictive examinations which, as Bourdieu and Passeron examined (1979, 1990), selected and excluded students from continuing on in higher education. "[Students] were rightly aware of the fact that 70 percent of them were eliminated by examinations" (95). Students also fought for sexual liberation, as the dormitories were separated by gender. Student protests against imperialism and capitalism's bureaucratic excesses happened in rhythm with particular demands for more inclusive and liberatory educational institutions. (These critiques became the subject of an intellectual dialogue between Althusser and Jacques Rancière between 1964 and 1969.) Les Enragés combined these two threads of critique in the spring of 1968. They formed a new movement called the Movement of March 22 (M22) during their occupation. M22's goals were "to use student discontent to detonate a general revolt in society" (Evans and Godin 2014: 161). It worked.

Nanterre's administration retaliated, arresting students. Some of the students arrested were from the Sorbonne campus of Paris University. Students at the Sorbonne then protested against how the administration treated their comrades in this incident. Administrators retaliated with police force at the Sorbonne against more protesters, the instability increasing over April. By May 2, administrators in Nanterre had had enough and they shut the university down, flooding the campus with police and threatening to expel leaders of the student movements. Students from the Sorbonne joined their peers at Nanterre to protest. Then a few days later the largest student union in France called for a march.

On May 6, twenty thousand students and teachers marched toward Nanterre. The police struck back violently. After this first encounter, high school students as well as young workers joined the growing fight (Gilcher-Holtey 2008: 111). Their demands were to drop charges against student activists, remove police from Nanterre, and reopen the university. Negotiations began and there was a report that the universities were reopening. It was a false report though, and students and their supporters found campuses still occupied with police forces, enraging them further.

The police blocked students from entering campuses, so the students put up barricades in the streets, harkening back to the Paris Commune of 1871. The police, following orders from the infamous chief Maurice Grimaud, then attacked in the middle of the night on May 10. The ensuing riot was televised and the police were blamed for inciting it. In solidarity with the students, federations of unions called a general strike. One million workers marched. The police and government retreated. They agreed to the new movement's demands, but students were emboldened. They occupied their universities, renaming them "people's universities," which then inspired workers to occupy their factories.

Against the wishes of the union leadership and the Communist Party, by the end of the month, nearly ten million workers, or 20 percent of the French population, were on strike. The events in France in 1968 surpassed other movements that had inspired them, like those in Germany and the United States (Gilcher-Holtey 2008: 113). Workers, defying their union leadership and the advice of the Communist leadership, shut down the French economy—all to support the student actions earlier in May. We might say, then, that the most significant disruption to modern capitalist social formations postwar started at school.

Louis Althusser missed these events. He was in the hospital. In the preface to the English translation of *On the Reproduction of Capitalism* (2014), his student Étienne Balibar tries to answer the question of where the Ideological State Apparatuses (ISAs) essay came from, specifically why Althusser would publish an excerpt of the larger book in 1970 before finishing it. The movements and worker strikes in May 1968, particularly the crucial role students played in them, made an impression on Althusser. As Balibar notes, "Even secondary students had mobilized" (Althusser 2014: x). The turn to schooling and education by Althusser and his students was an attempt to make sense of these events, of which the Parti Communiste Français (PCF) and union leadership (and Althusser himself) were critical.

To Balibar, the ISAs essay was Althusser trying to interpret the events despite his illness and his disagreements, incorporate the events' significance into his own previous theorizing, and get back to first principles of Marxism. Elliott (2006) concurs that the essay "might be seen as Althusser's attempt to integrate the lessons of 1968 in order to resolve the problems in his original system" (204). Althusser, having been hospitalized and overwhelmed with the wave of revolt, wanted to make sense of these events by reiterating some of the basic concepts of Marxist theory but also offer a version of that theory relevant for the moment. He had been writing *On the Reproduction of Capitalism* for exactly this purpose, but because he had not finished, he decided to publish an excerpt.

Having faced significant criticisms of his first ambitious and provocative philosophical works, and faced with deep rifts between the Old and New Left, this excerpted essay has an element of apprehension, with Althusser constantly hedging his bold claims by calling them suggestions in need of more examination. Even the subtitle of the essay is "Notes towards an Investigation," trying to affect some humility. Throughout, Althusser asks his readers to interpret his words as schematic and not fully formed. Yet perhaps emblematic of Althusser's instability, the essay is at the same time confident, strident, and almost aphoristic in its general proclamations. *On the Reproduction of Capitalism* (hereafter *OTRC*) manifests this dual tone even further, at times articulating esoteric arguments pushing the boundaries of Marxist thought, or gesturing toward tentativeness, while at other times berating anarchists for their differences of opinion.

The ISAs essay is important in Marxist intellectual history for its contributions to the theory of ideology, but is especially important for the history of critical educational research. In it, Althusser makes the claim that the school has replaced the church as the most effective ideological state apparatus, making it the most important arena for the reproduction of capitalist relations of production above even political parties, unions, sports, media, religion, and family. These passages on education, though widely cited, have not been examined in the context of the larger book from which they were excerpted. In this first part I derive eleven rules of thumb for understanding what it means when Althusser says education is an ideological state apparatus.

2

The Rule of Keys: Social Reproduction

At the beginning of the excerpt, Althusser signals an interest in youth and development. "As Marx said, every child knows that a social formation which did not reproduce the conditions of production at the same time as it produced them would not last a year" (Althusser 1971: 127). Mary McIntosh (1982) would later find that the phrase "reproduce the conditions of production" does not appear in the letter of Marx's that Althusser cites (1982: 116, cited in Barrett 2014: 269). Despite (or perhaps starting from) this creative mistranslation of Marx, Althusser's reference to children is a kind of rhetorical promise to focus on the world of reproduction, which he fulfills when he prioritizes schooling in ways rarely seen in Marxist theorizing until that point.

McIntosh suggests that we call Althusser's focus on reproduction a dictum, which reads: "The ultimate condition of production is ... the reproduction of the conditions of production" (Althusser 1971: 129). The sentence expresses what has become a distinct paradigm in the history of the Marxist tradition: the reproduction of conditions of production, or social reproduction. Althusser's dictum is that reproduction is an ultimate condition of production, the thing upon which production ultimately depends. Having embarked on a rereading of all three volumes of Marx's *Capital*, and writing that reproduction is the ultimate condition of production, Althusser is not—if we take him at his word—making a claim about social functions maintaining equilibrium such as might be argued in the functionalist tradition downstream from Emile Durkheim (though there are compelling cases which I review later, including [DiTomaso 1982]). Rather, Althusser's dictum and the claims following from it draw from specific ideas in Marx's *Capital* about how capitalists maintain the continuity of commodity production as part of the class struggle.

Social reproduction is about renewal. To Marx, this means the renewal of surplus value and capitalist relations. Marx first takes up this theme when analyzing how prices become commodities, which become money, and then turn (through exchange) into commodities with prices again (1956: 36). Marx calls this "periodical renewal of the functioning of capital" or its "self-expansion" a simple process of reproduction. David Harvey says this is when the same amount of value transfers between phases of production. The renewal covers productive capital, the capital that goes into paying for labor and equipment needed to complete the labor, as well as surplus value. He then examines the reproduction of social capital. Social reproduction refers to this third type. Social capital, for Marx in Volume Two, is just this "interlacing" of capitals, or all the capitals in their aggregate "as a totality" (Harvey 2013: 215). Social reproduction therefore is the renewal and self-expansion of these intertwined and interlaced kinds of capital.

When looking at productive capital's reproduction, Marx writes the term "preservation" to refer to what workers do when they nourish themselves to continue producing. "The wage-laborer lives only by the sale of his labour-power. Its preservation—his preservation—requires daily consumption." To do this, the worker has to "repeat the purchases needed for his self-preservation" (1956: 21). Others would use the term reproduction in reference to this nourishment (Munro 2019). Thus reproduction has at least two senses in the Marxist tradition: expansion of capital and preservation-nourishment of bodies that work. These two senses match up with three streams of social reproduction thinking. Distinguishing these streams clarifies the first rule for understanding education as an ideological state apparatus, what I call the rule of keys.

Étienne Balibar's contribution to *Reading Capital* is an articulation of an interlacing view of social reproduction. Balibar writes, with an unfortunate turn of phrase, that social reproduction is "the pregnancy of the structure" because reproduction ensures "the general form of permanence of the general modes of production" (Althusser 2016: 426). What exactly does the structure give birth to when it reproduces? What does it mean to ensure permanence? Balibar lists three things. First, the structure gives birth to "economic subjects" through "interlacing and intertwining" of individual people with individual capitals (426); the way people find, seek out, or become associated with wages, rents, or commodities. Second, the structure gives birth to different levels of society which aim to "sanctify the existing situation as law" (426). Finally, the structure reproduces the economic status of objects. In general, social reproduction, for Balibar, renews social relations: relations between people, between objects, and between people and objects (Backer 2017).

None of these texts, neither in Marx nor in Althusser and Balibar, links schooling to reproduction (yet). But this link was in the air. In 1979 Pierre Bourdieu and Jean Passeron published their first major study of the French university system in *The Inheritors: French Students and their Relation to Culture*. Their conclusion gestures toward social reproduction, inaugurating a different stream of social reproduction thinking. *The Inheritors* is a sociological analysis of how French universities "transmit" cultural privilege and "produce individuals who are selected and arranged in a hierarchy" (Bourdieu and Passeron 1979: 68). Bourdieu and Passeron elaborate this transmission view in *Reproduction in Culture, Society, and Education*, focusing on symbolic violence.

A final stream begins with Canadian theorist Margaret Benston's (1969) claim that the reproduction of labor power is how patriarchy relates to capitalist exploitation, as women do a vast majority of what she (following Marx) called reproductive labor: birthing and raising children, cooking, cleaning, and taking care of men so that they are ready for work. Mariarosa Dalla Costa and Selma James (1975), Silvia Federici (1975), Christine Delphy (2016), Lise Vogel (2013), and Michèle Barrett (2014) would follow this thread in a number of key texts. Their stream of thinking would become a social reproduction theory distinct from Bourdieu, Balibar, and Althusser's. These men ignored women's work, a marginalization clearest perhaps in Balibar's problematic pregnancy metaphor.

Recently, this tradition of social reproduction feminism is having a resurgence. Tithi Bhattacharya (2017) and others argue that it is a paradigm shift within Marxism itself. For this tradition of Marxist feminists like Benston, if workers do not reproduce themselves—sleep, eat, rest, dress, learn—then there would be no labor force and no production. Social reproduction is therefore the concrete form of care work traditionally done by women to maintain the bodies of the largely male workforce, alongside actually giving birth to children and raising them. This sense of reproduction is in line with Marx's concept of preservation in Volume Two mentioned earlier.

Each stream—the interlacing view, the transmission of privilege view, and the care work view—is an interpretation of Marx's original concept of reproduction. Althusser's dictum that social reproduction is the ultimate condition of production is best understood as the interlacings view with a hint of the care work view, each of which are explicitly oriented toward the maintenance of capitalist production. Bourdieu and Passeron's transmission view is further away from Althusser's. Remember that the dictum says that the foremost premise upon which production relies is whether and how the conditions of production or factors of production, like labor and economic relations are maintained over time. This reproduction is distinct from the transmission of cultural privileges to which Bourdieu and Passeron point. Further, Althusser's exegetical focus, and the whole of the theory, trains on Marx in Volume Two and not Durkheim or Weber (1971: 128). As Shelly Ronen and I have argued (Ronen and Backer 2018), social reproduction theory's claim is that reproduction is the key to the key to production. If labor is the key to production, reproduction is the key to labor. Call this the rule of keys.

This concept of reproduction as a key to production, or Althusser's dictum, is the excerpt's scope. "It is extremely hard, not to say impossible, to raise oneself to the *point of view of reproduction*" (1971: 128, all italics in quoted text are in the original unless mentioned otherwise). Althusser is overstating somewhat. He was part of a cohort of thinkers, like Balibar and those around Bourdieu and Benston, also doing the allegedly impossible. This is difficult to do, however. In *OTRC*, Althusser contrasts the point of view of reproduction with the "viewpoint of the *enterprise*" (2014: 48), which focuses only on the workplace or the point of production. The excerpt sets out to delimit this point of view, centering reproduction as the ultimate condition of production. Thus his eventual focus on schools, which are beyond the enterprise, outside the workplace, and are thus part of how a capitalist ruling class attempts to renew and maintain their favored relations of production.

3

The Rule of Hands: Relations of Production

But before examining the view from reproduction more closely, to make sure we are all on the same page, Althusser sets out his view from the enterprise. Readers must understand what a relation of production is before looking at how schools try to reproduce them. Therborn (1985) notes that relation of production is the most important concept in historical materialism. Althusser proceeds to examine it in the excerpt by rehearsing a handful of basic Marxist premises. Relations of production and productive forces are what a social formation arises from. Taken together, they form a mode of production. The excerpt runs through these terms quickly, but in *OTRC*, after an introductory chapter on philosophy's relationship to society, Althusser advances expanded definitions of these terms in a self-standing chapter titled "What is a Mode of Production?" The book is more instructive than the excerpt on this front.

First, Althusser lays out the typical Marxist definition of production as tackling nature. In the mode of production, or the manner of tackling nature, there are two main elements: productive forces and relations of production. Althusser writes that "tackling here means mobilizing productive forces under the aegis of relations of production" (Althusser 2014: 45). Mobilizing the means of production under the aegis of relations of production, he clarifies, means being set to work on the means of production, being put to work on them.

Relations of production, following the formulation above, bring people into relation with the means of production. Each mode of production does this differently. A capitalist mode of production sets people to work on the means of production by dividing them into two groups. One group owns and controls the means of production while the other does not. Having one group own and control the means of production and another group not control them is the "act of bringing wage-workers into relation with means of production belonging, not to them, but to the capitalist owner of those means of production" (32). The capitalist relation of production sets people to work on the means of production in this divided way.

It is easy to see the difference between relations of production using a hypothetical example of how the same people can be set into relation with the same means of production in different ways. The English analytic Marxist philosopher G. A. Cohen, who was influenced by Althusser's return to Marx, writes for example that "the Soviet collective farm and the American 'agribusiness', despite their difference of social form, display the same material ... of grain, if they plough, sow, and reap using similar methods and instruments of production" (2000: 80). The Soviet farm might have the same means of production as an American agribusiness in terms of ploughs, methods, and material. But, Cohen continues, the ways people are brought into relation with those productive forces—their control of that technology and raw material—are distinct. The communist farm will have a relation of production where workers control the means of production. When the relations change, so does the mode of production (85).

But what is a relation? Althusser's philosophical answer to this question is one of the most important and overlooked of his contributions to education. To Althusser, society is a social formation with a definite structure: groups of people who act in certain ways and relate to one another accordingly. To delimit what the term relation refers to, there is an important point to consider about what social structure is and is not. For this we have to return briefly to Althusser's philosophical work in *Reading Capital*. There, he writes that the definite structure of a society is immanent in the ways that groups of people act rather than transcendent on them (Althusser 2016: 344). Elsewhere, I have illustrated the difference between transcendent and immanent structure by drawing an analogy to the cartoon superheroes Captain Planet and Voltron (Backer 2019: 48). Humans call forth Captain Planet (King 1994), who is more powerful than any of them individually or combined. Yet Voltron (Koppel 2010) is a robot piloted by a group of humans, each responsible for a different body part. Any one of Voltron's movements are the result of specific coordination between humans, whereas Captain Planet's actions are the result of his separate agency. Voltron is an immanent hero while Captain Planet is a transcendent hero. Althusser's concept of structure is immanent, not transcendent, which has led to some interpreters' conclusion that his structuralism is not a structuralism (Montag 2018). I maintain that it is structuralism, but a distinct variant that understands structure as immanent.

Like Voltron, social structure only exists in the specific combination of its peculiar elements in determinate circumstances. Unlike Captain Planet, who has a distinctive personality over and above the planeteers that bring him into being, the name Voltron only refers to the coordination between drivers of the five separate robots that compose him. In the same way that Voltron is nothing outside of that coordination, social structure is immanent in its effects, or nothing outside the particular forms and relations composing it. 'Voltron' is the name that refers to an absent will that exists only in the coordinated movements of the robots composing him. Those places and roles of coordination between composite elements that are immanent effects of their absent structure are what Althusser intends by the term relation. Therefore, we should understand the term relations of production as a series of places and functions (actions) that exist among and between people (Althusser 2016: 335). The distinction between positions and the persons occupying them traces back in the French tradition to the Swiss linguist Ferdinand de Saussure. In his landmark work *Course in General Linguistics,* Saussure distinguishes language from speech, claiming that the former is a "well-defined object in the heterogeneous mass of speech facts" (2011: 14). He elaborates that language, as an object amid speech, "is the social side of speech, outside the individual who can never create nor modify it by himself; it exists only by virtue of a sort of contract signed by members of a community" (14).

Languages change, Saussure says, but not because any one speaker by themselves decides to change it. The language rather exists in the collectivity. Indeed, by thus separating language (well-defined object outside the individual that they cannot modify by themselves) from speech (mass of speech facts), Saussure can state that "language is not a function of the speaker; it is a product that is passively assimilated by the individual" (14). Althusser is participating in the tradition of this distinction but bringing it to bear on Marx's relation of production, making sure to distinguish his account as immanent (which Glucksmann (2014) recognizes as a distinct paradigm from Levi-Strauss's structuralism). Insofar as the tradition flowing downstream from Saussure is structuralist—language is a structure separate from speech—then Althusser fashions a structural concept of relations of production (Caws 1997). Rather than language and its speakers, in this case it is the division of labor and its workers.

Perhaps infamously, Althusser says that the agents of production are "never anything more than" (Althusser 2016: 344) their positions, or in French *ne sont jamais que*. Althusser is saying that when it comes to the relations of production, there is a clear difference between the person and the position. Further, an individual person can only ever fill that position. They can bear the function, support it; but when it comes to changing that position we have to take very different things into consideration. Just as Saussure notes that a speaker cannot change the language by themselves, an individual cannot change a position by themselves. The relation is rigid, having its own temporality and effectivity. It exerts a force on the person, but that force is a specific kind of force whose strength varies depending on certain conditions. Certainly the position's force can be much greater than the individual's, just as Saussure pointed out that an individual speaker cannot change the language all by themselves. This inequality in the effectivities need not imply more than that however; namely the resulting account of individual action is neither passive nor prohibitive of agency.

A clue comes from the word bearing. It may seem as though bearing the weight of an already-existing structure is passive. However, anyone who has carried heavy weights knows that supporting weight is active. It takes energy and perseverance to carry a heavyweight. It can be done well or poorly. Like learning a language, there are rules and best practices that make sense. Furthermore, the heavyweights themselves are made of material that decomposes, rusts, or breaks apart either over time or during pronounced exposure to outside forces. Being set to work on the means of production, bearing a relation of production, means holding up and regenerating the places and functions of the social structure through practices.

This active insight is not only present in later essays. Rather, this frequently overlooked understanding of immanent social structure as active is present throughout the ISAs essay and *On the Reproduction of Capitalism*, particularly in terms of resistance and struggle. Structure is both separate from any given individual, but also moveable and changeable. In other words, the place/function both preexists the individual and comes into being as that individual fills it.

A relation is therefore bearing a function in a definite social structure. An immanent concept of relation understands that structure as existing only in its effects. A relation of production is how people mobilize means of production. We can put these pieces together to get Althusser's immanent concept of relation of production. In Balibar's contribution to *Reading Capital*, "On the Basic Concepts of Historical Materialism," he provides a helpful illustration. Balibar says that to understand a given moment's relations of production (and whether/how it may transition to a different relation of production), one can look at what workers have their hands on. He writes that Marx's originality in theorizing the industrial revolution was to focus on "*the transformation of the relationship* which followed from the replacement of the means of labor," in the transition from workers operating tools by hand to machines operating those tools (Althusser 2016: 406).

Notice that this "relationship" of individual human beings to the tools they use to tackle nature is an example of a relation of production. Whether manufacture or industry, each labor process "occupies *the same place*" (406) in social structure as relations of production. The agents and objects of production, tools, and humans, are set to work on the means of production in distinctive ways in each case. Rather than a human being working with a set of tools to manufacture goods, machines do the work. People and objects in this transition are brought into relation with the means of production in such different ways that the transition from one to the other is a reorganization of the real appropriation of nature: "The machine which replaces the ensemble to tools and educated, specialized labour-power is in no way a production of the development of [manufacture] ... [i]t replaces the previous system" (407).

In manufacturing, skilled humans use tools to produce. In industry, humans manage machines that do the production. Thus what workers have their hands on matters in the Marxist perspective: the reorganization of real appropriation of nature is socially transformative. What Marxists do is think about how social upheavals derive to a great degree from what workers have their hands on, since that indicates a relation of production. Having your hands on something can also mean owning or controlling it. Workers do not have their hands on capital in the same way as capitalists. In industrial capitalism, workers have their hands on machines (they work on them) but do not own them. In financial capitalism, capitalists have their hands on finance capital more than industrial capital, indicating a change in the relation of production as well. I propose to call this general insight the rule of hands: a relation of production is what people have their hands on. When Althusser says that schools reproduce a relation of production, they are maintaining the continuity of how people have their hands on the material world.

4

The Competency Rule

Indeed, all this talk about social reproduction and relations of production lead up to Althusser's focus on education. In the excerpt, the transition comes somewhat abruptly. In *OTRC*, however, it comes from a careful consideration of how ruling classes maintain their preferred relations of production over time. Althusser does this by distinguishing two kinds of workers and, in so doing, shows the importance of knowledge in the division of labor. The focus on knowledge leads right to education.

On the one hand, there are proletarians, in the strict sense: common laborers, unskilled laborers, skilled laborers, "and (sometimes) a handful of technicians" (Althusser 2014: 41). These proletarians do the grunt work. From the point of view of the ruling class, these strictly proletarian workers were once thought of merely as hired hands but, given the technological transformation of the means of production, "become mere extensions of their machines" from the ruling class point of view (42). On the other hand, there are supervisors and goons that manage the proletarians, performing "*functions of repression*" within the relations of production (41). Supervisory and goonish activities include "surveillance … fines, demotions, the attribution or withholding of bonuses, and dismissals … police-like inquiries" and various "abuses" (41).

Observe here that Althusser makes the distinction between supervisors and strict proletarians in terms of their functions. The former serves functions of production while the latter performs functions of repression. Althusser elaborates the concept "function" here through practices, experience, and exploitation. When someone serves the function of a goon by engaging in police-like inquiries into factory workers who toil with machines, they are not reduced or determined by that function, but rather sell their labor for that purpose. From the point of view of the ruling class, via hiring contracts, these individuals are expected to perform these functions—that is, do the work—or they could lose their jobs. They are not reduced to that activity but rather are forced to do it for their livelihoods.

Notice too that grunt work and supervisory repression, toiling and gooning, are two kinds of relation of exploitation. Proletarians in the strict sense, Althusser writes, are brought into relation with the means of production because they have no other options for survival: they have to take night shifts, for example, and are beholden to the exhausting rhythms of machines and assembly lines. They relate to the means of production via repression from supervisors and goons, whose relations to the means of production are to surveil, fine, demote, give, and take away bonus pay, interrogate, and abuse the proletarians. We could extend this distinction to any subordinate-superior relationship while at work, and understand different kinds of workplace differences, and even abuses, in this context. It is here, in the analysis of hierarchies in the working-class division of labor, we find the first mention of education.

Althusser considers that these two kinds of work (toiling and gooning) are associated with "certain kinds of 'knowledge'" (Althusser 2014: 41). One group in particular holds a "*monopoly* on certain contents and forms of knowledge, and thus on a form of 'know-how', while others … are *'penned' in other contents* and forms of know-how" (38). The class struggle thus manifests in knowledge. These insights refer strictly to the point of production and workers' access to resources and position within hierarchies. Certainly, factory workers create culture, read widely, and are highly educated in other respects. However, when it comes to the relations of exploitation delimiting their pay and place in work hierarchies, existing regimes of qualification, know-how, and training pens them in. Thus the differences between toilers and goons fall along differences in knowledge. The differences in knowledge and training hold in place hierarchies in the division of labor. The strict proletarian gets penned into this kind of work because of her lack of knowledge and qualification. Education plays a significant role in perpetuating these distinctions.

As an example, in a footnote in *OTRC*, Althusser focuses on how a recruiter might hire a machine worker: "Any 'engineer' will tell you: … I need someone to run a milling machine, so I run an ad. A milling machine operator answers it. I hire him. Is it my fault that he's *just* a milling machine operator?' Literally, taken in its own limits, this is not 'wrong'" (38). In this hypothetical situation, Althusser notes that it is a kind of consciousness or understanding that sees a trained mill operator as just a plain old mill operator. This perspective understands the division of labor, or the stratification within the relations of production outlined above, as a strictly technical division of labor. There are milling machines. There are milling machine operators. People come to know how to operate the machines and then get jobs. Simple. There are better and worse ways to manage and supervise these operators. This picture of work is technical, functional, economistic. There are people. They get prepared for jobs. They get the jobs.

Yet Althusser has laid out an entirely different picture. When analyzing the world of work from a Marxist perspective, understanding economy as a mode of production with relations of production, the picture is not functional, technocratic, or economistic. Quite the opposite. At the very least we can say that there are relations of hierarchy within those relations of production: differences of rhythm, power, surveillance between supervisors and strict proletarians. These points alone show that the engineer's view of hiring a machine operator is quite limited. The supposedly technical division of labor is anything but. Rather, in Althusser's rendering of Marx, there is a "social" division of labor (34). People are distributed into certain places in the division of labor, people relate to the means of production in different ways, and further people imagine those relations of production differently. In other words, every position in the social structure requires people who have had certain experiences, have become proficient in certain practices, and have a certain kind of knowledge that compels them to mobilize the means of production. School is where people learn these kinds of knowledge.

As a precursor for the insight to come, consider Althusser's (1964) short essay "Student Problems" from 1964. In it, Althusser elaborates on the distinction between technical and social division of labor mentioned in the previous section, but focusing specifically the university's role in reproducing these divisions of labor. For him the university's role

> in the *technical* division of labour consists of undertaking the pedagogic training of future technical, scientific and social cadres of the society, and of participating in creative scientific work. Pedagogical training—that is, the transmission of knowledge that exists in society, knowledge which conditions the existence and development of the labour process of the society, is a vital necessity for every society. (11)

On Althusser's account, relations of hierarchy and relations of production come with differences in knowledge, inequalities of qualifications, and general preparation that fall along the complex echelons in the social formation. The majority of people get cornered in a certain kind of low-paid work, skills to work machines but not be supervisors. Most people are strict proletarians. They do grunt work for low pay in difficult circumstances. The way they come to get those jobs (which they largely hold for life except for the few of them that move up the ladder), has entirely to do with the reproduction that maintains the continuity of these relations of production. In other words, the mill operator mentioned before—as operator of a mill, in terms of her ability to have that job—comes from somewhere. Where does this division come from? Her pedagogical training: her instruction in requisite knowledges for completing the work.

In the footnote about the hiring agent, Althusser writes a key passage focusing on competencies:

> But, precisely, "competencies," that is, qualifications or the lack of them, *owe their direct existence not to the enterprise as such*, but to a system *external* to the enterprise, the school system that 'educates', more or less, different individuals ... in ways that vary with the milieu from which they come ... The reason [for the engineer's lack of understanding] is that the school system that supplies ready-made, at the national level, a predisposition for the "distribution-penning-in" of people that becomes concrete reality in the enterprise is the capitalist school system corresponding to the capitalist class's system of exploitation, *not some other school system*. (Althusser 2014: 38)

While the human resources agent looking for a mill operator seems to think mill operators appear out of thin air, Althusser points to action happening outside the firm, external to production, that prepares people for the job market. Education is that region outside production that provides the relevant competencies for the existing labor process, supplying a predisposition that corresponds to the system of exploitation (a thesis which, considering when Althusser was writing in the early 1970s, we may have to at least partly attribute to him along with Bowles and Gintis).

When thinking about how this mill operator came to have the competencies required for their job, it is not the enterprise or firm that handles this basic instruction. Rather, a school system outside the point of production does that. Althusser continues with another key passage: "[The school system] cannot be other than what it is, whether certain dreamers like that or not, as long as the foundations of capitalist exploitation remain in place, namely, capitalist relations of production" (Althusser 2014: 38). From a Marxist perspective, a school system in a capitalist social formation is a capitalist school system "and not some other school system," despite the dreams of those starting alternative schools (see Gramsci's critique of Free Schools in the *Prison Notebooks* (1971: 24), as well as Bowles and Gintis's (2011)). Schools in the social formation tend to serve the dominant mode of production.

A classic formulation of social reproduction theory in education, this argument is somewhat uncomfortable for teachers, students, parents and other people working in schools. At first it may seem Althusser is saying that schools in a capitalist social formation are determined to serve the interests of capital in some transcendent way beyond the powers and struggles of individuals or groups within it. Yet we know that Althusser's theory is one of immanence and not transcendence; one that takes struggle and contradiction into account. What Althusser means by the word "is" in the formulation above (the school system "cannot be other than what it *is*") is quite different than what it was made out to be by his critics. In this theory, the school system is an immanent structure, an ideological state apparatus that exerts a unique force in the social formation, but one that shapes those forces and is shaped by them in turn.

The key takeaway of Althusser's thinking on school is not to conclude that schools are determined by a god-like economy that forecloses freedom of action. The takeaway is rather to understand the kind of strategies and tactics that would be adequate for unseating the dominance of capitalist relations of production in the formation, and the role of schooling in that process of transition. This is why Althusser mentions Lenin's relentless focus on setting up polytechnical schools. The fact that Althusser mentions Lenin's thinking on education at this moment—which he cites from Nadezdha Krupskaya's writings (1957)—tells us that Althusser is primarily interested in struggle, revolution, and changing social structure.

At the start of a chapter called "The Reproduction of the Conditions of Production," Althusser (2014) elaborates further by distinguishing between simple and extended reproduction. Simple reproduction maintains the continuity of things like natural resources and machinery. Extended reproduction covers labor power. Labor power, or the requisite human force needed to operate the means of production, has to be "competent" (50): "it must be such that it can be put to work in the complex system of the productive process, in specific posts and specific forms of cooperation ... labor power must be (diversely) *skilled* ... as required by the social-technical division of labor, its different 'jobs' and 'posts'" (50). Althusser calls this instruction of diverse skills for the social-technical division of labor qualification. Whereas in a slavery or serfdom, this qualification may have happened "'on the job' (instruction during production itself)" (see Wolf 2013), in a modern capitalist society it occurs "*outside* production, by the capitalist school system" (Althusser

2014: 50). Althusser then asks, "But what do people learn in school?" Here we find another important passage:

> Everybody "knows" the answer: they stay in school for longer or shorter periods but, at all events, they learn reading, writing and arithmetic. That is, they learn a handful of techniques, and quite a few other things besides, including elements (rudimentary or, on the contrary, advanced) of "scientific culture" or "literary culture" that are of direct use in different jobs in production (one curriculum for workers, a third to engineers, still another for technicians, a final one for senior managers, and so on.) Thus they acquire "know-how." (51)

Althusser defines know-how as "simple *techniques* (knowing how to read, write, count, read a map, find one's way in chronology, recognize this or that object or reality, and so on)" as well as "knowledge, that is, the rudiments or elements (sometimes even relatively advanced) of scientific learning" (51). Labor power gets reproduced by teaching and learning such know-how, which can differ according to the qualifications necessary in different echelons in the division of labor: workers get different educations than technicians who get different educations than managers, and so on. Critical education has provided decades of evidence to this claim, perhaps most notably in its most recent iteration beginning in the United States with Jean Anyon's (1981) work on school knowledge in five different New Jersey high schools, each serving different fractions of the working class: unskilled, middle class, professional, and affluent.

Competence includes technical know-how but is not limited to it. Competence is more than just qualification, or know-how in the form of rudimentary science and simple techniques. Althusser notes that submission is a crucial part of the picture: "The reproduction of labor power requires not only that its *qualifications* be reproduced, but that its *submission* to the rules of respect for the established order be reproduced at the same time" (Althusser 2014: 51). This piece of the reproduction puzzle, he says, goes largely ignored because people do not really want to talk about it in education.

> What everybody also "knows," however—that is, what nobody *cares to know*—is that *alongside* these "techniques" … and this "learning" … people also learn, at school, the "rules" of good behavior … to put it plainly, rules of *respect* for the social and technical division of labor, and, in the final analysis, the rules of the *order established by class domination*. (51)

For educators, students, parents, and everyone else educated in modern capitalist society, it is not a happy thought that schools are what Althusser will call apparatuses that teach not just respect for persons, but respect for society as it is. A teacher may be effective in their instruction, empathize and connect with their students, but in the midst of that effective instruction and emotional connection are lessons about domination.

Classroom talk is a paradigm case of how students learn rules of respect and order alongside technical know-how for Althusser. In school, students have to "speak proper French" and "write properly" (51). Althusser applies his version of the correspondence principle here, saying that to speak and write proper French "in fact means (for future capitalists and their underlings) to 'order workers around properly', that in fact means (the ideal case) to 'talk properly' to them so as to intimidate or cajole them—in short, to 'con' them" (51). Getting students to speak properly instructs them how to con one another because it is a training for relations of exploitation. To be a proper manager, you have to speak properly. To be a proper underling, you have to speak properly. Speaking properly in a capitalist economy means speaking in such a way as to effectively engage in exploitation. To the extent that exploitation is a scam, then learning how to speak properly while engaging in exploitation is learning how to scam properly. Instructing students in speaking and writing properly, particularly in those schools that train future managers, teaches students to submit to the division of labor, thus enabling them to serve their function as exploiters and exploited, a process Althusser calls "*submission* to the rules of respect for the established order" (51).

And here Althusser turns to a flagship term in his theory of education. An instruction in submission, he writes, ensures future workers' "*capacity to handle the dominant ideology* properly" (51). Proper writing and speaking has the combined effect to teach know-how "but in forms that ensure *subjection to the dominant ideology*, or else the 'practice' of it" (52). School, in addition to teaching know-how, offers instruction in the capacity to handle the dominant ideology. Althusser unpacks this idea further:

> every agent of production ... has to be "steeped" in that ideology in one way or another in order conscientiously (and with no need to have his own personal gendarme breathing down his neck) to carry out his or her task: the task of the exploited (the proletarians), the exploiters (the capitalists), the auxiliaries of exploitation (supervisory personnel), or the high priests of the dominant ideology, its "functionaries," and so on. (52)

This passage readies the ground for many of the claims Althusser will make about ideology. Students get steeped in ideology at school through the process of becoming competent, learning both to become qualified and submissive to society as it is. Yet this process does not install some kind of machinery in their heads. The process of instructing submission to the dominant ideology is meant precisely to avoid the necessity of making sure students have their "own personal gendarme breathing down [their] necks." While they learn how to carry out tasks, they learn to trust the relations of production on their own, so they (as Althusser will say later) "go all by themselves."

Instruction in submission to dominant ideology is the primary way to reproduce labor power "for it is *in the forms and under the forms of ideological subjection that the reproduction of the qualification of labor-power is ensured*" (52). Whereas some might think that school's primary purpose in a capitalist society is to instruct qualification (skills and techniques), instruction in the dominant ideology (teaching respect for the society as it is) is just as important. Althusser's theory of competence places equal weight on qualification and submission. The competence rule says that reproducing the relations of production requires teaching and learning competencies that are both qualifications for the technical division of labor and submissiveness to the dominant ideology.

Yet this is all just the beginning of Althusser's theory of education. We know that capitalism renews the relations of production through school's instruction in competencies, both in terms of qualification and submission. But how? Althusser's famous notion of the ideological state apparatuses (ISAs), and their accompanying concept of ideology-as-interpellation, provide an answer.

5

The Rule of Special Thirds: Base and Superstructure

In the excerpt, under the subtitle "The State Ideological Apparatuses," Althusser (1971) points to the central term of the essay, ideological state apparatuses (ISAs). The ISAs are "realities which present themselves to the immediate observer in the form of distinct and specialized institutions" (142). He goes on to list "with reservation" a few ISAs that he says "will obviously have to be examined in detail, tested, corrected and re-organized." The first three are: "the religious ISA (the system of the different churches), the educational ISA (the system of the different public and private 'schools'), the family ISA" (142).

The term ideological state apparatus was a neologism at the time. Balibar notes in the preface to *On the Reproduction of Capitalism* that members of Althusser's seminar chose the term apparatus from Marx's (2008) *The 18th Brumaire of Louis Bonaparte*, as in the line "Taxes are the life source of the bureaucracy, the army, the priests, and the court—in short, of the entire apparatus of the executive power" (Marx 2008: 128). In this sense, as Althusser (1971) defines the term slightly later in a section on the State, an apparatus is "a 'machine' … which enables" a class to "ensure their domination over" another class (137). An apparatus is also a "force … of execution and intervention" (137) that one side uses against another as part of the struggle (an early version of a concept charted more recently by Agamben [2009]).

But before we can zoom into the ISAs themselves, we have to zoom out to see where they fit into the larger Marxist theory of society: the base-superstructure model. Althusser (2014) values this metaphor both theoretically and pedagogically, setting out an interpretation of it before detailing his notion of the ISAs (53). To understand his concept of apparatus, it is essential to see it in this context. The theoretical insight in the base-superstructure model is that society is held up by its base, just as the foundation holds up a house's floors. The upper floors, in this metaphor of society, are twofold: "the *superstructure*, which itself contains two 'levels' or 'instances': the politico-legal (law and the State) and ideology (the different ideologies, religious, ethical, legal, political, etc.)." What Althusser calls the pedagogical insight of the model is that it helps us think about cause, effect, and force in society, or what he calls the "*respective indices of effectivity*" of the base and superstructures as they determine one another (Althusser 1971: 134). Althusser offers more detail in *OTRC*, elaborating on these passing phrases found in the excerpt.

The base-superstructure model represents how social realities determine one another. Cohen (2000) elaborates this relationship between base and superstructure using a simple architectural metaphor:

> Four struts are driven into the ground, each protruding the same distance above it. They are unstable. They sway and wobble in winds of force 2. Then a roof is attached to the four struts, and now they stay firmly erect in all winds under force 6. Of this roof one can say: (i) it is supported by the struts, and (ii) it renders them more stable. (231)

In Cohen's telling of the base-superstructure topography, you can see that base and superstructure exert forces and are dependent upon one another, but in distinct ways. Each distinctive force has what Althusser calls an "index of effectivity" precisely for that reason: there is an indexed amount of determinative force exerted by different aspects of a social formation. A mode of production affects the social formation in a different way than the police, government, or school. These forces do not exist in a vacuum, but rather in relation to one another. We therefore can assign them an effectivity, or their determinative force, indexed to the larger balance of forces. Cohen assigns indices of effectivity with numbers to the struts and base, as well as the wind. He actually quantifies the wind's force, thereby assigning an index of effectivity to the base and superstructure of the hut in his metaphor. In "winds of force 2," the struts wobble. They have an index of two, in that case. Yet with a roof, the whole structure can stay erect in winds of "force 6," its new index of effectivity.

Althusser (2014) is careful to note: "We can say straight away, with no risk of error, that the upper floors of the superstructure [are] *determined* by *the effectivity* of the base" (54). Just as we see from Cohen, it is not accurate to say that the superstructures are merely determined by the base. They are determined by the effectivity of the base, or its particular force in relation to other forces in the structure. The base has a specific force, a particular effectivity in relation to the superstructures, not just an overall determining force on them. After noting the base has an effectivity specific to it, Althusser then reiterates one of his best-known formulations about that special force: "the object of the metaphor of the edifice is, above all, to represent 'determination *in the last instance*' by the economic base ... determination in the last instance of what happens in the 'upper floors' of the superstructure by what happens in the economic base" (54).

The base determines the superstructures in the last instance, but "in the last instance" is just a phrase from Engels. Althusser's conception of these words is that the base has a special force unique to it and this force is indexed to other forces in the social formation (54). So the base-superstructure model assigns the economic base a certain index of effectivity, a quality and quantity of unique force that the economy exerts in society. According to the base-superstructure model, because the economy is at the bottom we should assign its index of effectivity as a determinant in the last instance when it comes to what happens in the upper floors or the superstructures. Following Cohen's analogy of the simple structure with struts and roof, if the entire structure is able to withstand six units of wind force, but without the roof this structure can only withstand two units, then we would assign the base of that hut at least two units of force, and the roof four units. Those two units of force are determinative in the last instance because they are at the bottom of the structure, but they are far from determining the total force of the whole structure. Indeed, they are relatively autonomous.

The superstructures exert special forces of their own: "the 'floors' of the superstructures are obviously endowed with *different* indices of effectivity" (54). Furthermore, Althusser notes that these forces are related in a specific way to one another. Thus, the last instance thesis is "*thought* in two forms in the Marxist tradition": The unique and different index of effectivity in the superstructures is relatively autonomous with respect to the base and reacts back on the base (54). Continuing to use Cohen's simple structure, the roof both rests upon the struts and renders those struts more stable. The roof is therefore only *relatively* autonomous. The roof exerts its own kind of downward-facing stability force on the overall structure and that force is relatively independent and has its own unique character. But that stabilizing force ultimately rests upon that exerted by the struts. The superstructures' autonomy is relative as indexed to the other forces in the formation (namely the base), or, as Althusser puts it, the superstructure's force has a "'derivative' effectivity that is specific to the superstructure" (54). This is the rule of special thirds. The mode of production exerts a special third force in a society, as does each superstructure (on which more later). These thirds are special because they are qualitatively distinct from one another, nonreducible to each other, yet quantitatively they add up to a social formation's total social force.

In Althusser's rendering, there are two superstructures. Combined, these exert two-thirds worth of relatively autonomous force in society, resting and reacting back on the base. The two superstructures are based on a distinction in Marx between the "legal-political superstructure (law and the state)" and the "ideological superstructure (the various ideologies)" (Althusser 2014: 55). Althusser says the same relationship between the base and superstructure in the larger social formation holds between law, the state, and the various ideologies. While the legal-political superstructure is "as a rule, 'more' effective than the ideological superstructure" at the same time "the ideological superstructure, too, is endowed with 'relative autonomy' in its relations with the legal-political superstructure and is capable of 'reacting back' upon it" (55).

The ideological superstructure therefore largely rests upon the legal-political superstructure, but exerts a special index of effectivity without which the latter would remain unstable (just like the base and superstructure). The ideological superstructure is relatively autonomous and acts back on the legal-political superstructure, which in turn is relatively autonomous and acts back on the economic base. We can note here that there are at least two layers of relative autonomy in the theory: the relative autonomy between base and superstructure and the relative autonomy between legal-political and ideological superstructures. These are two clear aspects of the theory that make space for contingency, movement, and autonomy.

Rather than rely on the ambiguous compound noun legal-political superstructure, Althusser gets more specific and calls it a repressive state apparatus. Similarly, the term ideological superstructure transforms into ideological state apparatus. We can understand this state apparatus thesis, when it comes to the superstructures, as a way of theorizing indices of effectivity. As an example, Althusser notes briefly in the excerpt that any state apparatus, whether repressive or ideological, has a primary and secondary function. In other words, there is no such thing as a pure apparatus. Any given repressive apparatus has an ideological function. Similarly, any given ideological apparatus can, in a secondary way, function by repression. The excerpt famously mentions school, for example: "Schools and Churches use suitable methods of punishment, expulsion, selection, etc., to 'discipline' not only their shepherds, but also their flocks" (Althusser 1971: 145).

School discipline, in this sense, is a kind of repressive force exerted within an ideological state apparatus. Police and military academies, on the other hand, are ideological institutions within the repressive state apparatus. In the excerpt, the repressive state apparatus "contains: the Government, the Administration, the Army, the Police, the Courts, the Prisons, etc." (Althusser 1971: 145) and therefore "'functions by violence'—at least ultimately (since repression, e.g. administrative repression, may take non-physical forms)." In *OTRC*, we get more detail. The army, navy, armed units, police, courts, and prisons compose that apparatus (Althusser 2014: 108).

Althusser therefore writes that "'repressive' should be understood, at the limit (for there exist many, very varied and even very subtly occulted forms of *non-physical* repression), in the strong, precise sense of 'using *physical violence*' (direct or indirect, legal or 'illegal')" (Althusser 2014: 75). The repressive state apparatus (RSA) is a "single, centralized corps" (92) that exerts violent force, presenting itself as "an *organic whole* ... that is *consciously and directly led* from a *single center*" (135). He gives the example of Paris police chief Maurice Grimaud using both physical repression and persuasion to battle students and workers in the May 1968 rebellion. Thus repressive force—exerted by a cohesive group of institutions from army to police to courts, governments, and prisons—is preponderantly violent force that can rely on ideological force as well, but in a secondary way. In Cohen's simple structure, the RSA is the roof.

Conversely, ideological state apparatuses "function in *overwhelmingly preponderant fashion on ideology*, while functioning secondarily on repression" (86). Althusser gives an example of this mixture of ideology with repression in the ISAs, oft-cited in educational research:

> The school and the Church, to take only those two examples, "train" not just their officiants (teachers and priests), but also their wards (schoolchildren, the faithful, and so on) with the appropriate methods of punishment (once exclusively and often still physical and also, of course, "moral"): expulsion, selection, and so on. (86)

Naming the school and church explicitly, Althusser points to the fact that they train their authority figures with methods of punishment that can be physical, like corporal punishment or moral forms of punishment. Examples include expulsion and selection. Althusser concludes that "very subtle combinations of repression and ideologization, explicit or tacit, are forged *in and among all the state apparatuses*" (86). In capitalism, these forces seek to "guarantee the conditions for the exploitation of the exploited classes by the dominant classes, above all the reproduction of the relations of production" (93). Althusser next goes into detail regarding aspects of the repressive force, which are worth mentioning before he begins an explicit focus on schooling.

To review, an apparatus is a mode of intervention which classes use to further their purposes. Consistent with Gramsci's theory of hegemony he says that both ruling classes and subordinate classes can use apparatuses in the terrain of struggle, but of course the ruling classes have a leg up in the balance of forces. In *OTRC*, Althusser makes the crucial distinction between state power and state apparatus to clarify the constant struggle with and for hegemony between all groups of a social formation. On the one hand there is the "possession ... the seizure or conservation of *state power*" (73). On the other hand, there is the "state apparatus [which] can remain in place even after political events which affect *the possession of state power*" (73). Groups struggle with one another over state power for the use and control of state apparatuses.

He cites the Russian Revolution as an example. "Even after a social revolution, like that of 1917, a large part of the state apparatus remained in place after an alliance of the proletariat and poor peasantry seized state power" (73). In an even clearer articulation of the distinction, Althusser defines the "objective of the class struggle" as "the possession of state power and, consequently, use of the state" (74). Toeing a popular political line, Althusser's concept of class struggle is for the working class to get in the driver's seat of existing state apparatuses and use those apparatuses' reproductive and repressive forces to their benefit.

In *OTRC*, in the chapter, "Political and Associative Ideological State Apparatuses," which focuses on political parties and unions, he cites a speech of Lenin's from 1921, arguing that a trade union

> is not a *state organization; nor is it one designed for coercion*, but for education. It is an organization designed to draw in and train; the union is, in fact, a school: a school of administration, a school of economic management, a school of communism. It is a very unusual type of school because there are no teachers or pupils. (Althusser 2014: 105, in Lenin 1965: 20)

As educational researchers, the passage stands out for its mention of schooling. Yet Althusser's purpose in citing the passage is not to emphasize how schools and other ISAs exert a non-physical violent force of political coercion by swaying their members, whether students or union members, toward a particular line, communist or otherwise (as Lewis 2017 claims). Althusser is rather pointing out that unions and political parties are just the opposite: they are non-coercive, just like schools. The comparison of unions to schools is more a general point about the difference between repressive and reproductive force. People learn things in unions. They learn administration, economic management, and perhaps, communism. Unions, in principle at least, do not exert a preponderantly repressive force (like police action and a good part of the law) but rather a reproductive force, which Althusser equates with ideology and education. The ISAs do not exert repressive, violent, coercive force. They work with ideology. In Cohen's simple structure, the ISAs are the middle part where people live.

The rule of special thirds stipulates the proportions of force the two superstructures wield, as well as the combined force they exert with respect to the base, each part and subpart relatively autonomous from the others. Effectivities can vary within these proportions. There is no set amount that one practice, institution, or apparatus can exert within the bounds of its relative autonomy within the formation. And all of these apparatuses can change hands depending on the struggle for hegemony. Now we can turn to the famous ISAs and what it means to say that school is one such apparatus.

6

The System, Toe, and Anchor Rules: ISA Basics

In *OTRC*, Althusser points out something that "Marx, Lenin, Stalin, and Mao" already know "[from] *the terrain of political practice*" (Althusser 2014: 74). Writing as a rearguard theoretician, Althusser proposes to "sketch [the] corresponding theory" of what these communist political leaders already know. This tactic is in tune with the rest of *OTRC* and *Lenin and Philosophy and Other Essays*, but it is also a trend that runs throughout Althusser's work. As a theorist working both as a researcher, educator, and intellectual for a mainstream political party, his theory is rooted in mainstream communist political practice.

Althusser knows that theoretical work is subordinate to political organizing. He clearly says "we cannot put forward a single proposition *that is not already contained in the records of the political practice of the proletarian class struggle*" (74–5). He sees his work as "*giving theoretical form* to something that has already been recognized in the practice" (75). This rearguard process of giving theoretical form to political practice "is, or can be, *very important* for the class struggle itself. Without revolutionary theory (of the state), no revolutionary movement" (75). Revolutionary theory, for Althusser, must come from the history of political practice and not the other way around. Theorists do not produce a theory which organizers follow. Rather, organizers do their work and theorists' job is to give it form.

Althusser's contribution in this moment is that the Marxist theory of the state should include the ideological state apparatus. In the excerpt, those in power act "directly in the class struggle by means of the RSA and indirectly by means of the realization of the State Ideology in the ISAs" (138). Althusser's thinking in the excerpt is well-known, but the details in *OTRC* have only been available recently. First, a note about what the term ideology refers to at this moment in the text. While Althusser's full theory of ideology comes at the end of both the excerpt and *OTRC*, Althusser says the State Ideology sums up essential values that the ruling class needs everyone in a society to follow and makes everyone go all by themselves. In a capitalist society, those values are nationalism, liberalism, economism, and humanism (138–9).

In *OTRC*, Althusser provisionally lists eight ISAs: (1) the scholastic apparatus, (2) the familial apparatus, (3) the religious apparatus, (4) the political apparatus, (5) the associative apparatus, (6) the information and news apparatus, (7) the publishing and distribution apparatus, (8) the cultural apparatus (75). Again, the ISAs are diverse, relatively autonomous and are differently pliable when it comes to their use as tools of intervention (137). They are under different degrees of control by the state. And finally, these ISAs are in tension with one another, "grating" one another in ways that hinder, contradict, and complicate their work (137).

In fact, this is the first insight of a series of three remarks in *OTRC* that "arrive at a provisional but clear definition" (75) of ISAs. First, many organizations "correspond to each ISA" (76) and ultimately comprise the ISA. Althusser gives the scholastic ISA as an example: "the various schools and their various levels, from the primary to the tertiary, the various institutes, and so on" (76). He includes "the famous associations of parents of schoolchildren" in the familial ISA (76). Thus, for each ideological state apparatus there will be many organizations corresponding to it.

Yet these organizations are not diffused and unrelated when it comes to the corresponding ISA. Althusser's second remark is that the organizations comprising of the ISA "form a system" such that "we cannot discuss *any one component part* of an ISA without relating it to the *system* of which it is a part" (76). This is the system rule: an ISA is a system of institutions, not any singular institution. Political parties are organizations comprising the political ISA. The Democratic Party in the United States is part of the political ISA, as is the Republican Party. Trade unions are organizations comprising the associative ISA, but are part of the system of associations including social movements, and so on. Schools are organizations within the scholastic ISA, but are part of the system of that ISA, which includes bodies as diverse as universities, non-profits, and childcare facilities. We might speculate that any organization or institution whose mission is to provide instruction in the competencies of qualification and submission to ideology would comprise the scholastic ISA.

This insight that the ISA is a system of diverse institutions, organizations, and "activities" (78) is a response to what Althusser calls the "legalistic objection that might be raised against our concept of the Ideological State Apparatuses" (81). The objection is to the categorization of all ISAs as state ISAs. While some of the diverse institutions, organizations, and activities will be public sector institutions and others in the private sector, others (like schools) can be both depending on the country: "In certain capitalist countries, a large proportion of the schools (for example, two-thirds of higher education in the USA) ... belong, or can belong, to the private sector" (79). If some ISAs are in the private sector, how could they be state apparatuses? Althusser gives two responses that help clarify what ISAs are, particularly with respect to school.

First, singular legal institutions are not the type of thing we are talking about. An ISA is not this or that institution, but rather a system of organizations and institutions. Whereas public or private law would individuate institutions and organizations as being public or private, Althusser's theory picks out an entirely different kind of social thing, a system of institutions that may be public or private (81). Second, the designation of private and public sector "concerns only the status, that is, the definition, of the legal *persons* who hold formal title to this or that institution" (79). There are individual private legal persons (like a CEO), collective private legal persons (like a monastic order), and collective state legal persons ("our state educational system"), and so on (80). But the legal status of persons in charge of the ISA are beside the point and "not germane" (80). On the one hand, legal status is a formal consideration while the question about ISAs has to do with specific content, to which law is ambivalent. On the other hand, to get caught up in the legal status of certain organizations is to miss the point. Whether an ISA is administered and financed by private legal persons or public legal persons—whether by government or by individuals holding it as property—"they *know* perfectly well how to toe the bourgeois state's political line when they have to" (80). This is the toe rule: what it means for an apparatus to be a site and tool for intervention by a class is for the people in that apparatus to toe certain political lines.

The question is not whether an ISA is in the public or private sector, the question is which class fraction currently holds state power and makes interventions with the RSA and ISAs to maintain their dominance. In other words, what matters is who toes which lines. From the Marxist perspective, if the dominant relations of production are capitalist relations of exploitation, then the ruling class of a capitalist mode of production (the people who control the means of production) will, in diverse ways, understand the ISAs as a venue for making interventions on their behalf to reproduce those relations. They do this by making sure people in those apparatuses toe their line (Colin Kaepernick is one vivid contemporary example of what happens when the line is not toed). Nothing is guaranteed, of course, but such is dominance (81).

In summary, when it comes to the ISAs, whether they are public or private does not matter. Rather, "what matters is how they function. Private institutions can perfectly well 'function' as Ideological State Apparatuses." Charter schools in the United States are an interesting example. Insofar as private can mean marketized, or administered by a nongovernment entity, the exponential increase of charter schools in the United States is an increase in the extent to which schools are private. Charter schools are publicly-funded, privately-operated educational institutions.

If we follow Althusser on this point, then—at least when it comes to the way in which an institution or system of institutions contribute to class struggle—it should not matter whether a school is private, public, or charter: it still "functions" the same way. In one sense, Althusser is obviously wrong when it comes to charter schools. Recent history has shown that it makes a big difference, in terms of governance and finance, whether schools are controlled by non-profit organizations, for-profit corporations, or school boards or whose officials are either elected by the community or are appointed by elected representatives. Faculty and staff rights in the workplace, infrastructure, and the stability of the school institution hinge on who governs and funds schools. However, in another sense, Althusser is right in saying that the educational apparatus functions the same in the wider class struggle whether it is private or public or otherwise. A school will still be a school, in terms of the force it exerts when used by the ruling class, whether or not it is governed and financed in a certain way. There will still be some version of teaching, learning, and studying at the school. There will be some arrangement of students according to some curriculum, delivered with some pedagogy. From the point of view of the ISA, the school will still be a school, whether charter or non-charter. Charter schools and public schools exist within a system of diverse institutions that makes interventions to instruct young people in the requisite competencies (qualification and submission) for capitalist relations of exploitation.

A note about the term function. Althusser's focus is on the extent to which people in the state "toe the bourgeois state's political line when they have to" (2014: 80), and not a machine making them function in a deterministic way. His use of the terms function and machine are figurative rather than technical. An apparatus functions in this sense only when people in those institutions toe the dominant line, which in this case means engaging in a practice under duress from leadership. It means to act under pressure in accordance with those that have power, authority, or influence. ISAs function to the extent that people toe the line. They act under duress, feeling pressure from ruling class blocs to do and think certain ways. This does not mean that they only ever do and act in those certain ways. But it means that there are material consequences for not toeing that line (loss of a job, reprimand, docked pay, corporal punishment, shaming). When people toe the line in institutions, those institutions function to secure the interests of ruling classes. People and their institutions may resist, accommodate, or diverge from that line in all kinds of ways. It is thus possible to say that the apparatus functions without conceiving of it as an equilibrium maintenance machine devoid of class struggle. Again, I call this the toe rule: an apparatus functions insofar as people toe ruling class lines in its institutions and organizations, securing ruling class interests under pressure.

Crucially, Althusser specifies that what happens in schools is not reducible to this ideologization. In *OTRC* Althusser is explicit that cultural practices are not reducible to the ideology which they anchor. Rather, these practices serve as a support for ideology. Sports, film, theater, and literature are "not reducible to the ideology for which they serve as a support" (77). The same holds true for school, where schooling practices are irreducible to the ideology that those practices anchor. This insight is the anchor rule: culture anchors ideology but is not reducible to it.

Ideological state apparatuses, which are systems of institutions, function to maintain the continuity of the ruling class's preferred relations of production by pressuring people in institutions to toe the line. The cultural practices in these institutions anchor ideologies, but the practices themselves are not reducible to the ideologies (like humanism, nationalism, and economism). In *OTRC*, Althusser thus sets out a definition of ISAs as the following:

> An Ideological State Apparatus is a system of defined institutions, organizations, and the corresponding practices. Realized in the institutions, organizations, and practices of this system is all or part (generally speaking, a typical combination of certain elements) of the State Ideology. The ideology realized in an ISA ensures its systemic unity on the basis of an "anchoring" in material functions specific to each ISA; these functions are not reducible to that ideology, but serve it as a support. (77)

7

The Causality Rule: Grey Cows and Green Cheese

A philosophical question emerges here. What does it mean for an institution or practice to correspond to an ideology? One response is that institutions, organizations, and their practices enact a prefabricated ideology. This view would, as Althusser says, "grant that institutions could ... *follow* their ideology, that ideology could, in some sense, 'produce' institutions" (Althusser 2014: 81). In this case, ideology precedes practice or institution. Althusser is against this claim and chides Stalin's 1938 pamphlet *Dialectical and Historical Materialism* as advocating this position. The general secretary, he says, makes "an astonishing slip and, what is more, an *idealist* slip" (81) by arguing that ideology produces institutions.

Althusser articulates the materialist alternative to Stalin's idealist slip: "a right-thinking materialist should, putting the horse before the cart, have talked *first* about the institutions, and *then* (only afterwards, in the sense of derived) about the ideology corresponding to them" (82). So a second view, more materialist than the first, is that: "institutions do not 'produce' the ideologies corresponding to them. Rather, *certain elements of an ideology (the State Ideology) 'are realized in' or 'exist in' the corresponding institutions and their practices*" (82). In this case, practice precedes ideology. There is no ideology without the practices in which they exist.

Althusser goes so far as to say that it would put the cart before the horse to say that ideology precedes practice, thus clearly rejecting a Stalinist philosophical position about the relationship between ideology and practice. In the same breath, he mentions how this dynamic plays out in schools: "scholastic practice produces particular forms that may be termed *scholastic ideology* (the ideology of elementary school teachers, realized in the publications and initiatives of the SNI [the "main schoolteachers' union"], or teachers in secondary schools and higher education, and so on" (83). Rather than ideology producing certain practices in school, for Althusser, it is precisely the opposite: practices in schools produce particular forms of ideology.

To be more precise, Althusser claims that practices realize ideology. He mentions two kinds of ideology in this sense. First, there are ideologies from outside the apparatus realized in its practices. But there can also be "ideology that is 'produced' in this apparatus by its practices" (83). These ideologies emerge within the apparatus itself. Althusser names the former primary ideology and the latter secondary ideology. While practices realize elements of primary ideologies, secondary ideologies "are produced by a conjunction of complex causes" (83). They are a by-product of complex events, among which are "the effect of other, external ideologies, other external practices and, in the last instance, the effects—however veiled—of the *class struggle*, even its remote effects" (83). In other words, there are "ideological sub-formations 'secreted' by the practices of these institutions" (84). Those sub-formations are secondary ideologies.

These secondary ideologies emerge alongside the practice of the primary ideologies and can contradict and resist them. When people in ISAs toe the dominant line "this does not take place without 'contradictions'" (88), so we should not be surprised—in fact, Althusser says it is inevitable—that these secondary ideologies resist those of the ruling classes. "Produced in the apparatuses" such as they are, the secondary ideologies "sometimes 'make the gears grate and grind'" (88). When it comes to schools' relationship to class struggle, both primary and secondary ideologies are practiced in the institution. This insight is a key part of Althusser's anti-Stalinist theory of ideology.

Althusser returns to the student movements of 1968 to illustrate how schools and class struggle relate, but in a materialist way that does not put the cart before the horse and falls prey to Stalin's idealism: "no one will presume to deny [how the class struggle has effects in the form of secondary ideologies] if he pays a little attention to what has been going on now in the ideology ... in and around 'schools' (from May on)" (84). He continues:

> Everyone knows that, because "protest" is infectious, some ... teachers are balking, now that their pupils, those little devils, who (my God, but why?) no longer have any respect for "authority" and are no longer inclined to take the moon for green cheese—to the utter dismay of the Most Respectable Associations of Parents of Schoolchildren. (Althusser 2014: 88)

In this case we have both primary and secondary ideologies, each an effect of the class struggle. On the one hand, there is the official curriculum. In Althusser's acerbic phrasing, this means taking the moon for green cheese, or some content that toes the line favored by the bourgeoisie and their allies. Taking the moon for green cheese might be the happy story of pilgrims eating Thanksgiving dinner with indigenous peoples. It could be removing science from its problem-posing origins. In any case, the ruling class has an interest in certain curricular material and exerts its influence most likely via institutions in the scholastic ISA-like think tanks, for-profits, parent associations, university departments, and departments of education at the state and federal levels.

But then comes May 1968. Students (some of them in high school!) are setting bombs off in American corporate offices in Paris. The general strike happens. Suddenly protest is infectious and Parents Associations complain that students act like little devils and no longer have any respect for authority. The students do not immediately take the moon for green cheese. These are secondary ideological sub-formations that emerge internally to the institution, resistant to the official curriculum, pushing back against the ruling class's preferred practices. This is what it means for a school to be an ISA: school practices are part of the class struggle. Thus students living "every single day of [their] humdrum lives" (87) experience the class struggle firsthand at school.

Yet something is unclear. We know from the above analysis that the causal relationship between class struggle and school is not exactly linear. Ideology is realized in the institution. The issue of causality between school and class struggle, indeed the entire social formation of which it is a part, is still unsettled. The question for Althusser is how to put the horse in front of the cart and avoid Stalin's mistake when thinking about school and its corresponding ideologies. The causal relationship must not be that the ideology produces the institution. Using the example above, how should we think about the causal relationship between dominant relations of exploitation, the official curriculum, events like those of May 1968, and subsequent student resistance to the official curriculum? Are the parents associations right? Did the student rebellions cause incredulity in younger students, inspiring the kids to no longer swallow the official curriculum? For that, Althusser draws from a surprising resource.

Althusser is after a materialist account of the "relations between the primary ideological formations, which are external to the institutions" and the "secondary ideological sub-formations internal to them" (85). In distinguishing between materialist causality and idealist causality, at least in *OTRC*, Althusser relies on a critique Hegel made of Schelling's concept of the Absolute, namely whether and how to make distinctions within the Absolute. According to Hegel, Schelling understands the Absolute as "the night in which, as the saying goes, all cows are grey" (85). Each cow in a field is idiosyncratically patterned but, when viewed in the darkness, one might not be able to see these patterns. But just because it is night does not mean those patterns go away. The comment is an illustration of the philosophical mistake in attributing false sameness.

An unfamiliar partner (usually Hegel is a conceptual bogeyman for him), Althusser likens his position on causality to Hegel's comment on Schelling. Ultimately the insight here is about kinds of thinking. One kind of cognition fails to see the differences in patterns and another seeks those differences. The question then is about how one conceives of relationships between entities in reality. Althusser applies this distinction to class struggle and ISAs like schools. One form of thought sees all cows as grey in the night, which Hegel dismisses "as drivel" (84). According to this drivel, cause and effect is a simple reaction. Stalin, or some other idealist, would draw such simple linear causal connections between ideology and their corresponding institutions. The idealist wants to claim that one causes or produces the latter. Of course, this idealist would say, ideological formations cause primary ideologies, which in turn cause secondary ideologies that react back on the primary formations, because of the principle of interaction. Althusser agrees this "interaction scheme" (84) is drivel.

In *OTRC*, he calls this kind of idealist-determinist thinking fustian, referring to Hegel's critique of Schelling (84). Althusser is clear that the relationship between practices like education and class struggle is dialectical. So when the idealist says that secondary ideologies must react back upon primary ideologies, or claim that A causes B causes C, Althusser calls such thinking cloudy or turgid language (fustian) because it attributes a false sameness to the social events in question. Attributing a linear causality between ideological formations, secondary ideologies, and class struggle is a significant mistake in thinking, one that confuses important distinctions and their context. Deterministic thinking that poses simple causal relationships between social things is to refuse difficult, uneven, and complex features of social formation. This particular insight about unevenness and causality in society is one of the main currents in Althusser's thinking, the best expression of which is the 1965 essay *Contradiction and Overdetermination* (2005). When it comes to the Parents Associations, Althusser is therefore skeptical of their worries that young children were getting dangerous ideas in their heads and questioning authority because of May 1968. Indeed, children do not obey authority or swallow the official curriculum for a variety of reasons specific to their situations. It might be the case that some kids were more emboldened by the university students' actions of May 1968. But it could also have been the case that the teacher did not gain the respect of his students, or the students' families in that area were undergoing hardship, or a scandal had broken out in the school. Or, perhaps most likely, parents were displacing their anxieties about May 1968 onto what was just the evergreen issue of children misbehaving. Althusser is skeptical of their public worries about May 1968's influences because his concept of causality is complex, which permits his well-founded incredulity regarding their statements. In doing so, he defends May 1968 from detractors.

Althusser's rejection of simple deterministic causality has important implications for ISAs. There may very well exist "direct relations" between the primary ideological formations external to institutions and secondary ideological sub-formations internal to them (Althusser 2014: 85). But Althusser makes an important clarification that the causality inherent to the class struggle is distinct from the "so-called dialectical laws of interaction" advanced by idealists, like those following the Stalinist line (85). Althusser rejects the deterministic and perhaps functionalist notion that causality is transitive, linear, and simple. The class struggle and its ideological effects are not like a series of billiard balls (as the old analogy would have it), one event or action clearly hitting another and causing obvious impact. Class struggle is a different reality, one for which the laws of action and reaction cannot account.

Rather, school practices are overdetermined by multiple causes. We can point to another rule here, the causality rule. This rule says that any causal relationship in society must be structural. When it comes to correspondence between school structure and economic structure, each exerts a relatively autonomous force. The moon and green cheese example Althusser gives demonstrates his complex, uneven theorization of causality between school and class struggle.

Althusser then gives another example of structural causality and education: Lenin's focus on the scholastic apparatus. He says Lenin knew that the "future 'construction of socialism'" (91) depended on ultimately destroying the existing repressive state apparatus and replacing the ISAs, all of which—not only the scholastic apparatus—serve educational purposes. But ISAs are subject to the friction and conflicting movements of class struggle. The materialist reality of class struggle, to Althusser, requires a non-linear concept of causality, and Lenin knew this. ISAs like schools therefore undergo shocks of the class struggle where ideological sub-formations anchored in aspects of their practices can form. They are therefore "*relatively fragile* apparatuses" compared to the RSAs (89). ISAs are sensitive and get "shaken up by the conjuncture" (114). Thus ISAs can thus be grated and grinded (89) through contradictions emerging from social forces that cause secondary ideologies which find support in their practices.

Yet the fragility ISAs exhibit (the fact that secondary ideologies can even form at all) is misleading, for they are also "*extraordinarily strong and tough*" (89). Thus Lenin's worry about education. Those old-model ISAs leftover from before the revolution may remain in place such that "if the old ideology is not rooted out" its leftover roots might "survive, reproduce, and spawn a terribly dangerous effect, insinuating itself for good and all into one and another weak spot in the relations of production or the political relations of the socialist state" (91). If these weeds of the old ISAs are not pulled then one can lose the revolution. Althusser concludes that Lenin knew, in his approach to schools, that "things could not be settled by 'decree' from on high" but rather this project of replanting revolution's garden requires long experimentation with new ISAs (91). Rather, this kind of education requires persuasion and explanation rooted in a knowledge that is at once detailed and emerges from experimentation outside the vanguard. Building socialism requires planting new ISAs and uprooting the old ones through intentional planning, the process cannot be done in a top-down way, with "coercive administrative measures" (91). Rather, "it has to come through a struggle that plays to mass appeal but removes the old ISAs … This involves education, persuasion, and constant explanation" (91). The process is complex. The results will be uneven.

This particular kind of non-coercive, revolutionary education which gives exploitation no quarter also depends on appeals to mass judgment, action, initiative, and invention. Althusser is explicit: a vanguard will not hand down the precious knowledge of revolution to the people. Rather organizers will understand, take up, and take seriously what everyday people think, appealing to their inventions and actions and initiatives. Historically, Althusser gestures toward Stalin's practical mishandling of this project. He writes that Stalin "neglected these questions" (92). He rhetorically asks "Where are the Soviets, the trade unions, and the proletarian school system today, after Stalin, in the USSR?" (92).

In a footnote of the excerpt, Althusser mentions an essay by Nadezhda Krupskaya, Lenin's wife and comrade, on the history of this attempt to secure the future of the Soviet proletariat's ruling status in the Russian social formation through school. The essay Althusser might be referring to (he does not cite the work itself) is "Lenin's Role in the Struggle for Polytechnical Schools," dated originally from 1932, which *OTRC* cites explicitly. Althusser mentions this essay to drive home the point that securing control of a state apparatus in the long-term requires taking control of ISAs like schools as well as repressive state apparatuses. Krupskaya's essay also gives a good example of how the school apparatus exerts a reproductive force in communist thinking.

In *OTRC*, Althusser mentions that, if there were a different dominant mode of production, then the law might not exist in any recognizable form. If there were no difference in who controls the means of production, for example, then perhaps the law would "wither away" (2014: 61). Yet education does not wither away. Lenin believed that polytechnical education would make students capable of coping with their tasks in a society without relations of capitalist exploitation. This difference between inculcating capabilities to cope with socialist relations of production and thus perhaps law's "withering away" shows the difference between repressive and reproductive force. While the schools exert a largely reproductive force when creating the capabilities that furnish socialist relations of production (they renew those relations), when those relations of production take hold in a social formation, the law, as it is practiced to ensure capitalist relations of production, would wither away (since their purpose is to ensure capitalist relations of production's proper functioning).

Lenin's education policy is an example of how important the ISAs are in social change, and also an example of institutions producing ideology rather than vice versa since they are subject to struggle. They are not machines but rather sensitive organisms. The ISAs are like weeds, both fragile and tough. Their sensitivity is an example of the complex concept of causality at play in Althusser's thinking, as well as the uneven, overdetermined, and subtle ways that practices can anchor different ideologies.

8

The Struggle Rule: The Necessity of Contingency

After mentioning the example of Lenin and Krupskaya's work on Soviet schooling, Althusser makes a point in the excerpt that many critical educational researchers might find surprising. He states that ISAs are a site for "bitter class struggles" because workers resist, fight, and win significant gains there:

> The class (or class alliance) in power cannot lay down the law in the ISAs as easily as it can in the (repressive) State apparatus, not only because the former ruling classes are able to retain strong positions there for a long time, but also because the resistance of the exploited classes is able to find means and occasions to express itself there, either by the utilization of their contradictions, or by conquering combat positions in them in struggle. (Althusser 1971: 46)

Much critique of Althusser in critical education focuses on how his theory does not make room for working-class agency, yet this passage clearly says that the exploited classes can conquer positions against the ruling class while struggling against them, just as Lenin and Krupskaya note in their writings on education. He even uses the word resistance to name the project of workers' victorious struggle against capitalists in the ISAs. The ISAs, in fact, are harder for the ruling class to control and are ripe for the exploited class to find means and occasions to express itself there, and even win victories in struggle.

This passage is evidence of what was always true about social reproduction theories like Althusser's: social forces exerted by ruling class practices always attempt to maintain ruling class power in the context of struggle. Forces are never successful by definition and no group's power is absolute. Groups in a struggle fight with one another, winning and losing on different terrains under differing circumstances. Worker resistance, specifically in ideological reproduction, was always built into the Marxist theory (Backer 2017).

In a footnote, citing Marx's own words on class struggle and ideology, Althusser goes further to say that exploited classes can "turn the weapon of ideology against the classes in power" (Althusser 1971: 147). In *OTRC*, Althusser goes into more detail by providing numerous examples of resistance. He cites workers' unions battles for recognition (Althusser 2014: 116), as well as an example from Spain, where Carlos Franco's fascist government set up trade unions to advocate their political line, though the unions pushed back (97). In "Student Problems," Althusser makes this case explicitly for schools. He writes that teachers are a front line against ideological content. Their knowledge can be "weapons of scientific learning" (Althusser 1964: 15) and they offer "scientific and critical training" that the "government fears" (15). Whether unions, antifascist struggle, or classrooms, the fact of the matter is that people organize to exert counterforces against the ruling class on ideological terrain. That "fact" is the fact of class struggle, which is at the heart of Althusser's theory of the ISAs.

Indeed, in his discussion of political and associative ISAs, like parties and trade unions, in *OTRC* Althusser lays out an argument for ISAs as a terrain in the class struggle. He does so by articulating what appears to be a paradox. Even if a social formation's dominant mode of production is capitalist, proletarian parties and trade unions can and do exist. They are not just puppets of the social structure. At the same time, political parties and trade unions are "component parts of the ISAs in a social formation dominated by the bourgeoisie." Althusser says this looks like a paradox: "How can a component part of the system of an ISA figure in the system of a bourgeois ISA, while being the realization of an ideology of proletarian class struggle?" (Althusser 2014: 95). It should be the case in principle that either an ISA is working for the dominant relations of production or not. But the paradox is not a paradox at all if one considers class struggle.

> The answer is simple. It has to do, not with the "logic" of the system of corresponding ISAs, but, rather, with the logic of a long *class struggle* that *imposed* legal recognition of the party and ... trade unions as well as their inscription in the ISAs in question. It was as organizations of proletarian class struggle that these organizations, by dint of their struggle in the history of the French social formation, imposed this recognition and this inscription: *hence by force*. It is by dint of class struggle that they are able to preserve their proletarian class ideology in the ISAs in question. (95)

Dominant groups sometimes have to compromise with subordinate groups because of the force the latter can marshal in struggle. By dint of that class struggle, the supposed paradox of proletarian groups succeeding within bourgeoisie apparatuses dissolves. But we should be humble about the difficulty of this struggle. Take the example of political parties and trade unions. What holds for these ISAs is instructive for understanding class struggle in schools.

Organizers working to fight a class struggle internal to an ISA will confront a unique terrain whose dynamic is influenced by the larger society but is not reducible to it. When they organize, they can exert a unique nonzero force with its own character, one that cannot be reduced to the struggle in the mode of production, for example. This insight is consistent with the special thirds rule, as well as the causality rule. But the insight is distinct. So we have another rule: the rule of struggle says that ISAs are in the class struggle such that forces act on them and they act on the larger balance of which they are a part. Struggle does not guarantee successful action or full determination. Rather, being in class struggle (and understanding social stuff through class struggle) means facing different terrains that may reflect one another, but only in very limited ways. Indeed, Althusser says there is a "(sometimes grating) 'harmony'" (141) between regions of society, erupting in events like revolutions.

Schools can be part of that grating. They form an ISA like the political and associative ISAs, yet the force they exert is distinctive in the wider formation. Just like there is no paradox in saying that socialist organizations and institutions can exist within bourgeois ISAs, there is no paradox in saying that socialist schools, practices, or policies can exist within the bourgeois school ISA. In a footnote about schools and engineers from *OTRC*, Althusser makes this point clearly and foreshadows his thinking about ideology, showing again the influence of May 1968 on his thinking about schooling in capitalist social formations.

> The fact that engineers, even young engineers, who are stuffed with a heavy dose of economistic-humanist ideology in their school years, really "experience" (for themselves, and even when they have the "best of intentions") their status and work as *purely technical* makes no difference here. Given that they are educated in their schools in conformity with an ideology which, by a happy coincidence (such is not always the case: hence the "friction" that can indeed go quite far when "circumstances" are favorable, as happened in May, for example), also holds sway in the enterprises in which they are employed, how can anyone expect them not to "experience" their ideology as if it were the "nature of things"? (Althusser 2014: 36)

It might seem like these engineering students are passive receptacles of dominant knowledge, their curriculum corresponding rigidly to the existing division of labor. Yet the parenthetical about May 1968 is there in the text, injecting contingency, agency, and struggle into the apparently rigid relationship between school and capitalism. The ruling class certainly has students and teachers toeing the line in the official engineering curriculum, but such is not always the case as there is significant friction as well in the form of resistance, organizing, and movement.

When it comes to schools, Althusser notes that we should not get ahead ourselves. Schools are not necessarily what will bring about revolution. Rather "*what the bourgeoisie fears above all things* is (listed in order of increasing importance): 1) political unity between the workers' parties; 2) trade union unity between workers' unions; 3) and, *above all, above all,* unity between these two forms of unity" (122). Each of these are stages which have thresholds after which the bourgeoisie react. When it comes to stage one, the bourgeoisie have a "*state of alert*"; stage two inspires a "*state of emergency*"; while stage three "reaches the level of '*martial law*'" (122).

School is absent from these levels of alert. In fact, the bourgeoisie can tolerate "the simultaneous ideological revolt of the young people in school (in one segment of the scholastic ISA)" (122). Yet Althusser also says that May 1968 "warned the bourgeoisie that it had to exercise extreme vigilance" (123). The difference between a warning, threat, emergency, and martial law are in their effectivity. While not necessarily a central threat or emergency for the ruling classes, if schools shut down it can serve as a warning to them. Thus we have one answer to the question about how schools can change society: according to Althusser's theory, schools can serve as a sharp warning to the ruling class through struggle. The working class warns them through disruptions at school because the ruling class has an interest in schools running smoothly. Thus, for Althusser, schools are the most powerful ISAs in modern capitalist societies. Few, if any, ISAs have this power.

9

The School Rule

In *OTRC*, in a chapter called "The Reproduction of the Relations of Production," Althusser expands on this claim about the school's unique power, famously made in the excerpt, that it is the dominant ideological state apparatus in modern social formations. I call this claim the school rule. It comes late in the book, after Althusser has established all the above insights about reproduction, the relations of production, the base-superstructure model, the difference between RSA and ISAs, and addressed the aspects of ISAs specifically. The claim comes comparatively early in the ISAs essay however. When read with the relevant background material from *OTRC*, the claim about schools being the dominant ISA in modern society stands out in ways not captured by traditional readings.

The first thing to establish is what it means for an ISA to be dominant. We have heard that the ISAs are "multiple, distinct, relatively autonomous," (Althusser 2014: 140), that they are both fragile and strong like weeds, and are "prone to providing an objective field of contradictions which express ... the effects of the clashes between the capitalist class struggle and the proletarian class struggle, as well as their subordinate forms." We have already heard a little about ranking these ISAs, in the sense that unions and political parties can have higher effectivities when marshaled by the working class, putting the ruling class into a state of alert and even marshal law. But when it comes to the ruling class and their waging of class struggle, Althusser's claim is that the scholastic ISA is the dominant ISA: it holds a position superior to other ISAs in terms of its effectivity for the ruling class project.

Althusser gives two reasons for this. First, historically, Althusser says the Church was the most powerful ISA. It served economic, educational, and media-related functions in a feudal society whose relations of production were characterized by serfdom (142). The Church therefore "patently existed [as] a dominant" ISA because it "concentrated within itself" these other aspects (142). To be a dominant ISA in this first sense is to be an ISA where multiple functions are concentrated within the ISA. Second, Althusser says dominance-as-concentration results in a concentration of struggle at the ISA. He uses a number to rank the dominance of the Church in pre-capitalist European societies. Because it concentrated so many functions into itself, the Church was "the number-one ISA" (143). The Church was a high-priority target of revolutionary activities because it was the number-one ISA in the social formation. To be a dominant ISA in this second sense is to be the site of concentrated social struggle.

We should note here that Althusser abstracts from very specific examples of French revolutions. The reason he believes he is "justified in advancing the ... thesis" that the scholastic ISA "has been elevated to the *dominant* position in mature capitalist social formations" is because, in those capitalist formations, there has been a "violent political and ideological class struggle against the old ISA" (143). The whole point of organizing parliamentary democracy during the revolutionary period in 1848, for example, was to "wrest [the Church's] ideological functions from it" (143) and thereby ensure political and ideological hegemony for the bourgeoisie. The Church had so many ideological functions concentrated within it that the property-owning classes had to wrest some of those functions from the Church to delegitimize the feudal order. Schools emerge as a kind of trophy in this struggle. The government educates rather than the church after secular governments came to power. (Whether this narrative is historically accurate is important, but outside the immediate bounds of our interpretation of Althusser's philosophical claim about ISA dominance as concentration.)

Note how his analysis here follows the rule of special thirds. Althusser is tracking changes in the superstructures and modes of production in the French social formation according to their indices of effectivity. Specifically, he is following the relationship between the political, religious, and the scholastic ISAs. In the feudal period, the scholastic ISA was subsumed under the religious ISA. The bourgeoisie's interest in wresting the schools from the church using parliamentary democracy is the premise on which he makes his case that the scholastic ISA is the dominant ISA in capitalist social formations. The bourgeoisie wanted education out from the Church and used the political ISAs to do it to ultimately ensure the reproduction of capitalist relations of production so the bourgeoisie could prevail over the aristocracy. In the excerpt, Althusser goes so far as to say that the school has been "installed ... against" the Church in modern social formations, that the school plays the same role as the church in its dominance (152).

The next move Althusser makes in arguing for the school rule is to disprove the notion that political systems like parliaments and congresses are the dominant ISAs. One might think that representative democracy, such as the United States has in its congress, or its separation of powers between judicial, legislative, and executive branches are dominant ISAs (143). But after running through a series of historical examples from France to England to Germany, he concludes that "the bourgeoisie has been and is still easily capable of accommodating highly variegated forms of its political ISA" (143) whether they be a constitutional monarchy, presidential democracy, parliamentary democracy, imperialist and nationalist apparatuses (144). Because the bourgeoisie does not appear to care very much about what political apparatus it uses (it can be anything from Bismarck to Hitler, or Louis XVII to Charles de Gaulle), Althusser claims as follows:

> We have solid reasons for thinking that, behind the "theatre" of the political struggles, which the bourgeoisie has offered the popular masses as a spectacle, or imposed on them as an ordeal, what it has established as its number-one, that is, its *dominant* ISA is *the scholastic apparatus*. (Althusser 2014: 144)

Their openness to various forms of government shows that the bourgeoisie has a capacious and flexible attitude about the political ISA. It could be this or that or some other system, as the history of bourgeoisie revolutions show. Capitalists can even stand robust social democracy, as the period after the Great Depression proved. In fact, this flexibility in the capitalist ruling class when it comes to governance is a kind of theater meant to distract the masses of people, either as entertainment (spectacle) or force (imposition). Government, Althusser says, is a kind of ordeal through which the majority of people have to go when seeking social change. The ruling class established the scholastic apparatus behind this theater of political struggle, putting a higher premium on it as an intervention but much less explicitly. Althusser elaborates on how the school lurks behind the rest of the political theater by using the metaphor of a symphony to describe schools' place in the ensemble. The school is this symphony's silent note. The famous claim in the excerpt reads: "In this concert, one ideological state apparatus certainly has the dominant role, although hardly anyone lends an ear to its music: it is so silent! This is the School" (Althusser 1971: 155).

The symphony metaphor sets the stage, so to speak, for another of Althusser's reasons why the scholastic ISA is the dominant ISA. Capitalists set a premium on securing educational functions during their various revolutions, getting the masses of people to pay more attention to political theater than other methods of intervention. Indeed, the ruling classes make sure to keep these educational functions hidden from view, like a silent note in a symphony. Maintaining that silence is part of how capitalists maintain hegemony: they keep their most powerful methods of intervention hidden from general attention. It would make sense for the scholastic apparatus to be the dominant ISA, in other words, precisely because it is so counterintuitive to think of it as such.

These arguments and metaphors, while interesting, may not be convincing by themselves. Sure, capitalists wrested educational functions from the Church with governance structures to win hegemony. And yes, they may have used the impressive variety of those forms of governance to create a distraction from the other ways they maintain that hegemony. But why should we think that the scholastic apparatus is dominant in the same way that the Church was dominant in pre-capitalist formations? Althusser provides more reasons, both in *OTRC* and the excerpt.

Looking at the excerpt first, the scholastic ISA—a system of organizations including everything from daycare to graduate school to educational nonprofits—works with three main steps: taking, drumming, and ejecting. Children are first taken at young ages (when they are most vulnerable). Next, with "new or old methods" the school "drums into them ... a certain amount of know-how, wrapped in the ruling ideology (French, arithmetic, natural history, the sciences, literature) or simply the ruling ideology in its pure state (ethics, civic instruction, philosophy)" (156). After so drumming them, "a huge mass of children are ejected 'into production'" (strict proletarians) while others more scholastically inclined continue further in education to become "small and middle technicians, white-collar workers, small and middle executives, petty bourgeois of all kinds." A small group becomes intellectuals, agents of exploitation (managers and capitalists), agents of repression (soldiers, policemen, politicians, administrators, etc.), and professional ideologists (priests of all sorts).

In general, the school ISA is the dominant ISA because "no other ideological state apparatus has the obligatory (and not least, free) audience of the totality of the children in the capitalist social formation, eight hours a day for five or six days of seven" (156). Through these three steps, for years and years, there is a "massive inculcation of the ideology of the ruling class" (156). This inculcation is how "the *relations of production* in a capitalist social formation, i.e. the relations of exploited to exploiters and exploiters to exploited" get reproduced. Althusser admits his Marxist analysis of the school may come as a surprise, since there is an ideology

> which represents the School as a neutral environment purged of ideology ... where teachers respectful of the "conscience" and "freedom" of the children who are entrusted to them (in complete confidence) by their "parents" (who are free, too, i.e. the owners of their children) open up for them the path to the freedom, morality, and responsibility of adults by their own example, by knowledge, literature and their "liberating" virtues. (Althusser 1971: 157)

This school ideology, which Establet and Baudelot (1973) would elaborate further in *The Capitalist School in France* a few years later, makes it the number-one ISA. As a conclusion, it is worth reading the extended passage in *OTRC* for its expanded language and claims:

> No other ISA, however, has a *captive* audience *of all the children of the capitalist social formation* at its beck and call (and—this is the least it can do—at no cost to them) *for as many years* as the schools do, eight hours a day, six days out of seven. *The relations of production* of a capitalist social formation, that is, the relations of exploited to exploiters and exploiters to exploited, are primarily reproduced in this process of acquiring what comes down, in the end, to a handful of limited types of know-how, accompanied by massive inculcation of the ideology of the dominant class. I here anticipate demonstrations that we shall soon be providing when I say that the mechanisms that produce this result, vital for the capitalist regime, are of course covered up and concealed by a *universally reigning ideology of the school*, since it is one of the essential forms of the dominant bourgeois ideology: an ideology which depicts the school as a neutral environment free of ideology (because it is ... not religious) where teachers respectful of the "conscience" and "freedom" of the children entrusted to them (in complete confidence) by their "parents" (who are free in their turn, that is, are the *owners* of their children) set them on the path to adult freedom, morality, and responsibility by their own example, and provide them access to learning, literature, and well-known "emancipatory" virtues of literary or scientific humanism ... [T]he school today [is] as "natural" and useful-indispensable or even beneficial for our contemporaries as the Church was "natural," indispensable and generous for our ancestors a few centuries ago. The fact is that *the Church has today been replaced by the school*: it has succeeded it and occupies its *dominant* sector, even if there are certain limitations on that sector. (Althusser 2014: 146–7)

We can say that the scholastic apparatus is the number one ISA because children experience schools (along with the family) for the longest period of time during the most vulnerable and plastic period of human life. Second, mainstream thinking about school tells us that it is natural, neutral, and indispensable for getting along in our society, in just the same way that church was considered natural and indispensable for getting along in society in a previous epoch.

The way schools take, drum, and eject students into production—and the duration and repetition of that process—combined with the commonsensical necessity of schooling for success in the economy, exerts a concentrated reproductive force through its practices. This unique concentration of reproductive force gives schools a pride of place in the ensemble of ISAs in modern capitalist societies. Therefore, a crisis in schools, on Althusser's analysis, "takes on a political meaning" because the institution plays "a determinant part in the reproduction of the relations of production of a mode of production threatened in its existence by the world class struggle" (157).

This conclusion is dark. Rather than paths to opportunity, safe spaces where students become citizens of a great nation and productive members of a flourishing society under the caring guidance of knowledgeable teachers, schools are places where people toe the ruling-class line to eventually get into relation with the means of production and maintain ruling-class dominance. Except for occasional contradictions, crises, and moments of friction where the process of schooling comes to a halt (like in May 1968), schools maintain and renew the ways people intertwine with various kinds of capital.

At this point in the argumentation, Althusser senses the darkness of this conclusion and, in a now-famous passage, asks teachers for a "pardon."

> I ask the pardon of those teachers who, in dreadful conditions, attempt to turn the few weapons they can find in the history and learning they "teach" against the ideology, the system and the practices in which they are trapped. They are a kind of hero. But they are rare and how many (the majority) do not even begin to suspect the "work" the system (which is bigger than they are and crushes them) forces them to do, or worse, put all their heart and ingenuity into performing it with the most advanced awareness (the famous new methods!). So little do they suspect it. (Althusser 2014: 157)

What to make of this plea to the few heroic teachers who, aware of the social forces surrounding them, attempt to teach against domination? On the one hand, a social structure exists. Further, that structure is rigid and crushing. Most teachers toe the ruling class's line without giving it a second thought (and many leave the profession after being thoroughly demoralized and overwhelmed). Indeed, anyone who has taught—particularly amidst poverty, inequality, and oppression—knows the crushing pressures Althusser mentions.

On the other hand, schools can exert a resistance in the structure. Teachers can use expert knowledge to undermine the official curriculum. Students can be little devils and refuse to swallow that curriculum. Students can even go into open revolt, warning the ruling classes. While these insurgent practices are subordinate to dominant ones, the force they can exert is far from nonzero. Althusser mentions that "since May, bourgeois families of the highest rank themselves know something about that—something irreversible that is shaking them up, and, often, even has them 'trembling'" (Althusser 2014: 147). While most do not participate in such shake ups, those that do can make the structure tremble with their actions. Althusser asks their pardon given the uphill battle they face.

The school rule is a kind of climax to Althusser's theory of education as an ideological apparatus. But a final question remains. How should teachers, students, and other school people understand their positions—specifically their own freedom—under these conditions? What does it mean to teach, learn, and study in a structure in dominance that, while big and crushing, also shifts? We can answer this question with another that Althusser has left unaddressed and to which he devotes the last chapter of *OTRC*. What is ideology?

10

The Go Rule

In the excerpt, just after Althusser's pardon to heroic teachers, comes the most cited part of the essay: "On Ideology" (Althusser 1970: 158). This juxtaposition by itself is interesting. From an educational point of view, we can read his path-breaking concept of ideology as juxtaposed with a pardon to heroic teachers, implying that the account to follow is an attempt to respond to the sad-seeming reality in which heroic teachers find themselves. So much ink has been spilled interpreting the ISAs essay and its claims about ideology that a literature review of secondary commentaries would take a book on its own (see at least Rehmann 2013 and Eagleton 2014). More is unnecessary. Instead, I shift focus in this final section to Althusser's account of interpellation in *OTRC*, pointing out key elements of that expanded account of ideology against the backdrop of the ten previous rules set out in this first part of the book.

Althusser's question in this final chapter of *OTRC* is: Why do people follow marching orders without being directly ordered to march (Althusser 2014: 181)? What makes them choose to march without anyone obviously making them? Why do people follow the rules "without there being a need to post a policeman behind each and every one of them?" (177). The answer is ideology. In the excerpt, he makes explicit reference to school in this regard. Althusser's concept of ideology—what it means to be made to go all by one's self—prioritizes "actions inserted into *practices*" within the "*material existence of an ideological apparatus*." Ideology is in the practices of a small mass, the rituals at a funeral, patterns of movement when people play sports, or during a school day (Althusser 1971: 168). In *OTRC*, Althusser provides much more detail and examples of what he means, many of which are educational and pedagogical.

Althusser first goes through several other concepts of ideology to distinguish the account he will eventually give. He rejects each of these previous positions in turn, showing what his theory of ideology is not before detailing what it is. One such theory is that ideology is like a dream (Althusser 2014: 174). In this case, ideology is "nugatory" or "sheer illusion," in the sense that it is empty and vain: a mere disordered or inverted version of reality. Brushing that theory aside, another position—again, not Althusser's—is that ideology is like the police (177). In this concept of ideology, every person is "doubled by a personal monitor" and watched over by some "Ubiquitous Grand Inquisitor" (178). Althusser calls out one particular phrasing of this police concept of ideology from social movements at the time. Students in an anarchist collective in Paris used the slogan "get rid of the cop in your head!" Althusser dismisses this idea of ideology as a cop in your head, as it confuses exploitation and repression, imbuing the repressive state apparatuses with too much authority and ultimately ignoring the role of ideology, since, as he previews his own account, everyone "'goes' all by themselves" by making ideological choices in "'good' conscience" (179). Finally, ideology for Althusser is not a set of "Beautiful Lies," (180) as in Plato's allegory of the cave. There is no "small handful of cynics" crafting ideology behind the scenes, as though a group of "priests are to blame" (182) for enshrouding the masses in shadowy half-truths.

Neither sheer illusion nor a cop in the head nor the beautiful lies of a handful of cynics, Althusser defines ideology as that which "represents individuals' imaginary relations to their real conditions of existence" (181). An image in this case is part illusion and part allusion (181). Images allude to reality because they are based on a set of real conditions of existence. Rather than sheer illusion, an image is an image of real conditions; not entirely inverted or false, it is rooted in reality. Though ideology is not just an image (like a dream, lie, or a cop in the head). To go all by one's self is precisely not to go according to someone or any one particular person or group's direction. Rather, subjects march freely without a cop behind them. The illusion however is in the speculary, or mirrored, relationship with abstract entities that endow those subject to them with choice.

As an example, Althusser mentions an individual who "believes in God, Duty, Justice, or the like" (185). In this case we have a "subject endowed with consciousness in which she freely forms or freely recognizes ideas in which she believes" (185). This subject who has freely chosen her beliefs in God or Duty goes on to "behave in such-and-such a way, adopts such-and-such a practical line of conduct and, what is more, participates in certain regulated practices, those of the ISA on which the ideas that she has as [a] subject, freely and in all 'good' conscience chosen" (185). This person freely accepts the regulated practices in the relevant ISAs (185), inscribing "her own ideas as a free subject in the acts of her material practice" (185).

To the extent that she is subject to the dominant ideologies of these ISAs is the extent to which she, or any of us, "are a (free, moral, responsible, and so on) subject"; Going all by ourselves according to these ISAs, toeing the dominant line, is thus an "ideological effect" (189). We should remember that causality in Althusser is not regular, run-of-the-mill causality. When Althusser writes "ideological effect" he does not mean that there is a thing or person simply causing that ideological effect. Rather, when it comes to social stuff single causes are absent, only present in their dispersed effects. Therefore, what you and I freely choose to do are indeed ideological effects, but the cause of those effects are only present in the effect themselves, or the material practices anchoring the ideology.

Althusser moves to another example, this time to the apostle Peter and religion. He writes that "religious ideology is indeed addressed to individuals in order to 'transform them into subjects' ... [like] Peter, in order to make him a subject free to obey or disobey the call" (195). In this example, God calls out Peter's name (or any other person so called, like Moses) to "hold the place it marks out for them in the world, a fixed abode ... in this vale of tears" (195). That fixed abode is their subject position, whether apostle or employee. Althusser writes that ideology holds places for all kinds of subject positions. People called and thus transformed into subjects by ideology are free to obey or disobey. This freedom to obey or disobey the call to be an apostle, worker, boss, or soldier (195) thus depends "on the *absolute* condition that there is a Unique, Absolute, *Other Subject*" (195).

In Peter's case, this Other Subject is God. But in the worker's case it may be the School, Economy, Nation, or even Revolution calling them to a subject position. A Big Other must call subjects into their positions to go all by themselves. Freedom for any subject depends on what Althusser (following Lacan) calls a speculary relation with a big-s Subject, a mirroring relationship between an absent cause present in the effects of material practices. For instance, "in legal ideology, the speculary relation is that of the Subject (Justice) and the subjects (men who are free and equal)" (198). Going all by one's self—to be a subject—is to enter into speculary relations with Subjects. Securing freedom means obeying or disobeying that Subject. Being free to obey or disobey in these particular ways, across ISAs, is to *marcher fait*.

This is what it means to say ideology is an imagined relation to real conditions. The image here is allusory and illusory, both rooted in reality and rooted in the presence of a Big Other with whom we enter into a kind of relationship. But relationship, in this case, does not just mean an abstract relationship. From the rule of hands, we know that relations of production are the ways people are set to work on things. Relations are how people have their hands on stuff; how they set to work together on the means of production. As such, we should understand the relation in this sense as inclusive of gestures, movements, actions, interactions, rituals. To say that ideology is an imagined relation to real condition is to say that ideologies are the ritual practices like those performed at funerals, sports, and school that give material support to images alluding to reality. In this sense, Althusser writes that relations "contain the cause" of imagined representations (183). Ideology is therefore in the way we "live and move and have our being" (189).

Put yet another way, saying that ideology is an imagined relation is to say that "ideology has a material existence" (184). Bringing in the ISAs, an imagined relation to real conditions "exists in an apparatus and in the practices of that apparatus" (184). An apparatus is a mode of intervention that classes use to advance their interests (ruling or subordinate). Ideologies are the specific practices people and groups enact as they go about the struggle.

Althusser illustrates with more examples, starting with the churchgoer: "If she believes in God, she goes to church to attend mass, kneels, prays, confesses, does penance" (185). In this case, the church is an ideological state apparatus, a mode of intervention wherein believers enact practices that anchor images related to God, spirituality, the soul, etc. Most people in that ISA toe the dominant line. They follow a dominant ideology by attending mass, kneeling, praying, confessing, and all the gestures associated with doing penance. Each of these material practices contain the cause of imagined representations that are both illusory and allude to real conditions of existence. Ideology is not the believer's beliefs. Ideology is their kneeling. Althusser cites Blaise Pascal's seventeenth century dictum 250 in the *Pensées*: "Kneel down, move your lips, and you will believe" (in Althusser 2014: 186). The practice of kneeling and praying contains the cause of religious belief. Kneeling gives material support to the imagined relation of religiosity. Once someone has repeatedly kneeled, prayed, and attended Church this person is a believer, a believing subject. They are a subject of God because, in their actions, they have established a speculary relationship with God. To the believer, it is "self-evident" (189) that they are a believer, putting them in a position to freely choose to obey or disobey accordingly.

Althusser goes so far as to say that there is no practice without an ideology, and no ideology without a subject (188). Every practice anchors one or more imagined relations to real conditions. And every imagined relation to real conditions recruits a subject. Being a subject, in this sense, means being subjected to ideology in the form of practices. Ideology is therefore how it functions. Ideology is as ideology does. Althusser names this doing-ness of ideology, or the action of ideological reproduction (when ideology propagates) "interpellation" (190): "all ideology hails or interpellates concrete individuals as concrete subjects" (190).

The French word *interpellation* did not have an English correlate and Ben Brewster, Althusser's first English translator, rendered the word directly from French. To interpellate in French is to question, interrogate, hail, or summon. An interpellation is a concrete moment of hailing, a practice that recruits individuals to become subjects of an imagined relation to real conditions. Althusser mentions in the excerpt how police hailing an immigrant, for example, makes them a subject of and subject to national law (191). When the policeman says "Hey, you there!" and the person turns around, Althusser claims that this turning is a moment of subjection. The example is well known, but there are many others in *OTRC* readers should examine.

Althusser details how he himself was interpellated by family, school, church, and political party (193). He mentions how God interpellated Moses in the Bible through the burning bush (194). He notes how babies are often interpellated into genders before they are even born, and also interpellated into family history through their names: "simply noting the ideological ritual that surrounds the expectation of a 'birth', that 'happy event'. Everyone knows how much, and how (a good deal could be said about 'how'), an unborn child is expected [to be]" and how "it will bear its father's name" (192).

Althusser explicitly states that schools, according to this concept of ideology, are "material ideological apparatuses, prescribing material practices" (Althusser 2014: 187). The school day is full of these practices. Every moment of the school day is rife with interpellations. From a ruling class perspective (and even subordinate classes), that is what ideological apparatuses, like schools and universities, are good for: to interpellate, or enact practices that contain the cause of imagined relations to real conditions, thereby recruiting people to those imagined relations. In other words, schools are supposed to make students go all by themselves: to become productive members of society.

I will put forward one last rule: the go rule. Althusser's theory of ideology is that ideology is what makes people go all by themselves. Ideology is not stuff in the head but rather actions and practices. It creates the very conditions for idiosyncratic choices within the complex and uneven balance of forces. People go all by themselves in ideology, as they live and move and have their being. Interpellations recruit them to ideologies, reproducing imagined relations to real conditions, and what emerges is an uneven social structure immanent in its dispersed effects.

In the last sections of *OTRC*, with disarming humor and detail, Althusser gives many examples of everyday human experiences to illustrate this theory of ideology as interpellation. Many critics would seize upon Althusser's alleged lack of emphasis on the personal and individual. Looking at *OTRC*, the opposite is true. The text is alive with profoundly mundane examples, like door-knocking, handshakes, and reading (189–90). While few of these mention schooling explicitly, they provide examples of the kind of everyday practices students, teachers, and other people in and around schools experience. Althusser's use of his own autobiography, starting from childhood, is a kind of educational memoir. Writing about himself in the third person, he notes the interpellations that formed him from birth to adulthood.

> When religious ideology begins to function directly by interpellating the little child Louis as a subject, little Louis is already-subject—not yet religious subject, but familial subject. When legal ideology (later, let us suppose) begins to interpellate little Louis by talking to him about, not Mama and Papa now, or God and the Little Lord Jesus, but Justice, he was already a subject, familial, religious, scholastic, and so on … Finally, when, later, thanks to auto-heterobiographical circumstances of the type Popular Front, Spanish Civil War, Hitler, 1940 Defeat, captivity, encounter with a communist, and so on, political ideology (in its different forms) begins to interpellate the now adult Louis as a subject, he has already long been, always-already been, a familial, moral, religious, scholastic, and legal subject … This political subject begins, once back from captivity, to make the transition from traditional Catholic activism to advanced—semi-heretical—Catholic activism, then begins reading Marx, then joins the Communist Party, and so on. So life goes. (Althusser 2014: 193)

Here Althusser weaves together the myriad choices, decisions, and vicissitudes he freely made, including revolutionary political choices. Yet the account also includes large structural forces Althusser could have had no power over: his family, their religious practice, and the repressive apparatus of the moment. He did not have control over big historical events like fascism in Spain or Nazi occupation. However, he did come into contact with communists and chose to pursue heretical Catholic activism, after which he pushed further left toward communism by reading Marx and then joining the Communist Party. Althusser does not cast himself or anyone else as an automaton robbed of agency, determined wholly by a set of mechanical functions. Rather, through his own theory, he understands himself as having been made subject to differential social forces exerted by complex structures, each of which interpellated him differently at different times, creating pressures which created the conditions for him to make particular choices.

Thus, a clearer account of the agency inherent in Althusser's theory of interpellation emerges. There is agency in structure precisely because of the complex, uneven, and differential forces at play in it. Consider the sheer number of forces at work in a social formation. In most situations, Althusser points to inevitable "conflicts of duties" where "familial, moral, religious, political or other duties" have to be "reconciled when 'certain' circumstances present themselves" (200). In such cases, he says explicitly: "one has to make a choice." He uses the examples of the French leaders fleeing the country rather than engaging in antifascist organizing during the Nazi occupation (200). It is a clear reference to the ways subjects make choices in situations of conflicting obligations, where uneven social forces exert pressures on subjects, who then decide one way or another. In response to the fascist threat people in leadership fled, while some citizens stayed and fought.

Althusser gives political examples as well. A notable one is the struggle over contraception and reproductive rights in the Catholic Church, focusing specifically on the pill (200). Whether Catholics should think of their families or religion first is a clear conflict between ideologies, and the battle over contraception, circa 1970, forced the issue. Catholics had to make difficult choices given the presence of new medical advances. Ideology is how people go all by themselves and make these difficult choices under complex circumstances.

A final example is worth citing at length, as its humanity and texture are a wonderful illustration of Althusser's distinct structural concept of freedom at play in this section. In *OTRC*, Althusser includes an entire section called "A Concrete Example," where he reports a "faithful transcription of a conversation with a comrade who is a lathe operator in a Citroen factory" (205).

> The proletarian, when his workday is over (the moment he has been waiting for since morning), drops everything, without further ado, when the whistle blows, and heads for the lavatories and lockers. He washes up, changes his clothes, combs his hair, and becomes another man: the one who is going to join his wife and children at home. Once he gets home, he is in a completely different world that has nothing at all to do with the hell of the factory and its production rhythms. At the same time, however, he finds himself caught up in another ritual, the ritual of the practices and acts (free and voluntary, of course) of *familial* ideology: his relations with his wife, the kids, the neighbors, parents, friends—and on Sunday, still other rituals, those of his fantasies and favorite pastimes (likewise free and voluntary): the weekend in the forest of Fontainbleau or (in a few cases) his little garden in the suburbs, and sport, and telly, and radio, God knows what; and then holidays, with still other rituals (fishing, camping, Tourism and Work, People, and Culture, God knows what). Caught up in these other "systems," my comrade added, how could he be expected not to become someone other than the man he is at the factory—for example, someone altogether different from the union militant or CGT member he is? This other "system" is, for example, (this is very often the case), the ritual of the petty-bourgeois family. Might that mean that this proletarian, "conscious and organized"' when he attends union meetings with his fellow workers, is caught in another, petty-bourgeois ideological system when he gets back home? Why not? Such things happen ... All the fuss with the kids, who have problems at school, naturally; and some very odd political goings-on, of the sort that can culminate in certain "unexpected" electoral results ... But it's hard to be a union militant and even harder to be a revolutionary militant all your life. (Althusser 2014: 206)

This portrait of a comrade is effervescent with detailed, conflicting, and complex human experience. The worker is caught up in the capitalist mode of production selling his labor, but he is a union militant working against the exploitation of those dominant relations of production. In addition to that system, he is active in the petty-bourgeois family as a father. He engages in various cultural practices, follows politics, and tries to work through the problems his kids have in school. Althusser gives this example—devotes an entire section to it—to illustrate the unevenness and complexity of ideology. The worker is free to make his choices, yet he is caught up in layers upon layers of practices anchoring imagined relations to real conditions. His agency exists in and through the balance of forces within which he finds himself. He is a subject that goes all by himself in an immanent structure.

This concept of agency is inherent in Althusser's theory of ideology as interpellation. Furthermore, it is consistent with the arguments in *OTRC* and earlier philosophical texts. Structural causality posits an immanent structure only present in its effects. There is no transcendent structure that mechanically reproduces itself and determines individual freedom. Rather, ideology is as ideology does. Subjects go all by themselves in the balance of forces, making choices amidst the many pressures coming at them from the social structure. They bear the functions set out for them in this structure. But the structure is so massive, complex, and ultimately absent, that bearing, in this sense, is an activity. The lathe operator bears his place in the social structure through his free and voluntary decisions to be active in the union, work his job, and be a father in his family. The antifascists bear their places by staying and fighting the occupiers. Women and families bear their positions by considering whether or not to take the pill and avail themselves of birth control.

People go all by themselves when they become subject to dominant or subordinate ideology, making their way in the structure through decision points amid unevenness. Dominance does not preclude subordinate, insurgent, and resistant projects. Society is churning and trembling with the struggle-laden friction inherent in the tension between dominant and subordinate forces. The struggle happens through practices that provide material support for imagined relations, all of which can maintain the continuity of dominant relations of production or challenge that dominance. Learning, schooling, and teaching are caught up in the mess with everything else.

Schools are an important part of this structure but, like every other practice, their effectivity will be indexed to other ISAs as well as the entire social structure. While education fades from view at the end of *OTRC*, Althusser makes one last mention of it in the final paragraphs of the excerpt, which summarize the go rule and other features of his theory of education.

> The ideology of the ruling class does not become the ruling ideology by the grace of God, nor even by virtue of the seizure of State power alone. It is by the installation of the ISAs in which this ideology is realized and realizes itself that it becomes the ruling ideology. But this installation is not achieved all by itself; on the contrary, it is the stake in a very bitter and continuous class struggle: first against the former ruling classes and their positions in the old and new ISAs, then against the exploited class.

> But this point of view of the class struggle in the ISAs is still an abstract one. In fact, the class struggle in the ISAs is indeed an aspect of the class struggle, sometimes an important and symptomatic one: e.g. the anti-religious struggle in the eighteenth century, or the "crisis" of the educational ISA in every capitalist country today. But the class struggles in the ISAs is only one aspect of a class struggle which goes beyond the ISAs. The ideology that a class in power makes the ruling ideology in its ISAs is indeed "realized" in those ISAs, but it goes beyond them, for it comes from elsewhere. Similarly, the ideology that a ruled class manages to defend in and against such ISAs goes beyond them, for it comes from elsewhere.
>
> It is only from the point of view of the classes, i.e. of the class struggle, that it is possible to explain the ideolog*ies* existing in a social formation. Not only is it from this starting-point that it is possible to explain the realization of the ruling ideology in the ISAs and of the forms of class struggle for which the ISAs are the seat and the stake. (Althusser 1971: 189)

Althusser's theory of ideology, as a part of his overall interpretation of Marxism, is a theory of class struggle, large social forces, and contingency; but it is also rooted in existing movements, like educational crises throughout the world in the late 1960s. The ISAs are a seat and stake of class struggle where bitter battles are fought between capital and labor, but there are forces beyond the ISAs that are crucial to consider when understanding schools and their place in society. The layers and plates of social structure grind against one another in constant friction, changes coming suddenly and intensely in the form of rebellion and revolution. The last passage of "On Ideology" from *OTRC* states the case plainly:

> When nothing is happening, the Ideological State Apparatuses have worked to perfection. When they no longer manage to function, to reproduce the relations of production in the "consciousness" of all subjects, "events" happen, as the phrase goes, more or less serious events, as in May, the commencement of a first dress rehearsal. With, at the end, some day or the other, after a long march, the revolution. (Althusser 2014: 206)

11

Conclusion

Throughout this part of the book I have set out eleven rules of thumb for understanding Althusser's theory of education, centered on the idea that education is an ideological state apparatus (ISA). These rules refer to important features of the theory and their philosophical background as articulated in *OTRC*.

1. The ISAs essay is an excerpt from a longer book project born out of Althusser's experience during May 1968. It was also meant as a concrete application of his earlier philosophical work.
2. Reproduction is the key to production. *The rule of keys* says that without the reproduction of productive forces and relations of production, the ruling class cannot maintain the continuity of their preferred mode of production. Althusser says the preservation of productive forces has received attention in Marxism, yet the preservation of relations of production gets less attention. Althusser takes the view from reproduction for this reason. His overall project in *OTRC* is to articulate this view.
3. Relations of production are how people set to work on the means of production. *The rule of hands* states that you can tell a relation of production by what people have their hands on while they make material life. In capitalist modes of production, there are relations of exploitation that divide populations into two groups: some who exploit others' labor and have their hands on the surplus-value thus expropriated, while others are exploited and lay their hands on the means of production for work.
4. In the division of labor, competencies determine differences both between exploited and exploiters, and differences among the exploited. Those competencies come in the form of knowledge learned at school; knowledge of basic skills and submission to the dominant ideology. *The rule of competence* states that such competency is necessary for the division of labor and must include both know-how and submission to ideology.
5. In Marxist theory, we depict society topographically with a metaphor: the mode of production is a base that holds up and is held down by a superstructure. Preserving the relations of production happens to a degree in production itself, but large capitalist societies tend to do their reproduction outside of the firm. The superstructures—or the State—are responsible for maintaining the

continuity of the relations of production. Society is therefore a formation, a balance of forces whose effectivities are indexed to one another. *The rule of special thirds* states that for any social formation, the production force exerts a special third of the total social force in that formation. That base force is determinate in the last instance, while the superstructures exert a special two-thirds of the social force through repression and reproduction. Each force is thus relatively autonomous viz. the others.

6. There are two superstructures: a repressive state apparatus (RSA) which ensures the proper functioning of relations of production through violence (be it physical or otherwise), and a set of ideological state apparatuses (ISAs) which instruct the right competencies (know-how and submission) for enacting the relations of production, thereby reproducing them. The latter operates by ideology rather than violence. The RSA is a more rigidly coherent apparatus while the ISAs are diffuse. *The system rule* says that an ISA is a system of organizations and institutions. For instance, the scholastic ISA is made up of everything from childcare facilities to K-12 schools to universities to non-profit organizations which support these institutions. Any given school or organization is a component part of the scholastic ISA. ISAs realize ideology through practices that anchor the know-how and submission required for reproducing relations of production. *The anchor rule* says that these practices provide material support for reproducing the relations of production, but also anchor secondary ideologies unique to the ISA (which people can use in creative ways). *The toe rule* says that when people in ISAs toe the dominant line, they are following a dominant ideology.

7. When it comes to determination, *the causality rule* says that social structure is immanent, dispersed in and through its many effects. The practices enacted in an ISA produce ideology, not the other way around. It would be an idealist, deterministic, Stalinist mistake to say that ideology produces institutions. Such a claim puts the cart before the horse and commits fustian thinking. By extension, it would also be a mistake to draw linear causal chains between social events. We should not draw easy causal claims between curricula, pedagogy, and social structure, for instance.

8. Schools, as we saw in May 1968, play an important role in stabilizing/destabilizing the dominance of the ruling class, at least serving warnings to the ruling class and at most exerting more force than political parties, unions and parliaments (though the effectivities of these ISAs are typically indexed higher). Resistance is possible, inevitable, and effective; though difficult. Teachers' knowledge is dangerous. Students can act like little devils. Movements make their way through the institutions. Schools can deliver massive warnings to the ruling class. The history of the USSR, Lenin's focus on schooling specifically, is an example here, as are trade unions in fascist Spain. ISAs are therefore a battlefield where ruling classes establish their hegemony, but can be made to tremble. Masses of children go to school for long periods of time, giving the state access to a teachable population for a significant portion of their formative years. Given the school's commonsensical indispensability, and

the concentration of impactful practices at schools in modern societies, the school has replaced the church as the number one, or dominant ISA in modern capitalist social formations. *The school rule* says that the scholastic apparatus is the number one ideological state apparatus in capitalist societies.
9. While the social structure of ISAs is rigid, nothing is certain by dint of class struggle. There is no paradox in saying that bourgeois ISAs contain working-class organizations. *The struggle rule* says that the only necessity in social structure is contingency. The fact of class struggle is that things shift and ISAs are one such terrain of struggle where subordinate groups can and do win victories in the balance of forces.
10. Individual people live and move and have their being in this struggle, subjected to multiple uneven forces that present them with difficult choices to make. *The go rule* says that ideology is what makes people go all by themselves in social formations. They get recruited to dominant and subordinate ideologies through interpellations that shape their life histories and create the conditions for them to make choices in a context of multiple pressures.

OTRC was not available in full translation until 2014. This interpretation of Althusser's theory of education was far from common in the years after he published the excerpt, which caused a furious debate among Marxists. In those debates and the generation of scholarship that followed, Althusser's theory was interpreted very differently by educational researchers and organizers. In the next part, I revisit those interpretations, focusing on the founders of critical education and tracing the provenance of their reading of Althusser to a specific set of texts whose critiques forged part of the presumptions underlying critical education at its inception.

Part II

The Common Sense about Althusser: Reassessing Critical Education

12

The Three Critiques

Raymond Morrow's (2014) encyclopedia entry on Althusser, with which I opened this book's introduction, has two main parts. The first part, contained in the first sentence, is a pretty good summary of Althusser's project: a non-economistic theory of how the relations of production get reproduced. Althusser's way of getting around economism is to focus on the relative autonomy of the superstructures in his understanding of the base-superstructure model. That account of relative autonomy relies on a distinction between the RSA which is violent and ISAs that work through ideology, including a groundbreaking theory of education. Yet the second part of the entry characterizes Althusser's project as failed. Since the economy is determinate in the last instance, Morrow says, Althusser's ahistorical structuralist methodology is functionalist and denies the agency of individual people, who are mere puppets of the ISAs.

It would be easy to argue against Morrow's interpretation using the eleven rules of thumb from Part I. The rule of special thirds states that the economy exerts a special third of social force in a formation, but its special quality at the base does not imply the ability (in principle or in practice) to overpower the other two-thirds of social force from the superstructures. While its quality is basic, it is the minority of total social force. The base has a particular kind of effectivity that is always indexed to other forces in the formation. One of the chief findings of Althusser's research is to reject the principle, as Althusser wrote in *For Marx*, that there is a Royal Road of the Economy, or an economic essence of which superstructural stuff are phenomena.

Further, apparatuses are modes of intervention that class groups use to secure their interests, but not like a machine. The interventions happen when people working in institutions toe a dominant line through various pressures. The struggle rule states that everything happens within the contingent push-pull of dominant and subordinate groups struggling. The causal relationship between struggle and educational institutions, practices, and people is uneven and complex according to the causality rule. We know from the go rule that subjects are made to go all by themselves and make free choices in the midst of social forces. The unevenness and complexity of these forces, their fluctuating indices of effectivity, exerted by ensembles of ISAs and layered RSA, makes it easy to theorize agency, choice, and movement. Althusser explicitly rejects the idea that ideology determines institutions, that ideology requires an overseer or cop in the head, and he has the theoretical justification to do so in his concepts of immanent structure and structural causality. This is an explicit rejection of Stalinist idealism. Finally, Althusser draws from myriad historical examples in his argumentation, including personal and political examples of individuals making free choices as part of social movements. Ultimately, he intends his theory to be applied to specific circumstances for revolutionary purposes so that socialists, for example, can make good decisions about how to work for a transition to socialism in their specific historical contexts.

Morrow's entry does not hold up well against this reading. But his entry is just one instance of a widely accepted interpretation of Althusser's theory in critical education, a field of leftist educational research and organizing including critical pedagogy, social foundations of education, education studies, and others. Morrow's interpretation and variations of it are common sense in the field. Generally, the common sense has three main parts. The first is a critique from agency: Althusser's theory does not properly account for individual freedom. The second is a critique from functionalism: Althusser's theory is not Marxist but is rather better understood as an example of the sociological tradition of functionalism where social practices are defined by their capacity to maintain equilibrium, cohesion, and order. The third critique is that from tragedy: Althusser's theory is tragic because it set out to do something worthy (e.g., de-Stalinize Marxism) but ultimately undermines itself. Morrow's entry on Althusser exhibits all three of the critiques.

Like any common sense, critical education researchers' understanding of Althusser rarely gets articulated explicitly (Morrow's entry is an exception). I have encountered the common sense in conversations, oblique references, and side comments rather than full expression in the literature. Having worked through a good portion of that literature I contend that, beyond entries in encyclopedias like Morrow's, one can see evidence of the common sense about Althusser in basic presumptions of the field of critical education, such as the dichotomy between reproduction and resistance (recent cases include Uljens and Ylimaki (2017) and Hattam and Smyth (2014)).

The dichotomy has two parts. First, there were the reproduction theories. Important though they were in pointing out how capitalist, patriarchal, racist, and other kinds of structures impact schools, these theories did not leave room for the right kind of individual agency to change those structures; that is, in the reproduction schema, there was no way to theorize resistance. Then, the story continues, resistance theorists stepped in and issued the crucial corrective, shifting emphasis to agency. When it comes to critical pedagogy, social foundations of education, and Marxist educational theory, it is common sense to understand Althusser's theory as one such social reproduction theory in this sense; in other words, deterministic. The dichotomy is not a settled matter of course and has inspired much debate in the last twenty years (Apple 2012, 2015; Farahmandpur 2004; Hill 2001; Kelsh and Hill 2006; Malott 2011; Rikowski 2006; McGrew 2011).

The reproduction-resistance dichotomy is thus one instance of the common sense about Althusser in critical education, yet upon closer examination I find that, given the way the founders of critical education articulated their ideas, the dichotomy actually relies on the notion that Althusser's theory is functionalist and deterministic. How did this happen? Furthermore, when compared with the eleven rules set out in Part I, do these critiques hold up? In this part, I answer these questions by reconstructing the intellectual history of the common sense about Althusser in critical education to see how it crystallized and, juxtaposing it with the eleven rules, assess its charges.

First, I look at the tradition of critical education to see how Morrow and Torres (1995) arrived at their reading of Althusser's social reproduction theory. Their citations, as well as Gottesman (2016)'s recent history of the field, point to critical education researchers Michael W. Apple (1978 1982, 1985, 2012, 2015) and Henry A. Giroux (1976, 1980a, 1984, 2001) as influential sources. I therefore examine Apple and Giroux's thinking about Althusser during the late 1970s and early 1980s, when their research configured a decisive phase of what Gottesman calls the critical turn in education. In reconstructing their readings of Althusser I find, along with the common sense, an inconsistent mix of reverence and repulsion. I also find that Apple and Giroux rarely take on Althusser in a sustained way, but rather engage his thinking in passing by relying on other interpretations for their understanding so that they can move on to their own more general claims.

Gottesman has recommended that critical education, to remain critical, must be more discerning about its sources. My next step is therefore to reconstruct the arguments found in Apple and Giroux's citations when it came to Althusser, as well as the context around each of them. These texts include Rancière (2011), Erben and Gleeson (1975), Hirst (1976), Callinicos (1976), Thompson (1978), Connell (1979), and Willis (1981a). Examining these arguments, I find a treasure trove of intellectual history, but ultimately much left to be desired in terms of arguments, particularly those of the English historian E. P. Thompson's (1978) flagship rejection of Althusser, *The Poverty of Theory*. By revisiting Apple and Giroux's interpretations of Althusser and then reconstructing the arguments on which those interpretations rest, I reassess the common sense about Althusser in critical education, following the line of critique to its origins and responding to its three aspects.

This part also serves as an intellectual history of critical education more broadly. Revisiting Giroux and Apple's interpretations of Althusser in the late 1970s and early 1980s along with the source interpretations from which they drew, revisits some conceptual foundations of critical education, namely presumptions about social reproduction and resistance. The reassessment of this line of critique against Althusser and the common sense resulting from it thus also serves as a reassessment of critical education as a whole, providing context for ideas at its foundations and an assessment of those ideas.

As a methodological note, when I assess the critiques I use two tests. The first test is one of argument. If the critique has premises that lead to a conclusion—that is, if it provides reasons for believing a statement rather than merely proposing, suggesting, or observing that statement—then the critique passes the first test. In that case, I use a second test. If the eleven rules detailed in Part I cannot handle the argument, either because the critique points to an absence or an inconsistency in them or otherwise, then the critique is successful. Only one of the accounts in the line of critique passes both tests.

13

Foundations of Critical Education: Apple and Giroux's Indecision

Raised by communists and having been a classroom teacher, school principal, and union leader, Michael Apple was inspired by (but critical of) neo-Marxist approaches to education, namely that of Samuel Bowles and Herbert Gintis (2011). While studying phenomenology, critical theory, and education at the New School for Social Research in New York City, Apple established a connection with the British sociologist of language Basil Bernstein at the Open University-Milton Keynes in the mid-1970s. Bernstein, whose framework to understand pedagogies as class codes took from Marx and Durkheim, had seen Apple's work on curriculum and reached out to him. Apple began attending the Westhill Conference in England, connecting with a lively scene of left-critical education research whose proceedings were published by Len Barton and Stephen Walker (2013). This relationship initiated a dialogue between British sociological and cultural studies research on education and American left educational research that would, along with other influences, ready the ground for critical education (2018, personal communication).

Apple would go on to connect with Henry A. Giroux in the United States, who was on a similar trajectory. Giroux, who studied education and history at Carnegie-Mellon University, began working with labor organizer-turned-intellectual Stanley Aronowitz in 1973. Giroux (1976) would also bring left perspectives to education. Giroux attended Westhill Conferences at Apple's suggestion. This cohort would introduce British left thinking about education to a wide audience of American intellectuals and activists. These voices would be added to those Marxist and leftist voices that emerged as the McCarthyist freeze on leftist thinking thawed and Third World revolutions erupted onto the world stage. Bowles and Gintis, Gramscian historian Michael B. Katz, and socialist economist of education Martin Carnoy (and his collaborator Henry Levin) are just a few examples of that earlier perspective.

Not only would Apple and Giroux's voices get added to this mix of neo-Marxists, but they would also—albeit in different ways—contrast themselves with those voices. The term "critical," inspired by the critical theory tradition of the Frankfurt School, signaled the break. Centering their thinking on concepts like experience, culture, and agency, Apple and Giroux drew from their experiences and connections at Westhill, like those with Paul Willis, to distinguish their position from social reproduction theorists like Bowles and Gintis, Bernstein, Bourdieu, and Althusser.

Althusser was caught up in this transition, but not at first. Early publications are telling. Looking at Apple's (1978) early essay "Ideology, Reproduction and Educational Reform," Althusser is barely on his radar. The first reference to Althusser in Apple's canon occurs in a discussion of the hidden curriculum and "the criteria of validity and truth" educators employ in reform efforts. Apple includes a footnote here. In it, he makes reference to Miriam Glucksmann's (2014) *Structuralist Analysis in Contemporary Social Thought*, referring to Althusser in passing as a "French Marxist philosopher of science" whose work may be of interest regarding this question of validity and truth. The reference is neutral, reading Althusser as someone interested in theories of science, like the positivist Karl Popper.

Gluckmann's (2014) understanding of structuralism and her treatment of Althusser, even in the first pages of the introduction to *Structuralist Analysis*, does not cast Althusser as a philosopher of science. Her opening paragraph mentions how structuralism met the needs of the new student movements, providing them a militant mode of analysis (xi). She characterizes Althusser's thinking as a rigorous, militant framework for understanding social structure and its internal contradictions, which were of value to student organizers (xii). There is a distance between Apple's thinking on Althusser and his citation of Glucksmann from the beginning. Perhaps Glucksmann's text, which is a comparison of Althusser and the French anthropologist Claude Levi-Strauss's structuralism (the two of which she finds "poles apart" from one another (xiii)) was circulating at the time, and Apple felt it relevant to cite. In any case, the line of critique's three parts are notably absent, both in Glucksmann and Apple. This distance between Althusser's theory and Apple's thinking about it would remain, but in a much different form following Giroux's less neutral early reading.

The first paragraph of Giroux's (1980b) early essay "Teacher Education and the Ideology of Social Control" states that schools are "a significant agency for the reproduction and legitimation of a society characterized by a high degree of social and economic inequality" (cited in Giroux's (1980b)). Here is a classic statement of social reproduction theory: that schools legitimize and reproduce inequality; along with one of its best-known articulations by Bowles and Gintis. (It also includes an interesting use of the term agency, in this case denoting an institution rather than freedom, which was always an oddity about the English word (Fritsch, O'Connor, and Thompson 2016)).

Giroux (1980b) notably cites a study of urban teachers in the United Kingdom by Gerald Grace (1978), who defines a Marxist view of education as one that views schools as "reproducing the capitalist relations of production and constituting a crucial part of the 'ideological state apparatus' (see, for instance, Bowles and Gintis, 1976; Althusser, 1972)" (Giroux 1980b: 55). Grace cites both Althusser and Bowles and Gintis together as promoting the view from reproduction, creating an equivalence between the theories. Later, as Grace is examining head teachers' attachment to liberal theories of schooling, he describes them as potentially having a "false consciousness" about their situation, and cites the "Pardon to the Heroes" passage from the excerpt where Althusser asks the pardon of heroic teachers. Grace reads this passage as attributing false consciousness to teachers, a "deficit theory and as such counter-productive" (Grace 1978: 168). (He actually cites that passage, including a full pull-out quote on 102 as well.) Throughout the book, Grace is worried that Althusser casts teachers as "professional ideologists" who transmit ruling class content. His explicitly stated concern is false consciousness, however. We will see where these concerns come from in the next section.

Giroux continues his introduction by elaborating the importance of schooling to that reproduction process: "Schools and their various programs exist within a constellation of economic, social, and political institutions that make them a fundamental part of the power structure (Althusser, 1971; Bourdieu and Passeron, 1979/1990)" (5). I leave Giroux's in-text citations for readers to get a sense of whom Giroux is citing and how. Althusser, for him, is one of several social reproduction theorists who would come to be mentioned in the same breath due to Willis's (1981a) blanket excoriation of their frameworks. Giroux (1980a) followed Willis's thinking and published a more explicit critique of Althusser that same year. One example is in "Beyond the Correspondence Theory: Notes on the Dynamics of Educational Reproduction and Transformation," in a section called "Myth of 'Total' Domination," Giroux claims that Althusser's notion of domination is an "oversimplified view" that infects his theory of schooling. Giroux explains:

> Iin Althusser's (1971) Hobbesian vision of schooling there is little recognition of the dialectical interplay of power, ideology, and resistance. In Althusser's view, the school functions to transmit the necessary skills and discipline required to socialize students passively into their future work roles. Domination appears so total in this type of perspective that teachers and students "appear as unwitting servants of such an ideology and have little choice in avoiding the service of its interests (Erben and Gleeson [1975])." (Giroux 1980a: 232)

Again, I leave in-text citations to show Giroux citing British sociologists of education Michael Erben and Denis Gleeson's critique of Althusser, first published in 1975, which was one of the first of such critiques of Althusser's thinking about education in English. Drawing from Jacques Rancière's (2011) book-length polemic *Althusser's Lesson*, their arguments would inform many of Giroux's and others' readings of Althusser thereafter. I will go into these critiques in detail later (we will see where Erben and Gleeson get the idea that Althusser is "Hobbesian," for instance).

For Giroux, Althusser's concept of domination is totalizing because Althusser understands students as passive blocks of clay for the division of labor to mold. Such total domination is a version of the critique from agency. In a theory that does not recognize dialectics, power, and resistance, there can be no freedom of movement or action. Giroux continues later in the essay to say that, for theories like Althusser's, "structures of reproduction ... exist outside of the actions of educators to change them. For instance, writers such as Althusser see teachers and students as no more than products of structures" (Giroux 1980a: 241). Giroux (1984) republished this exact interpretation in his first book *Ideology, Culture, and the Process of Schooling*. Yet he would shift his critique somewhat over the next few years after encountering Apple's more developed thinking on the subject.

Apple (1982) edited a collection of essays under the title *Cultural and Economic Reproduction in Education: Essays on Class, Ideology, and the State*, which showed a different engagement with Althusser's claims than in 1978. In the introduction to that collection, Apple's view is similar but more subtle than Giroux's. Focusing on cultural practices in schools, Apple famously critiques the "economic reproduction" paradigm for treating schools as "black boxes," by not examining what actually occurs in them. Treating schools as black boxes fails to engage "in in-depth analyses of how [reproductive] effects are created in the school" (1). The critique here is that reproduction theories do not go into the right kind of detail when talking about how reproduction actually occurs. Such theories are too abstract when it comes to students' and teachers' experiences. That reproduction theories are too abstract is a familiar comment about Althusser from which Apple drew and lends support to both the critiques from agency and functionalism.

In contrast to such abstract theories, Apple looks to emphasize "analysis of the formal and informal culture of schools and other educational institutions, and the knowledge that gets in and is taught in them, [which] is quite important" (1982: 2). Such analysis would be more concrete, he argues. But Apple also appreciates the other side, noting that "a good deal of the research on cultural reproduction has neglected the concerns and insights of those scholars investigating economic reproduction" (2). Rather than a firm rejection Apple sees value in both sides of the distinction he is building between economic and cultural reproduction. A focus on culture, in this case, means focusing on the actual experiences of people in schools whereas a focus on economy does not. Yet he also notes that scholars looking at culture leave out insights made by those studying economic reproduction.

Three things to note about this text. First, Apple's black-box critique, combined with an interest in cultural practices, is a version of the critique from functionalism. The black-box metaphor points to reproduction theory's apparent inability to capture and analyze particular cultural practices due to its focus on economic structure. Second, Apple posits a dichotomy between culture and the economy when writing that cultural reproduction differs substantively from economic reproduction. The economy is analytically distinct from culture rather than connected. Finally, while he posits it, Apple is ambivalent about this dichotomy between economy and culture. While he favors culture he is careful to note the importance of economic reproduction. He sees worth and flaws in each approach, but enforces the dichotomy between them nonetheless, and somewhat indecisively sides with culture when push comes to shove.

Althusser arrives shortly after this setup. Apple is against an economic "neglect of the concrete meanings and activities of culture and people as they interact in our institutions" (2), and is more interested in thinking "about how these institutions may reproduce the relations of domination and ideological conflicts" (3). You can see the use of terms such as reproduction of relations in this phrasing. Apple uses Althusserian language of "apparatus" and "social formation" as well (2). Apple even agrees that "as both Gramsci and Althusser remind us, 'ideology is a practice producing subjects' (Mouffe 1979: 187)." But Apple then poses the following questions about such an approach:

> Are schools—as important aspects of the State—simply "ideological state apparatuses" (to quote Althusser), ones whose primary role is to reproduce the

ideological and "manpower" requirements of the social relations of production? Or, do they also embody contradictory tendencies and provide sites where ideological struggles within and among classes, race, and sexes can and do occur? (Apple 1982: 14)

The first question is about school's role within a social formation (what some group or other want school to do). The second question is about what actually happens at school: contradictory struggles on an intersectional terrain. For us, what is most important about these questions is what they presuppose: a dichotomy between the theory of apparatus and the theory of struggle. The first theory says school simply reproduces labor power, while the second theory says schools are sites of ideological struggle. While I hope to have shown in the previous Part that these theories are not mutually exclusive in Althusser—apparatuses that reproduce relations of production are in and of class struggle—Apple's questions create a mutual exclusion between reproduction and struggle. In his scheme, Althusser's theory either says schools reproduce relations of production or the theory says schools are sites of contradictory struggles. Like Apple's dichotomy between economy and culture, Althusser's theory cannot do both.

But notice that Apple's stance is not so clear-cut. Interestingly, he is not fully committed to the dichotomy while simultaneously committing to it. Note his ambiguity in the formulation above. The second question asks whether schools are simply ISAs "or, do they also" embody contradictions and provide sites of ideological struggle. Apple writes with both disjunction (or) and a conjunction (and) when adjudicating between the concepts of schools as apparatuses and schools as sites of contradictory struggle. A school can only be a site of struggle or an apparatus, or it can be an apparatus and a site of struggle. Reproduction cannot be a struggle. This opaque dichotomization of reproduction and struggle is common in Apple and Giroux's critiques of Althusser.

Apple justifies the position with the critique from functionalism. In an earlier paragraph, Apple cites Richard Johnson's (2018) essay "Notes on an Impasse" to point to certain theories of structuralism that reduce "a good deal of the complexities of a social formation into a kind of functionalism" (14). In such theories "ideology and culture—while having a degree of relative autonomy to be sure—'are subsumed within a single function: the reproduction of the conditions of capitalist production' (Johnson 2018: 69; see also Connell 1979)" (14). Again, I leave Apple's in-text citations to show whom he relies upon for justification. I will examine Richard Johnson's arguments in Part III, and Connell (1979), the Australian sociologist of education, co-author of the groundbreaking *Making the Difference* (Connell et al. 1980), at the end of this part. At this juncture, it is enough to know that Apple is leaning on them citationally to justify a soft dichotomy between reproduction and struggle, noting that the reason reproduction cannot be a struggle concept is because it is functionalist.

Apple's dichotomy, justified by reference to Johnson and Connell, is also a critique of functionalism. Structuralism reduces complex practices, cultures, and other aspects of social formations to the functions they serve. Again, building on the indecisive dichotomy, Apple is careful to say that there is some account of relative autonomy in Althusser's theory, but then he reverses course and makes the broad claim that, ultimately, reproduction theory subsumes everything into a single function. The critique from functionalism can therefore sometimes rely on reductionism, which Apple summarizes by mentioning two other important earlier critics of Althusser:

> Individuals such as Paul Hirst and Barry Hindness have argued on epistemological grounds that most current Marxist investigations of culture, politics, and economy (in particular Lukács, Poulantzas, and Althusser) are themselves still too reductive. Even though these writers … strive to go beyond simplistic base/superstructure models … their final result is little more than the production "of a more of less complex economism involving both the recognition and the denial of the autonomy of politics and ideology viz. the economy (Hindness 1977: 102–3; Hirst 1976)." (Apple 1982: 15)

Barry Hindness and Paul Hirst were British communist political theorists. In the early 1970s they co-authored a widely read book on pre-capitalist social formations drawing on Althusser's framework. They went on to critique Althusser however, and these critiques were influential, particularly Hirst's (1976) long essay claiming Althusser's theory is a complex form of economism (while Hindness (1977)'s chapter in *Philosophy and Methodology in the Social Sciences* on Althusser was more summary of Althusser's critiques of empiricism).

Drawing from these texts, Apple makes the claim that such reductive accounts as Althusser's (and allegedly Poulantzas, who will we look at later, and Lukács, a theorist from a different generation) amount to a denial of autonomy between politics, ideology, and economy. These claims about denied autonomy and economism are versions of the critique from agency, as economism imbues the economy with an overpowering influence in society that overwhelms creative action. Yet we can also see the critique from tragedy here, as Apple says that authors like Althusser and those working in the Althusserian tradition strive to go beyond reductionism, but ultimately fail to do so. Their theories are little more than a tragically complex version of the thing they were trying to avoid. What makes Apple's read here in 1982 so indecisive is that, at first, he poses a soft dichotomy between reproduction and struggle in reference to Althusser, then claims there is some relative autonomy in the theory, but then ultimately, he says, there is not since the theory subsumes all social things under single functions. Giroux's early interpretations are similar, if more strongly worded, and focus exclusively on agency. The indecision and sharpness of their readings would only intensify in later writings.

Giroux's milestone work *Theory and Resistance in Education: Towards a Pedagogy of the Opposition* (2001) is a paradigm case. Notable for its forewords by both Paulo Freire and Stanley Aronowitz, *Theory and Resistance* became a key text for critical education, configuring resistance theory as a contrast to reproduction theory in left education research. Interpreting Althusser was part of that contrasting project. Giroux's treatment of Althusser is a few pages long, beginning with a brief summary of Althusser's ISAs essay. He points to Althusser's theory of competencies, drawing a connection from Althusser to Gramsci (79). Giroux then lists a few phrases attributable to Althusser's position ("production of values that support the relations of production"; "use of force and ideology to support dominant classes in all important spheres of control"; "production of knowledge and skills relevant to specific forms of work").

Giroux completes this brief summary by writing that "since this position [Althusser's] has been treated extensively elsewhere by others (Hirst 1976; Erben and Gleeson [1975]; Callinicos 1976; Aronowitz 2016), I will focus my analysis primarily on the conception of power and ideology that emerges from Althusser's position" (Giroux 2001: 79). This passage displays the interpretations Giroux cites to make his own interpretation. I look into those citations in the next section. More importantly, this passage demonstrates Giroux's interpretive approach to Althusser: namely, that we need not engage with Althusser further than citing a handful of earlier interpretations.

In addition to mentioning the British-African Trotskyist Alex Callinicos's (1976) precocious and early critique *Althusser's Marxism*, by 1983 Giroux had access to his mentor Aronowitz's *The Crisis of Historical Materialism* (2016). These ideas made their way into Giroux's (2001) book. He gestures toward these accounts' worthiness by calling them extensive treatments, lumps them together with critiques by Hirst and Erben and Gleeson, and moves on. Admittedly, his project is not an exhaustive interpretive one on Althusser. But it is notable that Giroux opts to move quickly through the summary by relying on a specific set of sources, for which he gives very little context.

Giroux's analysis of power and control in Althusser has new elements from his previous two accounts. He repeats a line from his earlier essay that Althusser's concepts of repressive and ideological apparatuses are "self-regulating practices of the state" (Giroux 2001: 79). He does not explain the significance of the term: self-regulation signals a functionalist theory where parts of society self-regulate an equilibrium rather than the complex and conflicted actions of groups and individuals. While this phrase is evidence of the critique from functionalism, Giroux continues on with a more positive treatment of Althusser's view of schools than the earlier essay. Rather than a myth of total domination, Giroux claims that Althusser's theory does endow schools with a relative autonomy since it has "a particular relation" with the economic base (rather than being reduced to it) (80). Schools also have their own practices that get modified, altered, and contradicted by other social forces. For Giroux, at least in this part of the text, Althusser's theory actually dispels the idea that schools are simple ethereal reflections of the economy. He goes on to summarize Althusser's theory of ideology. The theory is appealing because it politicizes space, time, and routine (82) and mentions several other strengths in its materiality, its focus on the unconscious, and its anti-reductionism (83).

The formulations here are surprising given Giroux and Apple's previous negative positions. Giroux's summary captures some subtleties of Althusser's thinking. We can most likely attribute those articulations to Aronowitz's (2016) more positive treatment of Althusser. Giroux understands Althusser's theory as providing schools with autonomy and offering a much-needed perspective on the actual, material practices that happen within schools. But Giroux takes a quick turn. After this more Aronowitz-ish summary, he returns back to his previous interpretation that Althusser's theory contains a myth of total domination. In this sudden turn, Giroux reverses the interpretation he has just offered, citing different authors to support the opposite reading. Even though schools in Althusser's theory are relatively autonomous, have their own practices, and are not the ethereal reflection of economic order, nevertheless

> As a number of critics have pointed out (Erben and Gleeson [1975]; Aronowitz [2016]; Willis 1981b), Althusser has fashioned a theory of domination in which the needs of capital become indistinct from the effects of capitalist social relations. In fact, Althusser's (1971) notion of domination has become so one-sided that it is impossible to deduce from this perspective the possibility of ideologies which are oppositional in nature (Hall [1985]). This is no small point, because it suggests that schools are *not* to be viewed as social sites marked by the interplay of domination, accommodation, and struggle, but rather as sites that function smoothly to reproduce a docile labor force. (Giroux 2001: 82)

Giroux's formulation that the theory casts the needs of capital as indistinct from the effects of capitalist social relations is an interesting line of thought. It could very well be that the relations of production take hold in ways that do not serve the needs of capital. This line of questioning has its roots in Erben and Gleeson, as Giroux notes. Althusser could very well be vulnerable to this critique from the relations of production (it also resonates with Lefebvre's (1976) comments). It is a fruitful one to explore. But Giroux drops it for clumsier articulations that contradict the insights from just a few pages before. He even notes later that comments such as the ones he writes in these paragraphs are exaggerations (Giroux 2001: 83). His previously subtle and complex interpretation of Althusser's position that casts schools as relatively autonomous now become accusations that Althusser's theory of domination is one-sided and precludes any possibility for thinking about opposition. Giroux returns to the critique from agency ("impossible to deduce, from this perspective ideologies that are oppositional in nature") and functionalism (schools are not sites of struggle but rather "function smoothly"), contradicting the previous reading.

Giroux once again lists a handful of British critiques in a long in-text citation. Indeed "a number of critics" make these points about agency and functionalism, the quantity of which, apparently, should convince us of the arguments' veracity beyond a doubt. But a close reading shows Giroux reversing his understanding of Althusser's theory. Why? His mentioning of Paul Willis's (1981b) is a clue. After publishing the landmark *Learning to Labour: How Working Class Kids Get Working Class Jobs*, Willis wrote a scathing polemic distancing himself from any position perceived to be reproductionist, vilifying such theories, and forcing the terms structuralist and functionalist to become synonymous with reductionist, determinist, and even totalitarian. As we will see later, for Willis (1981a), Althusser, along with Bernstein, Bowles and Gintis, and Bourdieu and Passeron, are all guilty of these intellectual crimes. Giroux would have encountered Willis's largesse as a scholar of education at the Westhill Conference and elsewhere in England. Apple was also influenced by him. But Willis himself was influenced by E. P. Thompson, who normalized this style of polemical discourse against structuralism and whose forcefulness comes with a commensurate lack of substance, as I show later.

But Giroux does not just rely on Willis's polemic. He gives reasons, of a kind, for his reversal on Althusser's position. Repeating his interpretation from 1980, Giroux says Althusser's concept of ideology is treated undialectically (i.e., ignores the interplay of power relations) for three reasons. First, in Althusser's theory, "ideology collapses into a theory of domination that restricts its meaning to such a degree that it appears as a 'force' able to invalidate or diffuse any resistance" (Giroux 2001: 82). Here we have a reiteration of the critique from agency. We should note that Giroux, whether in 1980 or 1983, has not provided evidence or proof that Althusser's theory implies an overwhelming force that invalidates resistance such that there is total domination. He has merely stated it in different ways, citing the quantity of previously existing critiques as sufficient evidence to demonstrate the conclusion.

Second is a point about ideology that repeats the critique from functionalism. Althusser's "ideology becomes an institutional medium of oppression that appears to function so efficiently that the state and its ISAs are presented as part of a static and administrative fantasy [where] schools and other social sites seem free from even the slightest vestige of conflict, contradiction, and struggle" (82). This repetition of the critique from functionalism is similar to Apple's (1982) claim that, to Althusser, school is struggle-free. Yet like the first reason Giroux provides, this smoothly functioning administrative fantasy is a repetition of a premise in provocative terms rather than a proven thing. There is little argument. (Note the word "static" here: Thompson (1978) gives this term pride of place in his polemic.) Like the critique from agency, Giroux merely states the case without looking at Althusser's writing on the question. Rather, he leans on a particular set of interpretations to this effect. There is a slight hesitation in Giroux's writing however, just as in Apple: the social sites "seem" free from struggle. Giroux is not quite confident in the claim, despite making the claim quite confidently.

The third and final step in Giroux's reversal is an even more strident statement of the critiques from agency and functionalism. Althusser

> has developed a notion of power that appears to eliminate human agency ... there is no theory of mediation in this perspective, nor is there any conception of how people appropriate, select, accommodate, or simply generate meaning. Instead, in Althusser's reductionist schema human beings are relegated to static role-bearers, carriers of pre-defined meanings, agents of hegemonic ideologies inscribed in their psyches like irremovable scars. Consequently, it is impossible to explain from this perspective what mechanisms are at work to allow or characterize schools as relatively autonomous institutions. (Giroux 2001: 83)

Giroux repeats the critiques from agency and functionalism using reductionism as a support (like Apple used abstraction). The crescendo of polemic rises: humans carry pre-defined meanings and hegemonic ideologies are inscribed in their psyches like irremovable scars. At the same time, we can see Giroux's confident lack of confidence in these bold (yet hedged) assertions. The theory "appears to eliminate human agency." Giroux's rhetoric crescendos further to a fever pitch. He says that Althusser's theory casts the working class as "dumb and inert" (83). Workers "hop and jump" into the division of labor. Giroux explains this "failure" (83) by firing off the other version of the critique from functionalism, which is to claim that the theory is too abstract.

Althusser's theory is "at a level of abstraction that appears uninformed by the concrete interplay of power relations" (83).

Finally, as if having reached a tonal climax, Giroux decrescendos with the critique from tragedy. Althusser's theory is tragic because it "appears to suffer from the very reification it analyzes" and "has enshrined [domination] in a formalistic system that is as insular as it is theoretically demeaning to the notions of struggle and human agency" (83). More repetitions of the critiques from agency and functionalism come, this time in the form of name-calling. Althusser's theory is insular, formalistic, and demeaning (83). We have not seen proof of these suppositions except through repetition, rhetoric, and reliance on previous readings.

Just as before, however, there is a hint of something interesting in Giroux's frenetic and inconsistent interpretation. He claims that in Althusser's theory it is impossible to explain how schools are relatively autonomous institutions. Like his point about the incongruence between relations of production and the needs of capital, this is a fair insight: it could be that Althusser merely stipulates a relative autonomy between schools and other social forces, but does not furnish enough in the theory to actually explain that relative autonomy. I disagree with this claim given the rule of special thirds and the struggle rule, which clearly specify the conditions for relative autonomy between social forces. The causality rule further prevents any simplistic flattening of the dynamic between social beings. But at least in this passage there are the beginnings of an argument in Giroux's account, something to disagree with. However, this line of substantive thinking gets lost in Giroux's blustery and unsubstantiated repetitions of the critiques of agency and functionalism, which Apple does follow in his next key text.

Apple's (1985) *Education and Power* came out two years after Giroux's *Theory and Resistance*. The book articulates similar critiques as Giroux, but more fluidly, condensing them in calmer, more careful, yet consistently indecisive expressions. Apple sets out to critically examine "claims about both the school's function as what Althusser has called an ideological state apparatus—one that produces agents (with the 'appropriate' dispositions, values, and ideologies taught through a hidden curriculum) to fill the needs of the social division of labor in society" rather than emphasizing cultural practices (91). The project is thus an examination of "correspondence theories" (67) that cast schools as "*wholly* determined and can do no more than mirror economic relations outside them" (68). Apple calls upon the critiques from agency and functionalism again. The italicization of the word *wholly* emphasizes the complete lack of agency in such theories as Althusser's.

The dichotomy between reproduction and struggle present in 1982 survives in *Education and Power*. Apple's understanding of ISAs is that the theory casts schools as functioning in a simple, one-way, and reductive manner to fulfill needs in the division of labor (67). The theory risks being a bare parody of actual practice, or missing concrete features, is distinct from the critique from agency (69). Like the black box critique Apple made a few years earlier (and that Giroux alludes to in 1983), this is a critique from abstraction, related to the critique from functionalism: Althusser's theory misses out on important particularities of culture and experience in favor of functionalist generalities (68).

Apple focuses on the mirror metaphor at the beginning of the book as a way to illustrate the problem with reproduction theories. In a section called "Beyond Simple Reproduction," he begins by talking about the physics of optical reflection (67). Just as a person stands in front of a mirror, with their features repeated back in significant detail, correspondence theories claim that schools mirror society. For such theories, "school is a determined institution" (68). Thus the mirror analogy is another way to phrase the critique from agency. If there is no variation between school and economy, just as there is no variation between an object and its reflection, then there can be no agency in schools.

But Apple does not take issue with the idea that schools are determined to some degree (68). He says that "there is another end to the rope which binds schools to outside agencies" (70), implying that while one end does in fact bind school there is another end that does not. Indeed, using yet another metaphor, Apple's claim is that there is "another side of this picture": theories of correspondence like that of the ISAs essay retain an "overly deterministic model of socialization" with an "exclusive focus on reproduction to the exclusion of other things that may be happening" (70). While one side of the picture legitimately focuses on reproduction when it comes to Althusser's theory, there is another side that it does not consider. Recalling his "or, do they also" phrasing in the 1982 text, rather than critiquing the reproduction theory wholesale, Apple seeks to augment reproduction by adding a missing element.

But Apple reverses. Rather than being one side of the picture, in the next breath, he claims that reproduction theories ultimately understand workers as *wholly* controlled automatons (69). Rather than the reproduction theory being one side of the picture, which would be a partial critique, Apple does in fact critique the theory wholesale by saying actors in such theories are wholly determined. Echoing Giroux's claim that such theories are tragic, Apple writes that correspondence theories actually reproduce dominance themselves (70). We should therefore throw that part of the picture away.

Is the problem with Althusser's theory of the ISAs that it needs augmentation, or is the theory fundamentally flawed? Apple sometimes says the former but then other times the latter. Sometimes Apple points out that reproduction theory does not include worker resistance (72). Workers' "ability to 'defy' the supervisor and 'expert'" (73) get left out of the picture. Saying that there are accounts missing implies that the existing account is necessary but insufficient. He provides anecdotes of work stoppages, like white crane workers showing solidarity with a mistreated black peer by operating their cranes more slowly (77), and women cashiers slowing their transactions to resist oppressive managers (81). In this case he takes issue with the reproduction theory leaving out any room for subtle resistance, since it characterizes individuals as automatons.

The critique from agency is present once again. Like in Giroux, Apple issues the critique without proof. He does not engage with Althusser's text directly but rather states the case as taken for granted. We have ample evidence from the first part of this book that Althusser explicitly focuses on fine-grained practices and experiences in OTRC, as well as declaring—both in OTRC and the excerpt—that worker struggle provides the theoretical backdrop of the theory. Neither Apple nor Giroux engage with that passage.

More examples. Apple writes, in a section called "Against Romanticism," reproduction theories of school have to mirror theories of management since there is no room for variation between school and the economy (82). Yet in the next sentence Apple writes that, rather than discarding reproduction theory, it should be augmented with investigations of other modes of determination since it provides something clearly important (82). This point is interesting. Apple's six modes of determination in schooling unpack what schools' relative autonomy can actually mean (which Althusser does not spell out). Yet Apple is indecisive about whether reproduction theory is a lost cause or if it can be fixed with some clarification, like unpacking the ways schools determine and are determined by society. The latter is a solid contribution to the discourse, and sometimes Apple advances it; but other times, he rejects reproduction wholesale.

Apple's conclusion is that there are always contradictory and mediated actions within the workplace and schools, such that "determinations are seen not as producing mirror images, but as setting contradictory limits, limits that at the level of practices are often mediated by (and can *potentially* transform) the informal (and sometimes conscious) action of groups of people" (90). While this conclusion about the importance of relative autonomy, transformation, and contradiction is very insightful and interesting—and serves as a near-perfect articulation of critical education research's paradigm for thinking about school in its social context that would influence a generation of scholars—Apple provides little evidence that the theories he critiques were making a claim to the contrary. There is no proof that Althusser's account is any different. There is good reason to believe that they are entirely compatible.

While Giroux does some interpretive work with Althusser, and even characterizes the theory as one that posits relative autonomy and transformation, Giroux reverses that characterization to advance the unsubstantiated critiques from agency and functionalism. Apple's account is also something of a reversal. While sometimes he claims reproduction theories like Althusser's can be fixed or augmented, other times he claims they are a lost cause. He also relies on unsubstantiated critiques from agency and functionalism.

Gottesman (2016: 1) shows that Apple and Giroux were influential in the nascent field of critical education. Their writing from this period configured a framework for thinking about schools from a left perspective that would set the agenda for several decades. In these texts from the 1980s, as part of that project, they emplace a common sense about Althusser in critical education. In a series of insights, reversals, and unsubstantiated critiques—all while leaning heavily on a specific set of earlier interpretations—they describe Althusser's theory as worth mentioning, going some way toward understanding relative autonomy between school and economy, but they conclude that the theory tragically fails due to its functionalism and its lack of proper attribution of agency to individuals and culture.

One thing to note about Apple and Giroux's treatment of Althusser. They did not set out to study him. Such a thorough examination was not their project. Rather, they sought to consolidate then-nascent left perspectives on education and center the cultural, experiential, and agentic framework they had encountered in England. They most likely moved through readings of Althusser quickly because there were larger fish to fry. So in looking at their texts I only find a partial answer to the question of where the common sense about Althusser in critical education came from and why it persisted.

One key takeaway from this tour through these influential texts is that Apple and Giroux rely heavily on earlier interpretations of Althusser for their own. They were influenced by these texts, so much so that Giroux explicitly justifies his own treatment of Althusser by pointing to them. Others had done the work. To really understand the provenance of the common sense about Althusser, to see how and why the critiques from agency and functionalism landed so well in education, we have to reassess those texts.

14

Roots of the Common Sense

We now turn to Apple and Giroux's sources. Doing so unearths the underlying arguments against Althusser to which Apple and Giroux allude and on which they rely for their configuration of the common sense about Althusser in critical education. Doing so also unearths a partial intellectual history of critical education, providing occasion to reflect on some of its most basic assumptions. In this next section, I go through the texts chronologically, examining the arguments upon which Giroux and Apple based their interpretations of Althusser. In each subsection I provide brief historical context for the source at hand and then examine the author's arguments.

As a kind of preface to the interpretations of Althusser that influenced Apple and Giroux, consider Leszek Kolakowski's (1971) essay "Althusser's Marx," published in the *Socialist Register*. Note the venue. The *Socialist Register* was a British socialist publication whose founders split with the more established journal *New Left Review* (*NLR*) in the late 1960s (Miliband 1994). The British Marxist historian Perry Anderson began his tenure as editor of *NLR* in that period and the split is largely attributed to his rise to that position. Anderson at that time had a great interest in Althusser's thinking and was a rival to Edward P. Thompson, also a British Marxist historian, author of the landmark text *The Making of the English Working Class* and a leader of postwar British socialist thinking from a previous generation. Thompson and Anderson had disagreed mightily with the direction of the British left in the years after 1968. The feud between these two historians, which created torsions throughout the British left like the split between *NLR* and the *Register* would, I show later, prove decisive in constructing the common sense about Althusser in critical education, since Giroux and Apple took Thompson's side in the debate.

Back to Kolakowski's essay. Like most readings of Althusser, the text was published in the Anderson-Thompson crucible. But it was written in a much different one. Kolakowski was a Polish philosopher, historian, and activist who would renounce his deep commitments to Marxism over the course of his long career (Jones 2009). An active member of the Polish United Worker's Party as a young man, his political and scholarly accomplishments earned him an opportunity to travel to the Soviet Union in 1950. There he encountered what he called "the enormity of material and spiritual desolation caused by the Stalinist system" (Kulish 2019), and thereafter, much like Althusser, attempted to revise Marxism to separate it as a line of thinking from its applications in Stalin's Russia. Kolakowski became an ardent critic of the Marxist tradition generally speaking, and focused particularly on the religious influences in Hegel's thinking and how they survived in Marxism.

Throughout the 1960s, these critiques of Marxism got him fired from his teaching position in communist Poland. He then left his home country in exile. After holding several faculty positions in the United States, he settled at Oxford University, England, in 1970. While writing his three-volume *Main Currents in Marxism*, Kolakowski published the essay on Althusser in *Socialist Register*, surveying Althusser's thinking. He found a willing audience in those pages given the feud with Anderson and the *NLR*. After a summary of the main arguments in Althusser's writing to date, he concludes that

> the whole of Althusser's theory is made up of the following elements: 1. common sense banalities expressed with the help of unnecessarily complicated neologisms; 2. traditional Marxist concepts that are vague and ambiguous in Marx himself (or in Engels) and which remain, after Althusser's explanation, exactly as vague and ambiguous as they were before; 3. some striking historical inexactitudes … and, finally, that the whole construction, in spite of the verbal claims to "scientificity" is a gratuitous ideological project intended to preserve a certain traditional model of Marxism typical of Stalinist Communism. The main design of Althusser reveals an ideological or simply a religious way of thinking. (Kolakowski 1978: 112)

Given his history, we can understand Kolakowski's tone. His style is curt and polemically sharp. The descriptions of Althusser are final, dismissive, and closed. Finally, we see the association of Althusser's thinking with Stalinism. Kolakowski uses the term as a political cudgel. The critique is simultaneously analytical, polemical, and distractingly partisan.

Yet Kolakowski spends many pages examining Althusser's writing, working carefully to cite and interpret and refute. He lays out an argument for his interpretation, but it is not within our scope to delve into Kolakowski's claims as they do not directly come to bear on how Althusser was taken up in critical education. Neither Apple nor Giroux cited Kolakowski nor have I found his work influential in the field of critical education. Yet this essay, particularly its style and orientation, resounded in the crucible of critique that influenced Apple and Giroux. The form and content of Kolakowski's analytical-polemical-partisan critique manifests in the work of Jacques Rancière (2011), Paul Q. Hirst (1976), Michael Erben and Denis Gleeson (1975), Alex Callinicos (1976), and E. P. Thompson (1978) (whom Kolakowski cites). And we can see how these critiques were taken up by eminent education researchers like sociologist R. W. Connell (1979) and ethnographer Paul Willis (1981b), as well as labor organizer and intellectual Stanley Aronowitz (2016)—each of whom would influence the direction of critical education through their influence on Apple and Giroux.

While Kolakowski eviscerates Althusser's theory, he spends many pages and words to do it. Indeed, there was a cottage industry of essays and books in English that emerged responding to Althusser. Althusser's theory, for authors like Kolakowski, was an extension of the failed communist state project to which they had devoted their young political lives. The size and shape of Kolakowski's anger is understandable, and his writing is a kind of feverish search for philosophical reasons to reject Althusser's theory as part of his larger project. Yet the amount of time and energy required to pursue this rejection belies a kind of reverence: Althusser's Marxism is obviously something worthy of response.

Apple and Giroux's repulsion and respect for Althusser's arguments is a residue of this dynamic. The founders of critical education were passing along this repulsion/respect for Althusser they found in their milieu. They absorbed it from a distinctly (though not entirely) British line of critique of Althusser that developed between 1970 and 1980. This line of critique is composed of intellectuals who—like Kolakowski—had personal, political, and intellectual reasons for rejecting Althusser with a certain vehemence. From our moment, generations later, those reasons can feel specific to their time, place, and personalities. These critiques each take polemical, analytic, and partisan forms that Apple and Giroux would ultimately rely upon for their own project of critical education. The critiques themselves therefore have much to teach us about the history of critical education and the common sense about Louis Althusser therein, particularly because they leave much to be desired upon reexamination.

15

A Frustrated Student: Rancière and the ISAs

A paradigm case of this sort of critique, and one that would set the stage for several others whom Apple and Giroux would cite, comes from Jacques Rancière. Rancière was a student of Althusser's and a co-author of the original edition of *Reading Capital*. Rancière's first full-length book *Althusser's Lesson* (2011) was a political, polemical, and philosophical rejection of his teacher. Published in French in 1974, it was not translated into English until 2011, though it was an important touchstone for many British education researchers in the wake of 1968.

Rancière admits in the preface that this book is not an objective account weighing the positives and negatives of Althusserian theory, but rather a personal account of the events of May 1968, Althusser's conflicted role in them, and the role Althusserianism played during and after those events (Rancière 2011: xiv). A text rooted in its time and place, the arguments against Althusser rely on the histories of specific movement groups, the dynamics of which are not within the scope of our purposes here. However, the book is notable as a concrete rebuke to Althusser's supposedly concrete thinking about education (Lampert [2014] concludes that Rancière is largely correct about Althusser in this regard). Rancière portrays the French university system, its leftist student movements, and the intellectual debates teeming within them with a powerful clarity—basically depicting the actual life of institutions within the scholastic ISA as a gesture toward a refutation of the theory of the ISAs.

I will limit myself to those points Rancière makes about ideology and the ISAs. *Althusser's Lesson* (*AL*), he admits, is a critique of Althusser's concept of ideology without focusing on the notion of ISAs (Rancière 2011: xiii). Yet there are other points of interest in the text, particularly Rancière's view—confirmed by Althusser himself years later—that he played a key role in producing the concept of ideology behind the ISAs essay. Rancière's insinuation is that it was his provocation in a 1969 essay that changed Althusser's mind about ideology toward the theory he eventually published in the ISAs essay. Rancière includes that 1969 essay as an appendix to *AL*. Therefore, not only is Rancière frustrated with Althusser's orientation to the student movements of 1968 while writing *AL* in 1974, but he is also frustrated as a student. From the outset, Rancière's perspective on Althusser's orientation to 1968 is different than what I have laid out in the first part. Balibar, in the preface to *OTRC*, explains Althusser's absence from the student movement by citing his mental health, and reports that the ISAs essay was an attempt to understand that movement. Rancière has a very different and less charitable take. In opposition to Balibar's view that the ISAs essay was an attempt to understand the events of 1968, Rancière sees Althusser "struggling, somewhat pitifully, to reconcile his old ideas with the lessons offered up by the events themselves" (xx).

Reading Rancière's early critique of Althusser's concept of ideology in 1969 along with the provocations in the main text of *AL*, we see that a portion of the creativity and novelty of Althusser's thinking about ideology as written in the ISAs essay, and thus *OTRC*, derives from Rancière's thinking. I also find that the early Rancière has reason to be critical of Althusser personally and politically, and makes several provocative— and insightful—points against Althusser's theory. Yet these points, emerging from that young frustration, would remain only partially argued, and that partiality would reverberate throughout the line of critique. *Althusser's Lesson* influenced Erben and Gleesen's (1975) critique of Althusser's sociology of education, which would then influence Giroux. I first present context and arguments from Rancière's 1969 essay critiquing Althusser's theory of ideology up to 1968, notably before Althusser published the ISAs essay, and continue to Rancière's gestural critiques of the ISAs.

"On the Theory of Ideology: Althusser's Politics" (Rancière 2011) was a write-up of a course Rancière taught at an autonomous student-led university born out of the events of May 1968. It was June of that year. The course was meant "primarily to comment on Marx's texts on ideology" but "quite quickly became the instrument for reflection on … the Althusserian theory of the battle of science against ideology" (127). Then a plan to publish the essay went in an unexpected direction.

> At the end of the semester, Saul Karsz, who had attended the course, asked me to write an article based on it for a collection of essays on Althusser to be published in Argentina. It is quite likely that he showed my piece to Althusser and possible also that it might have played a part in Althusser's introduction of the notion of ideological state apparatuses to his thought. (Rancière 2011: 127)

Althusser read Rancière's essay and composed the ISAs essay with it in mind the following year. Elliott (2006) notes that Althusser started writing the ISAs essay in March 1969, leaving ample time between Rancière's writing and the publication of the ISAs essay for that to be true. Elliott also cites an interview published in the German collection *Die Krise des Marxismus*, wherein Althusser indicates that he read Rancière's criticisms and that they had merit. Althusser's ideas in the ISAs read like a response to Rancière's critiques, or perhaps the incorporation of a constructive criticism.

"On the Theory of Ideology" is also a direct response to Althusser's 1964 essay "Student Problems," which argues against student calls for more participatory pedagogies in university classrooms. Rancière sets the scene. Althusser's early essay was an intervention in a disagreement on the left between the Party and students over demands to change French universities. Party officials made quantitative demands for more campuses and professors, while students made more qualitative demands like making pedagogy less alienating (Althusser 1964: 136).

Althusser (1964) disagreed with the students, recommending that they put curricular content before the form of teaching in their demands (12). How we teach, he said, matters less than what we teach. Putting content before form, he insists, is a strategic point that makes a bigger difference in class struggle (14). The university can change its pedagogy to modern methods, or even keep the old ones, and so students "risk committing themselves to a confusion" that misses how capitalism, via positivism, encourages researchers to be blind operatives for capital (15). Furthermore, teachers are a front line against ideological content. Their knowledge can be "weapons of scientific learning" and they offer "scientific and critical training" that the "government fears" (15).

Students who insist on "participationist" or "anarcho-democratic" forms of pedagogy might miss these learnings, leading to "half-knowledge" (15), a "weak knowledge" that makes them "easier to manipulate" (15). Teachers, as trained experts, can work against this reproduction by passing along their knowledge. But Althusser also insists on the more philosophical point that "*pedagogic equality* between teachers and students" is mistaken because "this does not correspond with the reality of the pedagogical function" (15). He points to a basic inequality between teacher and student that the student movements miss. That philosophical notion would inspire vociferous disagreement with student Rancière (and eventually inspire his landmark book *The Ignorant Schoolmaster* (1991)). Indeed, as I mention later, one of Rancière's stated goals in his theoretical work generally, in the preface to *AL*, is to show how liberatory theories oppress.

In the 1969 text, Rancière understands Althusser's 1964 essay as indicative of the "political consequences of [Althusser's] theory of ideology" and responds to his teacher, taking aim at Althusser's distinction between science and ideology. Rancière's critique of Althusser's concept of ideology and science—and the suggestions Rancière makes to change this concept—look like the account of the ISAs Althusser would produce later in 1970.

Rancière takes issue with a Marxist concept of science that casts it as the opposite or "Other" of ideology, which would be positivist. Rather, knowledge is caught up in class struggle (Rancière 2011: 143). Thus Althusser's latent positivism is counter to Marxism. Rancière says there is a strategic consideration here: "The system of knowledge, like state power, is an object of the class struggle and must, like state power itself, be destroyed" (143). Science is not a matter of producing positivistically true knowledge over false knowledge. Rather, science should be about destroying the knowledge produced by dominant classes. Knowledge is an object of class struggle, but the knowledge is more than just curricular content: it is the system of knowledge delivery itself. Rancière cites science instruction in the universities as an example. He argues that science classes are reactionary rather than revolutionary not because of the content of the course but rather the "structures within which these courses take place" (144): institutions, mechanisms, relations, and hierarchies in the university. Rancière points to consultants as one example of institutional practices that tinge knowledge with class struggle. It is therefore the configurations of structures within the institutions that "manifest" ideology (145), not knowledge that is positivistically true or false.

Readers would be right to see the seeds of Althusser's concept of the ISAs in Rancière's claim here, as he is all but saying that concrete practices provide material support for dominant ideologies and realize these ideologies within modern institutions, and as such reproduce capital. Even more of what Althusser would claim in the ISAs is clearly present in Rancière when he says ideology exists within concrete practices like testing, disciplinary divisions, and departmental configurations (142). These practices realize state power, says Rancière, which serves the interests of the ruling class. He even writes that this dominant ideology is organized in a collection or system of institutions, which includes the information system (142). Rancière goes so far as to articulate the idea that ideology is not consciousness or a social imaginary but rather practices enacted in diffuse apparatuses (74).

Thus it is Rancière's critique of Althusser's nonmaterialist concept of ideology, pre-1968, that Althusser absorbs via Saul Karsz in 1969, which pushes Althusser to fashion the concept of ISAs and its attendant ontology of struggle. Rancière does not call these systems of knowledge appropriation ideological state apparatuses, nor the individual process of reproduction and recruitment to those ideologies interpellation, but rather readies the ground for such claims. These neologisms, their theorization, and further application are Althusser's.

The back and forth between Althusser and Rancière began as a debate about pedagogy and continued as a conversation about schools and universities. The ISAs idea was born through we could call eristic dialogue between teacher and student, in a disagreement over the politics of teaching and learning amidst student organizing. But it was a bitter dialogue. Perhaps already annoyed that his contribution to *Reading Capital* had not been published several years earlier (only Balibar's had been included), Rancière had good reason to be even more frustrated with his teacher who, using his ideas, went on to write one of the most cited and talked-about essays on Marxism of that generation. Althusser only acknowledged this influence much later. Plus, a professor that does not side with students in the most electrifying movement in a century will not be popular among leaders of that movement.

We can understand Rancière's frustration, but it does not add up to critiques from functionalism and agency, though he launches them nonetheless. In "On the Theory of Ideology" Rancière critiques Althusser for a superimposition of concepts, implying a dubious union of two antagonistic frameworks: historical materialism and Durkheimian bourgeois sociology (Rancière 2011: 132). Going back further than Durkheim and into the history of political theory Rancière also proposes that Althusser's account "could very well be a renewal of the myth of an ideological state of nature" (134). Rancière's point is that Althusser focuses too much on cohesion (131), which implies a connection to the Hobbesian state of nature. By extension, bourgeois theories of cohesion and order leave out the class that is dominated and that class' own activity, foregrounding instead a monstrous social structure. Ultimately, the theory is one of "universal illusion": "the representation of an enormous, despotic machine that subjects every individual to its functioning" (Rancière 2011: 77). Here we have prototypes of the critiques from functionalism and agency that others would take up later.

Like Apple's (1985) point about missing details of worker and school resistance, Rancière says ten years earlier that Althusser neglects everyday life in institutions like churches (Rancière 2011: 76), which leads to an accusation that Althusser's theory imbues social life with passivity and a lack of action. For Rancière (2011), Althusser's theory is guilty of a kind of tenured Marxism (79) that subordinates the student movement and champions its own book-writing as class struggle. In one searing line, Rancière reverses Marx's famous eleventh thesis on Feuerbach to denounce Althusser. He writes that Althusser's armchair Marxism is a kind of impotence that "in the end [says] 'It's all in vain. We've tried in various ways to change the world; the point now is to interpret it'" (xiii). Rather than focus on student movements trying to change the world, Althusser is focused more on interpretation. Rancière says the risk is in the barricaded street, not the published article.

That abrogation of activism, particularly student activism, is a sticking point for Rancière. He thus has a unique take on Althusser's pardon to the heroes passage. Recognizing that Althusser, in that passage, imbues teachers with a heroic agency that can make change in a social formation, Rancière's complaint is that students are not part of the picture. He writes "the heroes are, of course, teachers. In Althusser's 'anti-historicist' history, no student has been able to pick out the low music of or turn any weapons against the system" (75). We know that Althusser does say that students can and do make the social structure tremble. But Rancière is insistent. After saying teachers get credit for social movement in Althuser's thinking, he also says they do not get their proper due in Althusser's theory, narrating a striking anecdote about a disruptive teacher in a French district controlled by the Communist Party.

> The fact is that Althusser is perfectly free to propose all the theses he wants. All his "subversive" theses, however, share the following interesting peculiarity: they never entail any disruptive practices. He is free to put forward the concept of ideological state apparatuses, and free to use this concept to mock, however gently, the reformist illusions of communist teachers. But when a teacher in a communist district is barred from teaching secondary school because he tried to disrupt the framework of the school apparatus, and when district authorities rally to the aid of the academic inspectors to denounce the troublemaker, it is obviously none of Althusser's business. (Rancière 2011: 112)

There is no note in the translation specifying whether this event actually happened, but it is easy to imagine. The Communist Party controlled entire districts in France at that time. Teachers lived and worked in those districts. So what to do with a teacher who disrupts the school apparatus when communists control that apparatus? A leftist aligning with Rancière would not rally to the aid of the academic inspectors to denounce the troublemaking. Althusser does, however (if we believe the anecdote), proving Rancière's general point that subversive theories can be used to oppress. He expresses bitter disappointment that such a disruption is none of Althusser's business. This anecdote dovetails with Rancière's earlier observation that Althusser is against the anti-authoritarian stream of the student movement.

But *AL*, by Rancière's own admission, is a polemic rather than a detailed argument. While Rancière has a legitimate claim to be frustrated that Althusser did not initially cite his 1969 essay as influential for the ISAs essay, and while Althusser's critiques of the student movement would make any student organizer frustrated, this frustration does not an argument make. Rancière says the theory could very well take from Hobbes's state of nature. But does it? Rather, the stability in Althusser's theory—the stability created by the apparatuses—is a stability of ruling-class dominance in the midst of class struggle rather than the order-focused stability nascent in Hobbes and more fully present in Comte and Durkheim. Here we can see a flaw in one of the first formulations of the critique from functionalism. When it comes to agency, Rancière says Althusser includes no disruptive practices, but he clearly does in the book length project. Thus the critiques from functionalism and agency in *AL* are polemical gestures written in a style of intellectual exasperation to which there are easy responses.

However, Rancière's intervention here should not be totally dismissed. Hudson-Miles (2020) points out correctly that one of his major contributions to educational theory is to show how supposedly liberatory traditions of pedagogy contain oppressive inequalities. The question of whether Althusser's theory of education falls prey to this critique is an important one and to which I return in the third part and conclusion. For now, I have shown that Rancière's critiques from agency and functionalism do not hold up and, furthermore and perhaps more importantly, he himself contributed crucial elements to the theory of the ISAs.

Despite their lack of deeper substance, these faulty premises regarding functionalism and agency would travel and take root in England. Scholars and organizers who were following the events of May 1968 read Rancière in French, inspiring publications on Althusser's theory of education that would influence Giroux.

16

Formalization of the Provocation: Erben and Gleesen

Michael Erben and Denis Gleeson were professors of sociology of education in England, which was a fertile ground for Marxist theory and critiques of Althusser. Erben and Gleeson (1975) published one of the first significant articles on Althusser's ideas about education in English in the journal *Educational Studies*. Called "Reproduction and Social Structure: Comments on Louis Althusser's Sociology of Education," the authors take up Rancière's gestural critiques from agency and functionalism, draping them in sociological discourse. Erben and Gleeson give Rancière's critiques more formal purchase in their essay, yet disorganization and looseness pervade the account.

The critique from agency forms one part of their case against Althusser. To Erben and Gleeson (1975), the ISAs essay "neglects the importance of the actions of teachers and students" (75). Althusser's theory leaves teachers "completely flattened and speechless" and "reinforces the idea that radical change is beyond their frames of reference" (75). Generally, the authors have reservations about "Althusser's overemphasis upon the 'crushing' influences of apparatuses, which condition man in his pursuit of the maintenance and reproduction of production" (74). The resonance with Rancière's critique is clear: Althusser's theory casts social structure as a monstrous machine, leaving no room for agency and resistance.

To Erben and Gleesen, Althusser understands students and teachers as passive in two ways: first in knowledge production and consumption, and second in the face of crushing, dominant apparatuses from which they cannot escape. In their reconstruction of Althusser's arguments in the ISAs essay, they understand his claim about instruction and competency, and therefore reproduction, as skill transmission and passive socialization (77). There is a step missing there, in the sense that transmission need not be passive by definition, though Erben and Gleeson stipulate that it is. By the same token of passivity, teachers are unwitting servants of ideology. Althusser does say specifically that students can be little devils, teachers can be heroic, and ISAs are sites of struggle, but Erben and Gleeson do not make reference to these passages.

In general, Althusser's analysis "can lead to a state of inaction, justifying the avoidance of areas exactly where there might be a weak link in the chain of capitalist coercion" (82). Citing Rancière, they make a claim that Apple and Giroux would repeat: that Althusser's project is a tragic failure. "Althusser does not fulfil the promise of his own rigor when the situation moves to action" (81). Indeed, rather than "engage with [teachers and students] in struggle" Althusser is "scuppering the ship while it is still in port" (81).

They give historical examples. The first example is May 1968, where Althusser was wrong about his critiques of the student movements (86). Erben and Gleeson can thus claim that Althusser provides no theory of causality or change, though they provide no other evidence. We know that the opposite is the case, that Althusser mentions several kinds of political struggles and their impacts (including 1968). They make the claim nonetheless. They also point to the Black Power movement in the United States, the language movement in Wales, and Chinese student demonstrations against Soviet-style control as further examples of how movement can change social structure (86). These are some examples of resistance and activity that Althusser supposedly forecloses in his account of crushing, passivizing ISAs.

Certainly Erben and Gleeson ask a valid question to Althusser and any Marxist theory: what makes a theory a class struggle theory? How can we know if a theory is one that centers struggle and agency? While Erben and Gleeson broach this important question, they do not provide any unique criteria that would help us distinguish a failed class struggle theory from a successful class struggle theory. Nor do they provide a counter-argument that proves Althusser's is not a class struggle theory. While they state that Althusser's theory is accordingly a failed one, they do not provide reasons for coming to this conclusion. Yet they do formalize Rancière's provocations, providing more language for them, particularly the critique from functionalism.

Erben and Gleeson say outright that "Althusser has a functionalist tendency" (83) that contradicts "his argument that the reproduction of the social relations of production can only be a class undertaking, realized through a class struggle" (80). Part of the problem is Althusser's thesis about the RSA and ISAs and the dynamic between the two. Like Rancière they claim that the theory is preoccupied with order as opposed to struggle (99), making reference to the state of nature tradition in political theory. Just as Rancière mixed a similar interpretation with that of political theory and the state of nature, Erben and Gleeson make the same move by invoking the English political theorist Thomas Hobbes and the notion of the body politic. They add a sociological citation to the reading however, pointing to a claim by John O'Neill (1972) to that effect (Erben and Gleeson 1975: 77). The status of O'Neill's interpretation is too far afield for present purposes, but the citation lends Rancière's reading legitimacy via English sociology.

In general the claim here, as Rancière put it also, is that Althusser's theory is not Marxist but rather functionalist. Whereas Rancière characterizes it as bourgeois sociology by citing Comte and Durkheim, Erben and Gleeson render the claim scrutable to British audiences by aligning it with the sociological discipline in English like Talcott Parsons and Erving Goffman and certain forbears in social contract theory. Erben and Gleesen argue that Althusser is out-of-sync with the Marxist tradition and more in-sync with this line of thinking, naming Hobbes, Rousseau, Weber, Durkheim, and Parsons as comparables (78). They go so far as to say that Althusser is "a repetition of Durkheim" (84), though they do not cite which part of Durkheim.

Their wording is seductively formal. They state the conclusion first (which we find in Rancière as well): "Althusser's reading of the nature of reproduction proceeds along a different path than Marx in that he assumes the consent implicit in social contract theories" (78). Yet they have not provided premises for this reading. They say Althusser's theory cannot account for how people deviate within social structure (despite the many examples Althusser gives of such deviation, and the basic concepts of the theory itself being conducive to such accounts), but do not go further to state how.

They do give some evidence for the connection with Parsons. They cite the introduction to Parsons's essay "The School Class as a Social System: Some of its Functions in American Society" (2017). Erben and Gleeson say both Althusser and Parsons base their theories on similar assumptions, using terms like system and socialization. Beyond saying that Parsons and Althusser use similar words, their clearest claim is that there are parallels between the ISAs and Parson's theory of pattern variables (Erben and Gleeson 1975: 79). If the ISAs and pattern variables are meaningfully similar concepts, then indeed we might conclude that the theories are similar. Erben and Gleeson do not elaborate on the premise or go into detail about whether ISAs and pattern variables are actually similar, but we can attempt a brief foray into Parsons and evaluate this proposal. Doing this evaluation is particularly important because the functionalist label stuck to Althusser's theory in such a durable way. If the two concepts were similar then there might be reason to believe this comparison.

What are pattern variables in Parsons's theory and are they similar to the ISAs? Early Parsons commentator Park (1967) sets the stage for pattern variables by linking them with Parson's theory of action. Parsons was chiefly concerned with creating a sociology of action, or a theory of why individual people do things that are social. People that do stuff (actors) do that stuff, he says, because the action has meaning for them. Actions become meaningful based on the situation and the possible orientations an individual can have in the situation. Parsons thinks that for any given situation people choose one of five meaning alternatives when thinking about what to do. These alternatives occur in pairs. He calls these pairs pattern variables (Park 1967: 187).

Indeed, Parsons and Shills (1962) write that pattern variables are a scheme that "defines a set of five dichotomies" (48). These dichotomies are a formulation of "the way each and every social action, long- or short-term, proposed or concrete, prescribed or carried out, can be analyzed into five choices (conscious or unconscious, implicit or explicit)" (48). An action's social meaning can thus be analyzed as a decision that individuals make between one of these five dichotomies: gratification/discipline, private/collective interest; transcendence/immanence; object modalities; and scope of significance (49). Parsons goes on to stipulate cultural, personal, and social system aspects for each of these pattern variables. He then differentiates each aspect into two further subcategories depending on the choice an actor makes in the pattern variable (Parsons and Shills 1962: 81–2). For example, the transcendence/immanence pattern variable is where "the actor faces the dilemma of whether to treat the objects in the situation in accordance with a general norm covering all objects in that class or whether to treat them in accordance with their standing in some particular relations to him or his collectivity, independently of the objects' subsumability under a general norm" (81). This pattern variable therefore breaks down into universalism or particularism in its cultural, personality, and social system aspects (82).

Pattern variables are thus a schema of five dilemmas that social actors must choose from when making their actions personally, culturally, and socially meaningful. The ideological state apparatuses are modes of intervention where the ruling class can maintain the continuity of their preferred relations of production nonviolently. Are these theories similar? The best account in the affirmative I can find is DiTomaso (1982), who argues that Parsons's and Althusser's theories are similar because they are sociologically reductionist: they do not specify how any action could be outside the bounds of social structure, giving no specification of the limits of structural effects (14). This is a fair point, though as we will see in Hirst's critique below, one can critique any theory for not specifying how a phenomenon is outside of it. Beyond metatheoretical concerns, the fundamental question for DiTomaso is whether Althusser's theory permits change (15). She says it does not on the ground just mentioned. While this is clearly an argument, it is easy to refute using the eleven rules. The struggle rule clearly lays out how changes to structure happen in the theory, for which Althusser gives many examples, some focusing directly on schools. The comparison with Parsons does not hold up.

Yet Erben and Gleeson pursue the case undaunted. After likening ISAs to pattern variables without explanation, their second premise for this argument makes mention of equilibrium. To Erben and Gleeson, Althusser's account is "an oversimplified equilibrium model in which the main features (ISAs and RSA) complement one another inter-dependently" (Erben and Gleeson 1975: 79). Erben and Gleeson use the metaphor of a machine to repeat the similarity. To them, the ISAs and RSA are like the hardware and software of a computer (79). Certainly the word apparatus can refer to machines, but we know that Althusser's use of the term comes from Marx's reference to French bourgeois tax structures and not the history of technology. While he uses the terms mechanism and function, the concept behind these words is one of class struggle and not the maintaining of equilibrium. Rather, Althusser's concept of maintenance (as with his concept of stability) refers to ruling-class dominance in class struggle. These concepts are quite distinct, even if similar words can be used to express them. Erben and Gleeson conclude, however, that "the questions Althusser sets himself [are] functionalist in nature [and] his use of language assumes a functionalist 'rhetoric'" (79). Mimicking Rancière's provocative style, they write that "not unlike Parsons, Althusser portrays a model of a man as a puppet or cultural fool constrained completely by agents or mechanisms of the system" (83). The image is provocative but the argument behind it is lacking.

With these characterizations in particular, it is easy to see where Giroux would find footing for his polemical treatment of Althusser. Like Rancière, Erben and Gleeson gesture toward a claim and articulate the conclusion with rhetorical force without going through a process of argument. They claim Althusser's theory makes no mention of action but do not cite passages where Althusser clearly does. They say that the ISAs are like pattern variables without showing it (which, when you try, the comparison does not work). They say Althusser is concerned with equilibrium in a functionalist tradition without evidence. Formalizing Rancière's gestures in *AL*, their writing has more of an accusatory structure than a logical one. Their contribution is to bring in disciplinary language to give the polemical gestures a more formal tone.

Hirst provided a different, stronger argument for functionalism in Althusser, though it fails on similar grounds.

17

Against Generality: Hirst

Paul Q. Hirst, professor of social theory at Birkbeck College, University of London, would take another direction. He wrote an incisive critique (1976) of Althusser's theory of ideology, focusing specifically on the reproduction of the relations of production. Hirst had co-authored a noted book *Pre-Capitalist Modes of Production* (1975) with Barry Hindness that drew from the Althusserian stream of structuralism. Thus Hirst and Hindness were seen by followers of the *Socialist Register*, notably E. P. Thompson, as defending the Althusserian paradigm on British shores (Corrigan and Sayer 1978). Yet they did not join Anderson and other sympathetic Althusserians at the *New Left Review*, but rather started their own journal called *Theoretical Practice* (Pimlott 2003). Hirst did not see himself as British-Althusserian and issued critiques of the theory, which Giroux and Apple would later cite.

Hirst's essays critiquing Althusser were published with his earlier work on Rancière in the book *On Law and Ideology* (1979). While heady, these critiques are robust and emerged within organizing contexts. His essays on French concepts of ideology were initially written as pamphlets for the Cambridge University Communist Party, and then presented to the first meeting of the Communist University of Cambridge (Hirst 1976: 411, n2). In the text, Hirst first takes issue with Althusser's question itself: the question of the reproduction of the relations of production.

In his view, there are several things wrong with this question. First, the question is too general and, for that reason, functionalist (388). Like Erben and Gleeson, Hirst does not provide much evidence for this claim. And like Erben and Gleeson, the jump from functionalism to agency is quick. Hirst writes that, in this functionalist view, individual agency "exists as such only as a result of the functionalist mode of posing the question" (388). Since the theory is functionalist the concept of individual agency in the theory is also functionalist (by which he means largely nonexistent). To Hirst, Althusser attempts to deal with this agency-denying functionalist generality "by reference . . . to 'concrete' conditions" (388), but doing so, he says, "is really just a matter of words rather than substance," a faulty attempt to "rectify a problem in discourse by reference to the non-discursive" (388). Thus Althusser's attempt to ground his overly abstract, functionalist, and deterministic theory fails.

These statements sound similar to the Rancierian line formalized by Erben and Gleeson: strongly worded accusations, draped in technical terminology, without much evidence or argument. But Hirst is different. He sets out premises and a conclusion.

His position is that any answer to the question about the reproduction of relations of production must be functionalist and deterministic because "there can be no general theory of the maintenance of capitalism" (389). While it is strange for a Marxist sociologist well-known for writing abstract general theories of capitalism to say that no such thing is possible, Hirst elaborates.

Reproduction, he says, is not the ultimate condition of production as Althusser says. It is rather the condition of existence of particular practices. Indeed, Hirst thinks there are only "definite capitalist social formations and the determinants of the conjunctures which are the forms of their existence or transformation" (389), nothing more. This means that no institution or organization or system of organizations can reproduce relations of production. These relations only exist under specific conditions. Nothing secures them (390). Since there is no general theory of the maintenance of capitalism, we cannot stipulate that certain organizations or entities reproduce the relations production. We can only do analyses of determinate moments of construction and destruction of particular relations (389). Thus Althusser's question about the reproduction of the relations of production is too general to have an answer at all. Furthermore, Hirst reminds us, the abstraction is such that any answer to this question will be functionalist and deterministic.

There are two flaws in this argument. First, any theory will involve some level of generality. Following this line of thinking against generality would lead to the rejection of any theory whatsoever, including Hirst's (a predicament that Thompson is happy to own as we will see later). Second, Hirst draws a distinction without a difference. It is a valid and interesting question to ask whether one can talk about the reproduction of relations of production at all, but contrasting that attempt with doing analyses of the construction and destruction of determinate relations is to make a distinction without a difference. What would an analysis of how determinate relations continue over time be other than an account of their reproduction?

But to Hirst, it is not just Althusser's question that is a problem. Althusser also gives a flawed response to his flawed question. Again, his response is functionalist (390) and Hirst specifies where the functionalism occurs. Althusser commits this error by equating "the *relations of production* with the distribution of agents to 'places' in the social division of labor" (390). In general, "divisions of the labor force," while not "inconsequential for the development of the relations of production" (392), are not themselves relations of production. Althusser mistakes one for the other.

Hirst points to China (392) and the Soviet Union (393) as examples. What Althusser would say constitutes the socialist relations of production in China—the forms of organization, the managerial hierarchies, the centralized administration—actually have nothing to do with socialist relations of production. More specifically, Althusser's concept of the relations of production conflates distinctions between administration, organization, and centralized policymaking, muddying what a relation of production in a social formation actually is (411). Giroux's stray thought that not all relations of production will be consistent or determined by the relations of exploitation is perhaps a reference to this interesting point.

Hirst's concern is that, on Althusser's theory, we would have to equate China's or the Soviet Union's actually existing division of the labor with their relations of production.

Hirst's general question here is legitimate. What is a relation of production? Is it just the existing structures in a labor force? Furthermore, what does it mean to have socialist relations of production and how do those differ from capitalist relations of exploitation? If a country has a government that identifies itself as socialist, does that mean its relations of production are socialist? Perhaps most importantly, does Althusser provide a good way of knowing in either case? These are important questions for Althusser's theory of education because ISAs reproduce the relations of production. Education as an ISA is supposed to reproduce these relations. But if we do not know what these are then it is difficult to advance the theory.

Hirst's is a challenge to the rule of hands. It is interesting and robust, but I do not think it is successful. The rule of hands does not say that managerial forms, hierarchical structures, and centralized administration comprise the relations of production. Rather a relation of production—if we follow Balibar—is how people have their hands on the means of production, not merely how they are managed as they do so. Althusser makes this point clearly in his distinction between the social and technical division of labor in reference to toiling and gooning.

At its strongest, Hirst's point is fertile ground for a substantive critique. Yet for Hirst's critique to land properly he would have to provide some positive account of relations of production. He would have to point to the social structures that do comprise relations of production and contrast these with what Althusser says. But he does not. Hirst does not go further in detailing what the relations of production are if not the division of the labor force. Without that positive account, he makes another distinction without a difference. Why must the division of the labor force be different than the relations of production? (Hussain [1976]) gestures toward a response to this question in his analysis of education and the labor market, though his text is quite similar to Althusser's account of competencies.) Thus while Hirst puts forward some of the strongest arguments for the critique from functionalism, the arguments do not hold up against the eleven rules.

18

A Trotskyite Calling Stalin: Callinicos

Like Hirst, the British Zimbabwean Marxist philosopher Alex Callinicos published a critique cited by Apple and Giroux, though it did not come to bear on education. His pamphlet *Althusser's Marxism* (1976) placed Althusser's theory in the broad scope of Marxist thinking. Callinicos was a graduate student at the time and active with the International Socialists, an iteration of the Socialist Worker's Party. Impressive in its precision, scope, and readability, Callinicos published the short book when he was only twenty-six years old. It is a deft retelling of the story of Marxist philosophy, from Engel's pursuit of a theoretical structure for Marx's thinking to the Second International's adoption of his mechanistic-scientific socialism to Stalin's metastasizing that account and the Hegelian Marxists' rejection of the latter.

Callinicos's overall assessment is that Althusser's work is "complex and contradictory" (1976: 102). He tells us it is important as a contribution but must ultimately be rejected because of "Althusser's closet Stalinism" (102). After a philosophical critique of Althusser's epistemology—namely, that Althusser offers no epistemology—Callinicos comes to the political conclusion that this lack of epistemology could potentially justify Eastern-bloc policy. Thus, Callinicos can claim that Althusser is a closet Stalinist. He does this by a juxtaposition of Althusser's theory and his political positions.

In a chapter called "The Politics of Ambiguity," Callinicos quickly but effectively gives historical context to Althusser's position within the French Communist Party (PCF), characterizing his intellectual project as the destalinization of Marxist theory (91). In a paragraph-long summary of Althusser's central project, Callinicos agrees that Althusser's is a Marxism that rejects economism, that is, one that rejects Stalinism but is still recognizable as Marxism. Yet while Althusser's philosophy is largely convincing for Callinicos, this philosophy is insufficient as a rejection of Stalinism. Why? Callinicos focuses on a distinction Althusser makes in *Essays in Self-Criticism* between a "right critique of Stalinism and a left critique of Stalinism." The former, Althusser says, is made by "the studies of 'totalitarianism' beloved of American political scientists" and also "the analyses of Russia produced by Trotskyists" (93). The left critique, we are told, is "'implicit' in the practice of the Chinese Cultural Revolution" (93). As a Trotskyite himself, Callinicos is not happy about this assessment. No Marxist likes to be deemed conservative, much less associated with American political scientists. Althusser's remark is a little slap in the face to his tendency. So Callinicos comes to Trotskyism's defense, noting that Althusser's critique of Trotskyism is flawed.

This may be so. But Callinicos slides into a barbed parenthetical that likens Althusser's critique of Trotskyism to Stalin's purges: Althusser "could of course expel the Trotskyists from the Marxist tradition, as Stalin did when he classified—and shot—them as fascists" (93). The comments are offhand but telling. Historically it is true that Stalin violently purged Trotsky's followers and then had Trotsky assassinated. While a written intellectual critique of Trotskyism is far from a violent purge, Althusser, Callinicos continues, is ambiguous about such Stalinist atrocities. Althusser is a Stalinist because he does not properly decry Stalin's crimes. He cannot critique Trotskyism and then fail to properly critique Stalin, lest he be a Stalinist.

Callinicos says Althusser's ambiguity about Stalin derives from a dilemma that Stalin's rule in the USSR created among socialists and communists. The dichotomy is between affirming Stalinism or the straightforward reforming thereof. Callinicos notes correctly that Althusser advances Maoist critiques of Stalinism in several places, yet this "serves merely as a certificate of revolutionary militancy that enables him to evade the real questions that are Stalin's heritage" (94). To Callinicos, a partisan Trotskyite, Althusser does not go far enough. Maoism is insufficient. Althusser's anti-Stalinism is inauthentic (an authentic disavowal, we imagine, would be leaving the PCF and joining the Socialist International, which Althusser never did). All this may be correct when it comes to Althusser's politics. But Callinicos makes a leap to equate this political dilemma with Althusser's theory.

"The ambiguity we encountered in *For Marx* on the question of Stalinism is, in fact, a structural feature of Althusser's political position" (94). A political observation, by the magic of the phrase "in fact," becomes connected to a structural feature of a theory. But Callinicos only substantiates his proposition that Althusser's political choice not to leave the PCF (despite numerous denunciations of Stalin and a clear statement that his project is destalinization of Marxism) comes to bear on features of his theory with ambiguous juxtapositions. The quick jump from political trajectory to structural feature of a theory does not hold up well as an argument against the theory itself. The causality rule is a firm philosophical rejection of Stalinist idealism, perhaps one of the most thorough Marxist rejections of Stalinism available. Althusser's repeated denunciations of Stalin and his characterization of his project as destalinizationist, which Callinicos recognizes, should be sufficient. Yet it appears that the dig at Trotskyism pushes Callinicos to call Stalinism on Althusser.

The Stalinist label would stick, leading to strong associations between Althusser's theory and totalitarianism. This particular critique would be taken up and disseminated by one of Althusser's most severe and influential critics, the celebrated British Marxist historian Edward P. Thompson.

19

The Eagle's Apostasy: E. P. Thompson

Edward P. Thompson was a celebrity of British Marxism. His writings, chiefly *The Making of the English Working Class* (1991), were and are hugely influential. He started the History Workshop, an initiative at the labor stronghold Ruskin College where workers researched and wrote histories of the working class. Thompson championed, in both his writing and his practice, notions of working-class agency and experience, which he expressed with an indomitable style and depth. The sociologist Scott Hamilton describes the dynamic between Thompson and Althusser as that between an eagle and a bustard (2013: 184). Avian analogies aside, there was actually little interaction between the two intellectuals. While the two never corresponded, Thompson's *The Poverty of Theory* (1978), *or An Orrery of Errors*, written "in two weeks in February 1978" (Hamilton 2013: 184) was to some degree a scathing open letter to Althusser and those taking up Althusser's ideas. It would be characterized as one of the most important Marxist essays of its moment and a devastating critique of Althusser.

According to philosopher Asad Haider (2020), the British historian Perry Anderson sent Althusser a copy of Thompson's manuscript and invited him to respond. Althusser, in the letters to Anderson, said that he found *The Poverty of Theory* an interesting text, but he lacked the requisite familiarity with historical methods and historiography to make a proper response. Haider also points out that *The Poverty of Theory*, wherein Althusser is nominally its main target, is actually aimed more at other scholars and activists in Thompson's milieu, like Anderson, with whom he vehemently disagreed over questions of leftist strategy in England. In fact, scholars of philosophy, history, and literature outside of education research understand *The Poverty of Theory* as Thompson's response to Anderson rather than Althusser.

Yet that context is largely absent in educational research where *The Poverty of Theory* is and was influential. Scholars following Thompson, like Paul Willis and Michael Apple, read the book as an intervention against Althusser and social reproduction theory, not chiefly as a political intervention in the British left. Indeed, Dworkin (1997) claims "the essay was the most influential critique of Althusser's thought ever produced in English" (225) and "was greeted with great enthusiasm and acclaimed not only by British Left-wing students and academics but by leftist intellectuals throughout the English-speaking world" (233).

Much like Rancière, Thompson describes his own text as "a polemical political intervention and not an academic exercise" (Thompson 1978: 260). In historian (and Thompson's wife) Dorothy Thompson's preface to it, she says the book "is a rarity in Edward's work" and "was intended as a polemical statement and written for a particular moment" (x). She notes:

> As a definitive work of "theory" the essay has many shortcomings. It is much more a defense of history than an exposition of an alternative to Althusser's views of Marxism. Edward saw the dispute not only as a scholarly one, but as the tackling of a set of intellectual assumptions which in politics could be taken to justify Stalinism and the discredited methods of the old Communist parties. (xi)

Stalinism is an important vector of the polemic, but even that line receives inconsistent treatment. In a section called "Afternote" written in August 1978, on the occasion of a devastating parliamentary defeat for French Communists (after which Althusser published several reflective articles again renouncing Stalinism), Thompson allows that "Althusser may prove to be more serious in his new-found anti-Stalinism than I suppose" (Thompson 1978: 284).

Yet, true to form, Thompson continues this hedgy sentence with a forceful thesis statement: "But if he is to be [anti-Stalin], then he must revoke the greater part of his own published theory. And this is what *The Poverty of Theory* is about" (284). Indeed, *The Poverty of Theory* is a polemical, sometimes toxic, sometimes brilliant attempt by a celebrity Marxist historian to revoke a Marxist philosophical position, but also, and perhaps more so, philosophy as a whole. The genre is similar to Rancière's *Althusser's Lesson* in that it contains—in a somewhat stream-of-consciousness style—a motley assortment of declarations, arguments, analyses, insults, in-the-weeds left movement politics, and invective. It is a text unlike any other, containing satirical collages of Victorian machines overlaid with Marxist terminology. Thompson made the satirical collages to illustrate Althusser's Victorian mechanical functionalism (Thompson 1978: 132–6).

While Thompson does not look explicitly at Althusser's claim that school is an ideological state apparatus, the place where he does mention the ISAs is a good sample of his tendency toward tantrum:

> Althusser's subsequent essay on "Ideology and Ideological State Apparatuses" … is, perhaps, the ugliest thing he has ever done, the crisis of the idealist delirium. I will spare myself the tedium of criticism, since in its naivety, its refusal of all relevant evidence, and its absurd ideality inventions, it exposes itself. (234)

This comment is just one of many in the text that combine insult, force, and lack of analysis. We see echoes of this style in not only Willis and Giroux, but also Erben and Gleeson and even Apple in some cases. Thompson's is a cobbling together of points made for the critiques from agency, functionalism, and tragedy yet the word critique may be a misnomer. While there are many points of interest throughout the book regarding the history of Marxism, from beginning to end, from his pseudo-theory of experience and agency to his otherwise fascinating history of structuralism, Thompson largely eschews critique for performatively negative declarations that, for him, are true by virtue of their being declared forcefully.

After establishing himself as an historian interested in the path and progress of historical materialism, Thompson alludes to Althusser as a "philosopher, who has only a casual acquaintance with historical practice" (Thompson 1978: 2). This disciplinary dichotomy comes early and repeats often throughout the essay. Using the metaphor of a road to progress in historical materialism, he introduces Althusser by saying "we have been suddenly struck from the rear ... From the quarter of Louis Althusser and his numerous followers" (2). We are told that "Althusserian 'Marxism' is an intellectual freak" that has "lodged itself firmly in a particular social *couche*, the bourgeois *lumpen-intelligentsia*" (3).

Thompson sets the tone and scope of the text in these opening salvos, whose viciousness only builds. Althusserians are "diversionists (enclosed and imprisoned within their own drama)" under the influence of the Althusserian freak, which they accept as "'a' Marxism" though they do not wholly understand it. The freak is "reprehensible because it is theoretically unprincipled" (4). Posing as a critique of humanism, empiricism, and economism, Althusser "and his acolytes ... offer an a-historical theoreticism which, at the first examination, discloses itself as idealism" (5). Althusser their leader is "the Aristotle of the new Marxist idealism" (5), leading them to folly. These blind followers misunderstand their master's mistaken doctrine, are imprisoned in their embarrassing ignorance, and only pretend to have something to do with revolutionary politics.

Beyond this introduction, which sets the tone for the book, Thompson's thinking about experience was influential for later educational researchers, as well as his points about how Althusser's structuralism disallows any thought about contradiction or class struggle (leading ultimately to Stalinism). I will focus on these aspects of *Poverty*.

Thompson thinks experience is "the mental and emotional response, whether of an individual or of a social group, to many interrelated events or to many repetitions of the same kind of event" (9–10). Indeed, the tension here (and in the debate between structuralism and humanism at that time generally) is between such events and individuals' response to them. Thompson writes that "experience is valid and effective but within determined limits: the farmer 'knows' his seasons, the sailor 'knows' his seas, but both may remain mystified about kingship and cosmology" (10). We then get more ideas about this tension between individuals' knowledge and the social events around them, or what Thompson calls social being and social consciousness (10).

A historian's concern, for Thompson, is the observation of the dynamic between these two things, or "dialogue" as he calls it between being and consciousness. He calls the dynamic dialogue a thrusting impingement: "Our concern, more commonly, is with multiple evidences, whose inter-relationship ... stirs, in the medium of time, before our eyes. These stirrings, these events, if they are within 'social being' seem often to impinge upon, thrust into, break against, existent social consciousness" (9). This thrust-impingement dialogue between social being and social consciousness "goes in both directions," which means that social consciousness is not a "passive recipient of 'reflections.'" Rather, "consciousness, whether as unselfconscious culture, or as myth, or as science, or law, or articulated ideology, thrusts back into being in its turn" (12).

Thompson further describes this dialogical dynamic in terms of the lived quality of being and vice versa (12). This dynamic is his framework for understanding history itself. He will later say, in describing historical logic, that "interrogative and response are mutually determining, and the relation can be understood only as *dialogue*" (54). The framework has the makings of an interesting theoretical account. Yet we hear little about what this dialogue is, philosophically speaking. Rather than develop the categories further, Thompson assesses the status of this question between social being and social consciousness in Western Marxism, claiming that intellectuals have "tilted the dialogue heavily back towards ideological domination" after a more habitual stress on "the determining pressures of being upon consciousness" (12).

Thompson has set up the classic philosophical question between individual and society very well, offering rich descriptive language for a theory of the dynamic between self and society from a Marxist perspective. He uses the terms impinging, thrust, and dialogue to describe the mutual determination of these two entities, social being and social consciousness. Yet at the precipice of providing content for these theoretical terms, and thus a theory that might stand up to Althusser's in some way, he punts. When he points to the further justification of these categories and their underlying presumptions, he says, "This difficult question ... may be left aside for the moment; it is in any case a question more usefully resolved by historical and cultural analysis than by theoretical pronouncements" (12). As we will see, studying history (or anything but philosophy) will always solve the problem for Thompson. He quickly turns back to excoriating Althusser, in this case for having "almost nothing to say about [the dynamic between social being and social consciousness] ... His silence here is both a guilty one and one necessary to his purpose" (12).

Thompson does provide more language for his own concepts later, asserting that "consciousness is *lived* as much as it is *known*" (235), illustrating the point by talking about values (236). Thompson gives examples and tries to elaborate on this point about lived experience and consciousness in relation to social being. Joining a picket line is about a choice in values (237) as well as interests, which emerge from peoples' "ways of life" (237). Social consciousness is thus lived experience, the people's way of life is lived according to what is nearest to the heart, learned within feeling, and expressed in their values (which are, of course, limited by determinate material conditions). Interests are, apparently, what interests people. Contrast this picture to Althusser's "ornate rationalist Victoriana" (237) that subsumes interests, lived experience, values, and the heart itself to utilitarianism's bad breath and Thompson has made his case.

Questions about this theory abound. What is Thompson's concept of experience? What does Thompson mean by interest and values, and where does he stand on the tradition of debates about which determines which and to what extent? (He defines interest circularly, for instance, by using the word interest.) What is the difference between being and consciousness, and what traditions of thinking does he draw from when using those loaded terms? Rather than elaborating this theory of thrusting impingement between social being and social consciousness, we hear instead about how Althusser "makes a virtue of his own theoretical imperialism" (Thompson

1978: 13) and how "the absurdity of Althusser consists in the ideological mode of his theoretical constructions. His thought is the child of economic determinism ravished by theoretical idealism" (16), and on and on. Indeed, Thompson explicitly refuses to "counter Althusser's paradigm of knowledge production with an alternative, universal paradigm, of my own" (18). Instead of elaboration, we get bluster and accusation. Tragically, Thompson opts to chastise Althusser's claim in *Reading Capital* that historians have no theory, while Thompson—historian extraordinaire—refuses to provide one. Equally tragic is the poverty of Thompson's theory in *The Poverty of Theory*.

Stuart Hall pushed Thompson on this underdeveloped theory of experience at the St. Paul's debate (on which more later), particularly whether and how experience is ideological. Thompson would unsuccessfully try to answer this question. Dworkin (1997) tells us that, at the debate

> Thompson distinguished between "experience I" (lived experience) and "experience II" (perceived experience). Thus a pattern of events in social being gave rise to "experience I," which was then not simply reflected in "experience II," but pressed upon "the whole field of consciousness" in such ways that it could not "be indefinitely diverted, postponed, falsified or suppressed by ideology." (Dworkin 1997: 238)

Yet the distinction, and theoretical depth, between lived and perceived experience would go largely undeveloped. This is not what *The Poverty of Theory* is about. Reading through *Poverty*, much of what Thompson writes concerns the difference between philosophical and historical practice: what it means to be a philosopher and what it means to be a historian are different, and Thompson plainly prefers the latter to the former. He holds theorists, theory, and philosophers in disdain. "Philosophy ought not to stand on every frontier like a huckster, offering spurious 'universal' banknotes current in all lands" (Thompson 1978: 63). Rather than a competing theory, Thompson opts to reject theory wholesale. He can thus only pursue critique of Althusser through history rather than theory, despite the fact that Althusser's is a theory (which perhaps explains Althusser's reaction when he read Thompson's claims).

Althusser's philosophy is quite the huckster in Thompson's estimation. *Poverty* unfurls with an angry flow, pointing to Althusser's epistemological shortcomings, his misreadings of Marx and Engels, his misunderstanding of historical practice, and how Althusser arrives at the "absurdities of a certain kind of static self-circulating 'Marxist' structuralism" (82). Here begins Thompson's story of Althusser's static structuralism.

The problem, Thompson says, actually starts with Marx himself, specifically the *Grundrisse* (83). Thompson reads Marx as having, in his economic works, an antihistorical mode of analysis where capital is seen structurally. Such an outlook does not allow for the impingement, influence, or modification of relations (Thompson 1978: 83). The resulting static social organism works out "its own self-fulfillment with inexorable idealist logic" where "many activities and relations (of power, of consciousness, sexual, cultural, normative) ... have been *defined out of* Political

Economy" (84). Thompson actually thinks that "Marx was *caught in a trap*: the trap baited by 'Political Economy' " (80).

The trap caused Marx, when writing *Capital*, to get "locked into" (80) a way of thinking that focused on the closed system of the logic of capital rather than struggle. He says the *Grundrisse* is "a product of theoretical miscegenation" (88) vulnerable to this closed, static structure. This perspective is the "*Grundrisse* face of Marx" (100), the first step toward Thompson's case that Althusser's structuralism is a theory of stasis with no concept of struggle, contradiction, or change. The next step then is to show the philosophical and historical reasons why Althusser's position falls prey to this face of Marx. Thompson says that, philosophically speaking, though Althusser's theory claims to be one that casts history as a process without a subject, no such thing is really possible within the theory (96). Instead of elaborating this point—he does not truck with theory—he looks at the historical reasons for Althusser's structuralism of stasis and its popularity.

Marxism retained an evolutionist concept before and after the First World War. The October Revolution in Russia gave this evolutionist concept a revolutionary incarnation (97). Yet the subsequent period, specifically the decade, 1936–46 slowed and even reversed this evolutionism toward voluntarism. Marxist vocabulary took on "more of the active verbs of agency, choice, individual initiative, resistance, heroism, and sacrifice" (97). The emergency of fascism called Marxists the world over to adopt such thinking and language. Thompson himself came of age in this voluntarist moment and he says he prefers it.

> I cannot disclaim the fact that my own vocabulary and sensibility was marked by this disgraceful formative moment. Even now I must hold myself steady as I feel myself revert to the poetry of voluntarism. It is a sad confession, but I prefer it even today to the "scientific" vocabulary of structuralism. (98)

The passage is illuminating. After the voluntaristic antifascism of Marxisms before the Second World War, structuralism was cold comfort, a kind of opposite to this voluntarism. Thus, much of Thompson's critiques boil down to stylistic preferences. But there is a deeper melancholy in Thompson as he writes that his beloved "voluntarism crashed against the wall of the Cold War" (99). He even sounds sympathetic to structuralists given their historical context, since "in the West our heads were thrown against the windscreen of capitalist society; and that screen felt like—*a structure*" (99). Painting in appealing but broad strokes, he claims that "for more than two decades each impulse towards independent forward movement … (Hungary 1956, Prague 1968, Chile 1973) has been suppressed with a brutality which has confirmed the paradigm of structural stasis" (99).

Structuralist stasis is therefore "Cold War stasis" writ theoretical (100). This is why structuralism appeals to Marxists during that moment. The agentic voluntarism of the antifascist days could not withstand the intrepidly cold screen of capitalist society in the Cold War, making the *Grundrisse* face of Marx appealing to a new generation of Marxists. Using his impinging theory of dialogue between social being and social consciousness, this transition from voluntarism to structuralism is an example of how the "pressure of real experience ... has seemed to license the adoption of a particular language of social and political analysis" (100). The history is helpful, but Thompson's sympathy is limited. Thompson says structuralism understands society as a reified thing-society, regulating itself, making its own thing-ways to achieve thing-conclusions (103). Rather than further his analysis though, Thompson opts for theatrics. He likens Althusser's theory of structure first to an overbearing woman with a stomachache, reducing her overall bad temper to indigestion (110) and second to a fake grandfather clock, whose superficial parts move mechanically and poorly (112).

In a break from analogies, Thompson says the issue with static structuralism is the fixedness of its categories (113). Indeed, static structuralism is static thinking itself. This thinking does not permit change or redefinition. Structuralist thinking, in a word, prohibits historical thinking. There is no process, only category. Staying true to the title of the book, Thompson's claim is not just that Althusser's theory is flawed. Theory itself is flawed. Theory cannot describe social change over time, only history can. "In the last analysis, the logic of process can only be described in terms of historical analysis" (114). Theory is static, fixed, predetermined—in a word, poor. Thus, the poverty of theory.

Again, rather than think through theory, Thompson takes the polemic to new levels. Playing satirically with Althusser's hypothetical woman in the ISAs essay, Thompson writes that instead of interrogating theory, "we will interrogate a woman" (201). For several pages, Thompson goes on to describe a hypothetical woman in England, elaborating her various love and kin and political and cultural and economic relationships. Angrily crafting this fictional character based loosely on his experiences, the woman goes on to read Althusser on a train. "She turns the pages. Enlightenment breaks through. She shouts out 'I'm not a bloody THING!' She throws the book at the foreman" (203). Playing out his own revocation of Althusser's theory (and theory in general), Thompson's fictional woman storms off and engages in all manner of emancipatory actions that are much more worthwhile than Althusser's static structuralism.

Althusser's hypothetical woman goes out to protest because her subjectivity is interpellated such that she goes all by herself according to an ideology of justice. Thompson finds this objectionable because it renders individuals into things incapable of dynamic agency. Historical analysis is the only disciplinary mode by which we can know the historical process. Althusser's theory comes from a mistake of Marx's (the trap of political economy) and an accident of history that caused certain Marxists to pick up on this mistake (the Cold War). The woman throws Althusser's book away on the train much as we would expect Thompson might.

While his rhetoric is funny and well-wrought, his history of structuralism fascinating, and his argument—such as it is—has an effective appeal, like most of the points Thompson makes, it cannot be taken seriously. If we were to believe Thompson we could not do theory at all. We could not think in categories but rather only history, which, we would have to assume, is never subject to categories. A weaker version is that any category surmised from Marx's political economy face is flawed because it is static, and the generation of Marxist thinkers—we could think of Anderson here—have been misled. This is not their fault, as it is an accident of history that they were not born in Thompson's voluntarist moment. But this would mean that the only acceptable categories would come from thinkers working during this moment. Even Thompson, in his footnotes, agrees that this argument does not make sense. He himself declares that it is his own melancholic preference that leads him to these statements about structuralism.

We know from the go rule and the struggle rule, as well as the causality rule, that Althusser's theory accounts for idiosyncratic decision-making amidst zigzagging social forces caught up in the contingency of history. No event, decision, or subjectivity is simply caused by another. Things are uneven, overdetermined. These categories permit dynamism. Yet, in a nod to Callinicos, Thompson also says Althusser is Stalinist. After reiterating some of Callinicos's points about Althusser's lack of epistemology, drawing a connection between Stalin and a sociologist named Smelser and then from Smelser to Althusser, Thompson concludes that "Althusserianism *is* Stalinism reduced to the paradigm of Theory. It is Stalinism at last, theorized as ideology" (246). Thompson goes on to give a kind of biographical proof of the conclusion, pointing to Althusser's own journey to Communist Party membership via Stalin's doctrine (109 and elsewhere). Readers can examine Thompson's text in more detail if they are interested in reconstructing the premises of this aspect of his account. I must admit some exasperation in trying to follow its twists and turns.

In any case, ultimately the theory with which he is so incensed remains unchallenged on its own terms. Thompson's notion of impinging dialogue is interesting, yet there is no good reason for us to think that it is at odds with an Althusserian theory of history. Thompson might be right about the clash of Marxist problematics between the antifascist and Cold War periods. But a preference is not a position. Thompson might prefer the voluntaristic problematic, its poetry and power, but this is no reason to revoke Althusser's philosophy in particular or theory in general. And finally, Thompson's claims about Althusser's Stalinism are thin extensions of Callincos's suggestion more than anything, which itself was flawed and partisan. Gregory Elliott's *The Detour of Theory* (2006), published four years later, is as good a response as any if readers are interested in Althusser's political positions and the impacts they may have had on his theoretical positions.

20

Ashes and Promiscuity: Willis and Connell

Despite their shortcomings, Thompson's tirade against Althusser would influence many left intellectuals and academics in the English-speaking world. While flawed, it was persuasive. Among those it influenced were Paul Willis, R. W. Connell, and Stanley Aronowitz, who would more directly impact Apple and Giroux.

Paul Willis was an ethnographer and sociologist of education active at the Birmingham Center for Contemporary Cultural Studies. Within Thompson's milieu, Willis's *Learning to Labour: How Working Class Kids Get Working Class Jobs* (1981b) made a significant impact in critical education research. While the initial book made very little mention of Althusser and was published a year before *The Poverty of Theory*, Willis wrote several long essays responding to critics in the early 1980s that configured Althusser (along with social reproduction theory writ large) according to the line of critique so blazingly set out by Thompson. Willis's formulations, which will sound familiar to readers of the previous chapter, were echoed by critical education researchers. We can see these critiques in Willis's essay "Cultural Production is Different from Cultural Reproduction is Different from Social Reproduction is Different from Reproduction" (1981a). This essay, perhaps more than any other, was the bridge from the line of critique directly into critical education.

Willis's purpose in the text is to show how "*Social Reproduction*," exemplified by Althusser, Bowles and Gintis, Bourdieu and Passeron, and Bernstein, operates "at a very high level of abstraction and specifies concretely very little." It is an "easy 'total'" theory, a "thin and crippled theory of the simple passive formation" (49). Callinicos, Hirst, and Thompson loom large in these formulations. Willis says that "it is of course Althusser (in the celebrated Ideology and Ideological State Apparatus) essay who develops this case in the clearest and most sophisticated manner. His arguments are too well-known to outline in detail" (51). Certainly by that time Althusser's arguments had been laid out in detail in numerous articles and essays. It is understandable that Willis would not engage in a reading given that so many others had. However, by making this reference, he opens the door for Giroux to make a similar move in 1983. That exegetical point is not the only precedent he sets for critical education and the resulting common sense about Althusser.

Willis claims that the theory "pictures the working class as totally dominated" (52). The phrase, so prominent from Rancière to Erben and Gleesen to Thompson, recurs in Giroux. Further, Althusser's concept of social structure understands society as a "hypostatized given in a quite unsocial world" (52). In the theory there is "no sense of structure being a contested medium as well as an outcome of social process" (52). With Thompson's similar flair, Willis concludes that Althusser's theory "is to take ashes not fire from history" (52). Giroux would cite these claims in his work—specifically the "myth of total domination" in 1983—and, given the broad sweep of the line of critique traced in this part, we can understand now how Willis came upon them. Willis was passing along a line of critique whose form and substance came from Thompson most proximately, but who himself was working with ideas and in a milieu that included Kolakowski, Rancière, Hirst, Erben and Gleeson, and Callinicos. Other educational researchers would carry this line forward but add new dimensions to it, like Raewyn Connell.

Connell is a leading socialist and educational researcher in Australia. Her collaboratively written *Making the Difference* (1982) was a groundbreaking work of sociology of education. Active in left politics and organizing as part of Australia's New Left, she encountered Althusser's writing both through New Left Books' publications and E. P. Thompson's general critique. Having visited England and seen Thompson give a talk on nuclear disarmament, working with a newer Labor Party formation in the wake of the New Left, and identifying with German activist Rudi Dutschke's concept of the long march through the institutions, Connell's organizing focused on secondary school teachers and university professors. Given that Althusser's writing arrived with Thompson's critique in hand, and those taking the theory seriously were sagging deeper and deeper into armchair militancy, the theory was more a threat than a tool (personal communication with author, 2019). Thus she produced a formidable essay "A Critique of the Althusserian Approach to Class" (1979), which repeats familiar critiques of functionalism, a lack of agency, and Stalinism in Althusser's theory.

Yet Connell adds something new. Despite Althusser's abstract categorical functionalism, operating as it does by definition and prohibiting concrete analysis, Connell also finds the theory "sportive" (324) and "unstable" (325). The theory "gives no guide to any systematic pattern in the extent of the 'dislocations'; it suggests on the contrary that these are always specific to the conjuncture" (325). The theory is thus both too abstract and too concrete. It is a "bipolar functionalism" (335). With exegetical poise, she dubs the theory promiscuous (327): "The characteristic combination of tight-laced conceptual system with a promiscuous application of class categories in practice. History becomes a kaleidoscope, whose pieces can be re-arranged by a twirl of the conceptual barrel" (327). She calls this promiscuous, sportive, unstable, and kaleidoscopic theory—the fact that it is too concrete and too abstract simultaneously—the "Althusserian Two-Step" (328). Sandwiched between two familiar and overdone critiques (functionalism up front and then Stalinism at the end), this particular argument contains premises with a conclusion and poses an issue for the rules for ISAs. It passes both tests. Is Althusserian theory too promiscuous? Is there a two-step promiscuity? I take up this question in the next part.

21

Conclusion

The common sense about Althusser in critical education makes three critiques: Althusser is functionalist, Althusser does not permit agency, and Althusser's theory tragically fails. While Apple and Giroux pass along this common sense, they did not articulate it originally. Their project was not a detailed examination of Althusser's theory. Rather they set out to configure a framework that contrasted with neo-Marxism, and to do this, they relied on a line of critique developed by other scholars who had great influence in their milieu.

Rancière was the first to suggest Althusser's theory is functionalist, though not in those terms exactly. His suggestion is that the theory of the ISAs focuses on self-regulating social machinery that maintains cohesion, a concept more associated with Comte and Hobbes than Marx. Hirst and Erben and Gleeson would build on this suggestion. The latter authors used the functionalist label and added authors like Parsons to the list of comparables, drawing a connection between Althusser and that non-Marxist sociological tradition via examples such as Parsons's pattern variables. But for them, like Rancière, the suggestion remains just that: a juxtaposition of authors, phrases, and associations rather than argument. Hirst makes an argument, however, that Althusser's theory is functionalist because the question is too abstract and that Althusser confuses the division of labor with relations of production.

Thompson would give historical reasons for these critiques. Althusser's functionalism is a function of his static structuralism, which is both a flaw in Marx's later writings and comes from an attempt to digest the Cold War's counter-revolution and the cold screen of capital's victory. The critique from functionalism is connected to that from agency. If all practices get reduced to their functionality, then humans are not free in their actions. They are automatons, as Erben and Gleeson (and Thompson) would say. Again, Rancière suggested this first, noting that Althusser's attitude toward people in general and students and teachers in particular in 1968 does not respect their activism, resistance, and antiauthoritarianism. Erben and Gleeson extended this suggestion, adding a layer of epistemology by saying Althusser undercuts the possibility of teachers and students' knowledge of society. They also give examples of movements Althusser leaves out.

Callinicos adds arguments to these suggestions. He claims Althusser's epistemology is a rejection of all knowledge. This is a philosophical premise in the critique from agency since it means no one can think for themselves. For Callinicos this epistemological point is a political premise as well since it justifies vanguardism and Eastern bloc policy. He concludes that Althusser is a closet Stalinist, which is not just a coincidental feature of Althusser's personal politics but rather a feature of his philosophy. Thompson takes up all these premises and packages them into a blustery polemic, lending them the legitimacy of his platform, making them impossible to ignore. Neither Willis nor Connell ignored them, and ultimately neither did Apple and Giroux.

Over the course of these examinations, I have found this line of critique leaves much to be desired, however. My method for assessing these arguments has been to determine first if there is an argument, by which I mean a series of premises that lead to a conclusion. On that test, Rancière, Erben and Gleeson, and Thompson do not fare well. Rancière and Thompson, by their own admission, do not intend their texts as arguments but rather polemics and provocations. It does not lessen the texts' importance or value or persuasive force, but does threaten their validity as arguments against Althusser's theory.

Hirst and Callinicos do, however. In such cases, I have used a second test composed of the eleven rules generated in the first part of the book. A successful argument against Althusser's theory of education would level a claim these rules could not handle. Hirst substantiates the critique from functionalism but his arguments do not pass the second test. Callinicos substantiates the critique from agency but, like Hirst, the rules can handle his conclusions. While there are opportunities for good arguments and critiques throughout the line I have examined, only one passes both tests: Connell's critique from promiscuity. I will respond to this critique after examining the line of advance in the next part.

I can answer the questions I set out with at the beginning of this part. The common sense about Althusser in critical education is a combination of reverence and repulsion based largely on persuasive, passionate, but ultimately lackluster critiques from agency and functionalism. Apple and Giroux followed British scholars' leads in their readings of Althusser (some of whom were following Rancière), passing along the reverence-repulsion as well as the underdeveloped arguments. Their proximity to these texts' and their authors' influence led to their uptake in the configuration of critical education. The common sense lingers on in the foundations of critical education, such as with the reproduction-resistance dichotomy. Thus the common sense about Althusser and its faulty line of critique has implications for critical education as a whole. One can see this legacy in the work of Canadian American theorist Peter McLaren, who worked closely with Henry Giroux during and after their time together at Miami University at Oxford, Ohio, and who would influence a generation of critical pedagogues while teaching at the University of California, Los Angeles.

McLaren's sweeping essay "Ideology and Education: Critical Pedagogy and the Politics of Empowerment" (1988) is a prominent example. On the way toward a post-Marxist, and even postmodern, account of ideology, McLaren notes in passing that Foucault's thinking adds "to the growing disillusionment with scientific Marxism" (155). McLaren then points to Althusser as an example, saying "it is difficult to see how, from this perspective, strategies of resistance can emerge if it is agreed that all ideologies are essentially oppressive … The works of Althusser possess a similar problem" (180).

This comment is a paradigm case of the line of critique. In it, McLaren takes Althusser's theory of ideology as essentially oppressive, preventing any resistance. He continues to say that Althusser's idea of overdetermination operates like a machine in positioning, placing, and reconciling people into the social order, preventing strategies of resistance (180). McLaren's reading is buried in passing references and footnotes, more evidence of these critiques of Althusser becoming a common sense. The line of critique, as common sense, is difficult to spot. Apple and Giroux instituted the resistance-reproduction dichotomy as a kind of axiom of American critical education research, and the common sense about Althusser was a key part of that process. Since the line of critique's project—as synthesized by Thompson—was to revoke Althusser as deterministic and Stalinist, and, according to Willis, Althusser was a social reproduction theorist, Apple and Giroux, while certainly appreciating and revering the theory for its aims if not some of its achievements, ultimately understood Althusser's theory of education as a paradigm case of deterministic, functionalist reproduction. Morrow and Torres's (1995) reading of Althusser is more evidence that the line of critique, flawed as it is, became a common sense in critical education.

There is one critique that stands out. I have said that I would return to Connell's critique from promiscuity. If it were true that Althusser's theory were promiscuous in the way Connell says, then we might expect it would be difficult to apply that theory. If the definitions are so constrained and its conceptual aspects so kaleidoscopically applicable, we would expect other scholars to not pick up the theory and advance its premises, use it fruitfully, or extend it in interest ways. Yet the opposite is true. While researching the line of critique against Althusser I uncovered a line of scholarship that, rather than critiquing Althusser for determinism or functionalism or Stalinism, advanced and applied his theory of education. Starting in the 1970s and continuing to today, educational researchers on the left have taken up Althusser's arguments in ways occluded by the common sense about him in critical education. I call that tradition structural education and trace its development in the next part.

Part III

Structural Education: Toward an Althusserian Pedagogy

Paulo Freire (1970), while writing *Pedagogy of the Oppressed* in exile from a dictatorship in his native Brazil, published the essay "Adult Literacy Process as Cultural Action." In a short reference to Althusser's concept of overdetermination, he notes that "cultural action occurs at the level of superstructure. It can only be understood by what Althusser calls 'the dialectic of overdetermination.' This analytic tool prevents us from falling into mechanistic explanations or, what is worse, mechanistic action" (216). What stands out about this brief reference is that, even before the ISAs essay was published, perhaps the most prominent educational theorist on the left recognized that Althusser's theory was an antidote to mechanistic thinking and action. In contrast to the line of critique elaborated in Part II, there is a very different line that took (and takes) up Althusser's work by augmenting and applying it to education. Rather than a line of critique, this line of advance is both wider in scope and more diverse in its authorship, though it remains less visible.

In this part I examine the line of advance. While these applications are not entirely uncritical of Althusser, they use and move his thinking in ways that do not end at critique. This line of advance has four main themes. The first set of texts elaborate Althusser's concept of structure when it comes to education, following Establet and Baudelot's examination of French schooling, Poulantzas's structural determination, and Martin Carnoy's work on the concept of mediation (readers should also see Lefebvre [1976], a fascinating text on the relations of production I did not have the space to include). These texts are framed by Richard Johnson and Stuart Hall's responses to Thompson's polemic. Indeed, Hall's influence runs like a current throughout the line of advance. The second theme follows Stuart Hall's development of Althusserian theory, particularly via the concept of articulation as it comes to bear on race and how Zeus Leonardo applied that development to education. The third traces a group of Marxist feminist scholars who took up Althusser's view on reproduction in education, from AnnMarie Wolpe's contributions on the structure of girls' education and Bantu education in South Africa to Michele Barrett's chapter on education in *Women's Oppression Today* to Madeleine Arnot, Rosemary Deem, and Linda Valli. Finally, the fourth theme is ideology. I look at a series of extensions of Althusser's concept of ideology, engaging Hall again but also the sequence of new concepts of mis-, dis-, and counter-interpellation. This line of advance shines a much different light on Althusser's theory of education than the line of critique. I argue that the line of advance configures a tradition of structural education that critical education has obscured, providing an array of resources for left thinking about education, specifically furnishing resources for developing a contemporary and properly Althusserian pedagogy.

22

Developments in Structure

Althusser's theory of education left a number of questions. What does it look like for a school to reproduce a relation of production, as determined by and determining the class struggle? A related question is what structural causality means for studying ideological state apparatuses, specifically education. What does this immanent theory of social structure mean for schools? A group of texts take on these issues and generally push Althusser's thinking on questions of structure. In this vein, I open with two commentators on Thompson's *Poverty*, Richard Johnson and Stuart Hall. Each of them attempted, in the face of Thompson's fury, to create a synthesis of what Johnson and his milieu called culturalism and structuralism. Johnson lays out the terrain of the debate very clearly and proposes a novel conception of reproduction-as-struggle, turning to Gramsci. Hall on the other hand offers a more profound reading of Althusser's interpretation of the base-superstructure model, specifically the causality between the two parts of society. Rather than a simple reflection theory, Hall's idea is that the causal relation is asymptotic, capturing the unevenness and complexity in Althusser's theory. Taking Thompson's suggestion to look back again at Marx, Hall's rethinking of the base-superstructure model both clarifies Althusser's position and lays a foundation for structural education.

The Greek Marxist state theorist Nicos Poulantzas develops this concept of structural determination further and applies it to schooling, claiming that apparatuses are condensations of relations of production. The South African organizer and education researcher AnnMarie Wolpe applied that development to gendered/class education research, while the American education economist Martin Carnoy, influenced by ant-imperialists working in Bobby Kennedy's 1968 presidential campaign, further developed the notion of condensation in his concept of education as mediation in base-superstructure theory. In light of this development of education as mediation of material interests in the base, Establet and Baudelot's early work on the *Schools* project comes into clearer focus. I begin with Johnson and Hall.

In the wake of Thompson's attack on Althusser/Anderson, a number of intellectuals attempted syntheses that looked for middle ground between what had emerged as a dichotomy between culture and structure. British sociologist Richard Johnson and British Jamaican cultural theorist Stuart Hall are two such scholars. They were both on stage with Thompson at the St. Paul's debate, each trying to move the dialogue forward by praising Thompson's work but also examining his ideas more carefully rather than adopting them (for which Thompson eviscerated them on stage, causing a scene and compelling many audience members, including a cohort of feminists, to leave the event before it was over).

It was Johnson's "Histories of Culture/Theories of Ideology" (2018) to which Thompson was responding in his polemic at St. Paul's Church. As a published response to *Poverty*, Johnson assesses the relative strengths and weaknesses of Thompson's and Althusser's tendencies, hashing out helpful synthetic notions by cobbling together the positives in each as well as what is absent. His goal is to "reach some general pointers towards a more adequate (that is, usable) theory of culture-ideology" (56). Johnson is therefore on the lookout for an adequate theory: one that includes the relative strengths of both the culturalist and structuralist positions.

First, he summarizes the debate by setting out the positions. Culturalist texts "take the form of specific histories" while he says structuralist writings are "philosophical, formalistic and pitched, unrelentingly, at a high level of abstraction." Different as they are, Johnson sees these two tendencies coexisting and interrupting each other and declares emphatically that "*neither culturalism nor structuralism will do!*" Different as they are, Johnson shows their common heritage in opposing Stalinism and economism in the context of the Cold War. They are both opposed to idealism. Each tendency uses load-bearing terminology, sharing a certain "catholicity" (58–9). He points to two such terms: culture and ideology. With these similarities set out, Johnson can point to each of their relative strengths.

Structuralism, Althusser's theory in particular, provides rigorously delimited concepts to talk about the very experiences, histories, and cultural practices that culturalism seeks to describe. Johnson goes so far as to say that culturalism lacks such a framework: Althusser "supplies us with notions that enrich historical understanding and our ability to analyze specific situations … in general, the theme of complex, structured and contradictory unities" (60). As an alternative to economism, Althusser's abstract method has "a clarity and adequacy … that all culturalist formulations lack" (64). Namely, Althusser's structuralism focuses on more objective social relations that do not depend or emerge idiosyncratically but rather remain obdurately over time (70).

But structuralism is flawed as well. The first flaw comes from the strength it could potentially lend culturalism: its rigid emphasis on theoretical form over specifics. Johnson calls for more detailed accounts rather than theories (55). Echoing one of culturalism's main lines against it, Johnson says structuralism's high level of abstraction can be violent (61). Furthermore, structuralism is reductive and can "slide into a functionalist account" (67). The functionalist slide happens, apparently, when structuralists "think of ideology or the ideological instance solely as a condition of existence for a given mode of production" (69). On the other hand, while culturalism grounds itself in the authentic stories of working-class experience (66), the tragedy of culturalism is that it subscribes to "the theory of no-theory" (63). One example is the concept of experience (65). If a framework's fundamental concept lacks proper theorization, confusion and inconsistencies crop up in the deepest parts of the framework.

Johnson's project is to reconcile these differences into a "more adequate account" (71). He proposes Gramsci as a compromise figure, focusing specifically on hegemony. Indeed, Gramsci and the concept of hegemony would become influential in critical education for precisely this reason. But Johnson makes an important point regarding hegemony before laying out that synthesis. "It is important to add that though Gramsci's 'hegemony' is now very familiar in English cultural theory, it has been appropriated, almost always, in a particular culturalist form." In this culturalist appropriation, hegemony "refers wholly to superstructural relations or cultural relations of authority" (74). His proposal is to take a synthetic approach to the concept of hegemony rather than proceed with this culturalist appropriation. (The implications for education as social reproduction are clear, e.g., when theorizing recitation pedagogy. See Backer [2017].)

He understands the term "in Gramsci's own usage" to mean "the *relation between* structure and superstructure" where the "relation is that of massive disjunctions and unevenness" (74). Johnson sees this interpretation as a compromise between culturalism and structuralism. He goes on to apply this compromise interpretation of Gramsci to the concept of reproduction, arguing the concept refers to political and ideological struggle against obstinate structural forces (74). This synthetic concept renders reproduction as a struggle. It collates the strengths of structuralism and humanism while accounting for their weaknesses. For example, with it he can claim that while capital is indifferent to some cultural practices, it has difficulty dealing with others (75). Reproduction-as-struggle, as a synthesis of structuralist and culturalist tendencies, thus compels us to "start by looking for contradictions, taboos, displacements rather than unities" (76), where the concern is "the precise *forms* of the determination" rather than the "*fact* of a powerful relation between class position and culture" (77). The causalities between ideology and culture, or structure and agency, is uneven and takes precise forms.

Johnson's reproduction-as-struggle gestures toward a development of Althusser's structuralism that Stuart Hall would build out further. Hall's work on the base-superstructure theory is a much more detailed theoretical account of this struggle-concept of structure. It thus provides a philosophical underpinning for structural education.

Hall was on the stage as well at the St. Paul debate where Thompson, nominally responding to critics of *Poverty*, insulted Johnson and others. By then, the British Jamaican Marxist was something of a left celebrity in his own right: co-founder of New Left Books and an editor of the *New Left Review*, former director of the Birmingham Centre for Contemporary Cultural Studies, and prolific author of texts both in Marxist theory and media studies. Like Johnson, Hall was looking to take lessons from Althusser's intervention and build on them rather than revoke them. In so doing, he made a lasting contribution to Marxist theory by clarifying Althusser's advances and then applying them, notably to the problem of racism but also in media, discourse, and ideology. He extended the theory of interpellation in significant ways by showing the play between encoding and decoding messages and ideology's lack of guarantees. I will touch on the theory of race and the theory of decoding later sections. For now, I examine Hall's interpretation of the base-superstructure model, specifically his understanding of Althusser's theory as one of articulation.

In "Rethinking the 'Base and Superstructure' Metaphor" (1977), Hall begins by tracing the ambiguities in Marx's own writings from *The German Ideology*, *Capital*, and correspondences with Engels, through Lenin and Gramsci's interpretations of the base-superstructure model. The ambiguity Hall finds is between a mechanical, simple, and reflective relationship between the base and superstructure, on the one hand, and a complex, differentiated, and uneven relationship between them on the other. Hall calls the mechanical, simple, and reflective relationship the "identity correspondence position" (160). We know this identity thesis well from the line of critique, as it is one of the main salvos against Althusser. Yet Hall takes an opposite stance, claiming Althusser did important work to advance the uneven, complex, and differentiated interpretation rather than the simple, reflective one.

The big question is determination, or what causes what in society and how (144). Hall lays out several options. First, there is the identity thesis, with its one-directional concept of a simple relationship between base and superstructure. Second, Hall delimits (but is not interested in) a relativistic sociological position that focuses on all kinds of differences "without primacy of determination given or specified at any point" (144). Hall then sets out a third position, culturalism: "the tendency to reduce determination, not to the economic, but to History itself—to *praxis*: to an undifferentiated *praxis* which rolls throughout the whole social formation, as its essential ground" (152). His interest is in Althusser's position, which is distinct from each of these.

If determination in the base-superstructure model is not an identity between base and superstructure, nor a relativistic sociological account of all differences, nor a perpetual river of undifferentiated praxis—then what is it? In another essay on ideology (about which more later), Hall (1985) declares that "Althusser persuaded me, and I remain persuaded, that Marx conceptualizes the ensemble of relations which make up a whole society ... as essentially a complex structure, not a simple one" (91). Hall sees Marx insisting on the non-identity thesis in *Capital* (Hall 1977: 161), where relations of production are "complementary but different, articulated with each other, but each still requiring its own conditions to be sustained. Hence the 'unity' which these processes exhibit is not a unity of identity, but 'unity of the diverse'—the concentration of many determinations" (161). In this sense, Marx (according to Hall) is "concerned ... with the *necessary complexity* of the social formations of advancing capitalism and the relations between its different levels" (156).

What Hall comes out with is a theory of society where diverse levels get articulated together in an uneven, complex, and relatively autonomous structure. Society is a set of corresponding matrices of relations that exert force in different trajectories. Importantly, for Hall, these trajectories nearly meet one another but never quite do. He likens this dynamic to an asymptote (151); social forces approach one another but never meet (or mathematically speaking, meeting at infinity). Conceiving of the double relationship of the base and superstructure as asymptotic lets Hall capture the way each force closely relates to one another in their differences, yet allowing that the meeting only occurs at an infinite point. We can read the mathematical analogy to infinity as a way to understand Althusser's concept that the relations of production determine society in the last instance, though that instance never arrives. Hall clearly says that

> Althusser conceives a social formation as composed of different *practices*— essentially the economic, political, and ideological (with, perhaps, a

fourth: theoretical practice?)—each of which is required for the production and reproduction of the relations of the capitalist mode: and each of which has its own inner constitution, its own specificity, its own dynamic and "relative autonomy" from the others. (Hall 1977: 167)

In the essay on Althusser's contribution to ideology, Hall states his understanding of relative autonomy as articulation, a unity-in-the-diverse, in clearer language:

> [Althusser] enabled me to live in and with *difference*. Althusser's break with a monistic conception of marxism demanded the theorization of difference—the recognition that there are different social contradictions with different origins; that the contradictions which drive the historical process forward do not always appear in the same place, and will not always have the same historical effects. We have to think about the articulation between different contradictions; about the different specificities and temporal durations through which they operate, about the different modalities through which they function. (Hall 1985: 92)

For Hall, living in and with difference as articulated unities means understanding differential dynamics between parts of society, with causalities indexed at specific effectivities, forces relating to one another asymptotically. Indeed, this is what makes Althusser's concept of the ISAs such a "generative idea" (Hall 1977: 167). Hall's theory of articulation—that social forces form unities-in-difference with one another in complex and uneven ways, making causality between them asymptotic—provides a basis for the line of advance and structural education. Just as Johnson's concept of reproduction-as-struggle is an advancement of Althusser's particular variety of structuralism, Hall clarifies important philosophical premises underlying that framework. Indeed, the philosophical basis for the rule of struggle is the never-ending contingency existing between diversely arrayed practices and forces in society. This contingency applies to reproduction in education. These clarifications make it easier to understand structural interpretations of education, like those we find in the work of AnnMarie Wolpe and Nicos Poulantzas.

The Greek French Marxist Poulantzas was known for applying, elaborating, and extending Althusser's theory in ways that made his work almost synonymous with Althusser. But the two were actually peers influencing one another. Althusser cited Poulantzas's first work on the state, *Political Power and Social Classes* (1973), published in French in 1968, in the ISAs essay. Poulantzas's conclusion in that book is that the repressive state apparatus and the ruling class controlling it are not simple, uniform entities working as mechanical instruments to advance the interests of capital. Rather, the ruling class is a complex bloc of factions, fractions, and groups whose interests and histories do not always align; thus the state is an uneven condensation of complex class relations rather than a simple instrument.

Poulantzas's next book was *Classes in Contemporary Capitalism* (1978), a series of essays that clarify his own work and reconstructs claims in Althusser's ISAs essay. Notably, the introduction to *Classes* uses school as an example to illustrate the theoretical implications of Althusser's viewpoint from reproduction. Having established that reproduction happens in struggle (Johnson) and that Althusser's theory is one of articulated unities in difference (Hall), we can look to Poulantzas for a fuller picture of what it means to say that schools are an ideological state apparatus determined by and determining class struggle.

For Poulantzas, class exists in an ensemble of practices (1978: 14). Class emerges as one's position in this ensemble. This is what Althusser means by immanent structure. If struggle is just the moves that people and groups of people make as they contentiously enact practices, class is their place within that ensemble of practices. It follows that the kind of causality within class struggle should be appropriately immanent as well. Structural determination is the extent to which the relations of production thus emerge as places within class practices as people struggle (14). ISAs and RSAs, for example, are "the materialization and condensation of class relations" (25). They are modifications of the class struggle substance (27). These modifications are actually themselves relations, which, contrary to the line of critique, do not "consist of a self-regulating automatism by which social capital is accumulated" (27). A condensed class relation emerging from practices in a struggle is very different than a function performing an action in a mechanism. Poulantzas calls this condensation-concept of causality the structural determination of class.

The thesis leads to a number of insights. One is that there is a difference between agents and places (29), as it implies that class struggle is the change in structure and not individual actions within it (16). Relations are not interpersonal relations and classes are not empirical groups composed of individuals (17). Relations are structural positions that individuals come in and out of. Thus "the distribution of agents does not depend on their own choices or aspirations" (29). But so what? The structural determination of class thesis actually reverses a key bourgeois idea of inequality. For Poulantzas, inequality is an effect of a capitalist social structure, not a cause of certain unequal distributions of people or resources. According to this structural thesis, inequality is "not a matter of some inequality of 'opportunity' between 'individuals'" (17). This idea has implications for how we think about education and inequality.

Poulantzas says that schools, as an ideological apparatus, "do not create divisions, but they contribute to them" (28). Yet there is "an idealist and institutionalist view" (29) that says the opposite, namely that "social classes and the class struggle are the product of the apparatuses" (29) like schools. In the case of schools, this idealist institutionalist view would say that education increases or decreases certain forms of categorization, or that the apparatus determines the working class and its struggle. However, the structural determination of class thesis says something very different.

Schools—including their internal struggles, contradictions, and frictions—are indeed determined by the economic, political, and ideological class struggle. This determination is not functionalist but rather uneven and immanent. Schools' "concrete forms depend on the history of the social formation," which means that "it is therefore only possible to locate the apparatuses in this reproduction by referring to this struggle" (30). Schools do not create inequality. Schools contribute to an already-existing structure that is unequal. For example, take schools' relationship to a changing job market during the urbanization of peasant lands (34). The amount or kind of schooling that a peasant population gets does not compel them to leave farmlands and get jobs in a growing nearby city. It is the other way around. Peasants move into the city to get jobs and wages to make their livelihoods. Getting an education serves that purpose. Urbanization thus impacts schooling, not the other way around.

Idealists think that schools cause inequality. Structuralists on the other hand think the opposite: inequality in society creates schools such as they are. To use a counterfactual, in a society where workers are not alienated from the means of production, we would expect schools to look quite different in terms of their funding, administration, curriculum, and perhaps pedagogy. Schools in socialist and communist countries may take similar shapes to those in capitalist countries. But there will be fundamental differences. Those differences are not effects of mere schooling practices or policies. These differences between schools in socialist and capitalist countries are effects of different social structures. Poulantzas cryptically illustrates the point with a reference to Weber: "Thus Max Weber was wrong in claiming that the Church creates and perpetuates religion: rather it is religion which creates and perpetuates the Church" (31).

What does this cryptic thesis about causality tell us about school? Poulantzas does not mince words in bringing the message home. Structural determination of class helps us "understand the stupidity of the bourgeois problematic of social mobility" (33). This stupid problematic presumes that the "origin" of "'social stratification' ... is that of the 'circulation' or 'mobility' of individuals between strata" (33). He speculates that if workers replace the bourgeoisie and vice versa in a capitalist society, the society is still capitalist (33). To fight for equality, you have to fight the right causes of inequality: the relations of production.

Taking the institutionalist, stupid bourgeois view "we would fall into the same type of one-way regressive explanation" that fixes our categories and limits our understanding of class struggle. "Capitalist classes are not educational castes any more than they are hereditary castes" (33). Positions are fluid, unique, and complex. Poulantzas talks about the experience of "young people and ... old people" and further that of "women, which is of a different order and besides, more complex": "in the case of women, what is involved is not simply certain over-determined effects on them of the division of society into classes, but, more precisely, a specific articulation, within the social division of labor, of the class division and the sexual division" (Poulantzas 1978: 31). While Althusser is sorely lacking reference to marginalized and oppressed groups, Poulantzas makes room for what Crenshaw, Collins, and the Combahee River Collective would come to call intersections of gender and class. And this is precisely where the South African socialist feminist scholar of education, AnnMarie Wolpe, picked up the Althusserian thread and applied it to the sociology of girls' schooling in capitalist societies, a clear extension of Poulantzas's point about structural determination.

In her contribution to the collection of essays *Feminism and Materialism: Women and Modes of Production*, which she co-edited, Wolpe (1978) applies Poulantzas's reading of Althusser to challenge the stupidity of the bourgeois problematic in sociology of education, specifically with regard to gender. She takes up the inequality debate in the 1970s over "the role that the educational system plays in the production of the disparities which exist within society" (Wolpe 1978: 291). She combs through then-recent developments in social stratification theory to call out its "fundamental limitations" and "pose the question of the position of women in a different way and to indicate tentatively the concepts which may be necessary for the development of an alternative analysis" (291). That alternative analysis turns out to be a unique contribution to Marxist sociology of gendered education building on Poulantzas's thinking.

The concept of causality matters to Wolpe: "Analysis of the specific position of women in the educational system and in the division of labour depends in the first place on adequate conceptualization of the complex relationship between capitalist production, the division of labour, the family, and the educational system" (308). Stratification theories of school inequality are fundamentally flawed because in them there is an "absence of discussion of these relations, except in an extremely partial and simplistic way" (308). She finds it helpful that Marxist contributions look at "the process of the reproduction of agents—as economic, ideological, political, social agents—and their allocation into 'places' in the system of social relations" (308). Her goal is to elaborate how this reproduction of agents and places works for gendered education in capitalism. More on her contributions to Marxist feminism and education later.

For now, Poulantzas leaves us with an answer and a question. The answer is a clarification on what structural causality means for education. His response is that structural causality reverses the bourgeois, idealist, and institutionalist view of inequality. Schools do not create inequality. Schools contribute to existing inequality as part of a larger class struggle, but are not the source of it. The theoretical justification for this position on structural determination is that apparatuses like schools are condensations of relations of production. Such condensations emerge from class struggle, which itself is immanent in material practices throughout society. Thus Poulantzas also answers the more general question about what it means to reproduce the relations of production. To reproduce the relations of production is to condense class relations, a relationship Hall would call asymptotic such that one never reduces to the other.

Yet these concepts of condensation and asymptote are abstract. Martin Carnoy, the American political economist of education, made them more concrete. Trained in economics but influenced by anti-imperialists in the late 1960s, his work has ranged from education and cultural imperialism (1974), why Cuban students do better than most other students in literacy (2007), education and transitions to socialism in the third world (2014), and globalization (1999). After distinguishing himself by working as an organizer for Robert Kennedy's presidential campaign in the late 1960s, he completed an economic study of education in Mexican labor markets by doing direct field work (rare among economists). Carnoy then turned his attention to Marxist theory and education. In *Schooling and Work in the Democratic State* (Carnoy and Levin 1985), a book focusing on the United States, Carnoy and Levin characterize Michael Apple's and Henry Giroux's frameworks as a "critical autonomy view" that "reacted sharply to Bowles and Gintis's economic determinism and, by implication, to Althusser's structuralism" (22). Agreeing somewhat with Apple and Giroux but still apprehensive about their framework, Carnoy and Levin would articulate their own approach in a section called "Toward a Model of Educational Change," which tracks closely with the reading of Althusser in Part I of this book, that schools are ISAs and are thus "an arena of struggles over ideology and resources" (24).

Their focus is less on belief systems and political power, and more on "the conflict over resources—who will get them and who will control the way they are used" (24). In their eyes, "conflicts in schools are not primarily over the principle of capitalism, but over its practices" (24–5). Carnoy and Levin see contradiction in education as "intimately related to production" (25), and that intimate relation takes into account the importance of culture and autonomy as espoused by Apple and Giroux, but also maintains that schools are ideological state apparatuses that reproduce the relations of production as part of class struggle. This is structural education in a nutshell. Carnoy's contribution is not just carving out space for structural education in contrast to Giroux and Apple's critical education, but also clarifying the concept of reproduction further by building on Johnson, Hall, Wolpe, and Poulantzas.

In the same collection that Michael Apple edited, where Apple's essay dichotomizing reproduction and resistance figured prominently in the line of critique, Carnoy published a long chapter called "Education, Economy, and the State" (1982). After a deft intellectual history of Marxist theories of the state from Marx to Lenin to Gramsci, Althusser, and Poultanzas, and locating schooling within each of these, Carnoy offers a theory to answer the question about how schools both reproduce the relations of production and are relatively autonomous condensations of class relations. His answer is that schools are mediators of contradictions in society's base.

Simply put, this theory of mediation is that "struggle in the base leads to attempts to 'mediate' that struggle, and one of the ways that mediation takes place is through the public education system" (114). Thus the superstructure "softens" (122) the contradictions in the base. School is part of that softening effect, mediating contradictions in class struggle. We can see this theory of mediation developing the line of advance further, building on and clarifying insights by Poulantzas, Wolpe, Hall, and Johnson. Schools contribute to the ruling class' side of the class struggle by mediating contradictions in the base. Reproduction is thus a key part of the struggle in a complex and differentiated formation. Contradictions are present in schools from the wider class struggle but they are not an overpowering presence. The schools can and do exert a force with, through, and even against those pressures from the struggle. The way they exert their force is through mediation. This concept of mediation provides another way of understanding Poulantzas's condensation theory. Apparatuses like schools are condensations of class relations. This condensation emerges from the chemical dynamics in the class struggle and takes off pressure here, absorbs tension there, and extends surface torsion elsewhere.

The question becomes what that mediation looks like in the context of struggle. What are some examples where schools mediate contradictions in the base as part of the wider class struggle? To be clear, mediation is always contingent on complex circumstances. Carnoy points to four examples of how mediation can occur but also face obstacles. The first is over-education. This is not the idea that, generally speaking, a populace has too much education. Rather, Carnoy's concept of over-education is relative to the economy. Over-education happens when the kind and amount of education supersedes labor market openings. In this case there is a mismatch between existing job opportunities and the school system set up to train, certify, and develop people to be ready for job opportunities. One way to think about this contradictory mismatch of over-education is the common sense that education leads to opportunity. This is "correct to some extent" (119) because, to secure a position, you need education. At the same time, it is true that you do not get a job just because you are educated. Over-education is when a population attains a certain amount of skills through education while their economy does not have jobs available for them. Schools can mediate a contracting labor market through shifts in curriculum, teaching methods, technology or other messages from the ruling class. Yet sometimes that mediation fails due to significant economic issues or the ruling class's inability to compensate.

The second example of mediation in struggle has to do with democracy, namely that in school democracy is a symbol. While Carnoy observes that most schools themselves are not democratically run, students learn about democracy and "come to accept the abstract nature of democracy in their post-school, everyday lives" (121). As students many of us come to understand this hypocrisy between our supposedly democratic country and the obviously non-democratic structures in the school. The contradiction occurs as this symbol of democracy promises equality and participation but does not fulfill that promise. Yet the symbol of democracy remains a horizon toward which students can always orient themselves. That horizon will always be dangerous for bourgeois hegemony, because it "does promote an ideology of individual and human rights. This mass ideology can be and is directed against big business as well as big government" (121–2).

My own research on the democratic connotations of classroom discussion is a pedagogical case of school mediating this contradiction (Backer 2018). On the one hand, discussion has a democratic meaning—it connotes participation and equality—while on the other hand, actual discussions are observably quite rare. Teachers largely maintain central control of classroom discussion, making these interactions more like recitations or question-answer sessions. The word discussion promises a democracy that goes unfulfilled. Yet the symbol of democracy can be taken up if teachers facilitate discussion in such a way as to increase participation and equality, dangerous as it might be.

Carnoy's third example of mediation in struggle is that school is a legitimate institution whose purpose is largely understood as reproducing society. People recognize that school is where young people go to become productive members of society. Rather than limiting schools' autonomy in society, this legitimacy—an institution charged with preparing a society's future generations—imbues schools with a unique power. Everyone in society respects school to some degree, even if sometimes oppositionally. This widespread legitimacy permits teachers, students, and others in the school community to extend the boundaries of what the capitalist economy or government can accomplish, and even its mediating role itself. The intensity of the connection to its surrounding society, and its importance in maintaining that society, "gives the schools a formal autonomy from the base and the private hegemonic apparatuses," and this autonomy "allows teachers, administrators, and students to follow independent strategies which are not consistent with the mediation functions required for softening contradictions in the base" (Carnoy 1982: 122).

Fourth, as the long tradition of youth subculture studies has shown, Carnoy claims youth culture itself is an example of mediation struggle in schooling. "The very bringing together of large numbers of youth in the same institution promotes the development of youth culture which may be inconsistent with social reproduction" (122). Althusser noticed that schools bring together teachable young people into one institution that can, effectively, control the message. Yet in so doing the institution takes a risk in bringing together large numbers of untrained youth who can, as Paul Willis (1981b) famously observed, block and break up that message.

Each of the four examples—over-education, democracy-as-symbol, reproduction, and youth culture—are condensations of class relations, struggle-laden moments of mediation. But schools are not a smoothly functioning machine keeping social cohesion. Each of these examples has serious consequences for the material life of a society. When the number or kind of jobs available to an educated populace underwhelm its education levels, that populace can feel a dissatisfaction. When a society promises democracy but delivers top-down control, its denizens might feel brow-beaten and disappointed. When young people get corralled into institutions whose purpose is unclear and does not consider their daily experiences, they might revolt or reject its programming. Dissatisfaction, disappointment, revolt, rejection, and anger permeate and fester in a social formation leading to "absenteeism, worker turnover, wildcat strikes, alcoholism and drug usage, deterioration of production quality" (122). In our moment, the opioid epidemic would be an interesting case to examine. To what extent does such an epidemic owe its magnitude to over-education and these other mediation struggles?

These mediation struggles have consequences within school as well. Over-education can cause "relaxation of educational standards" (123) since, in a shrinking job market, what an education means deflates in value. Such relaxed standards can lead to a lack of discipline (123). Relaxing standards and lack of discipline then threatens the legitimacy of the grading system, causing grade inflation, or "higher grades for relatively poorer quality work" (123) and erosion of the school's legitimacy. There can be a concomitant "falling commodity value of education" (123). These impacts in schooling come back around in the world of work, when it comes to discipline in the workplace, for example.

Carnoy's theory of mediation answers, with fine-grained detail, the question of how schools contribute to the class struggle as apparatuses. They are mediators in struggle. The contradictions mentioned are manifestations of that class struggle in schools. They are examples of condensed class relations. Education is part of the class struggle because it is a terrain in the balance of forces "by dint of the organic relation between struggle in superstructure and struggle in the base" (124). Importantly, mediation is uneven. To Carnoy "actions in the schools have the potential to contribute positively to labor's position in the class struggle" (124). Rather than a stultifying, flattening passivity, there is "a constellation of relations between the schools and the workplace," which means that schools can offer "either reinforcement or disruptive potential" due to "the independent dynamic of schools and their internal contradictions" (124). While the idealist, institutionalist, and bourgeois theory of stratification sees schools as creating inequality, the structural framework of education downstream from Althusser claims that schools contribute to the larger class struggle, impacting and impacted by the social structure.

These insights about structure, articulation, condensation, and mediation are all advancements and applications of Althusser's theory of education. In fact, Althusser's students produced a book-length manuscript examining these dynamics in the French schooling system. Baudelot and Establet's *The Capitalist School in France* (1973), published years before Bowles and Gintis's *Schooling in Capitalist America*, is a paradigm case of structural educational research.

Althusser had some unfinished business after 1968 broke out in the streets of Paris. As I mentioned in Part I, there had been an ongoing conversation about schooling in leftist French sociology since the early sixties. That conversation focused mainly on universities, the Fourchet Plan and college students' displeasure with the form and content of knowledge available in their classrooms. Althusser's essay "Student Problems" and Pierre Bourdieu and Jean Passeron's early work on university education were part of the conversation that student movements had started with their professors and administrators. That dialogue about pedagogy and university policy paved the way for the events of May 1968. But before the March 22 group formed, members of Althusser's seminar—well-known for their collectively written text *Reading Capital*—were working on a project tentatively called *Schools*. Bourdieu and Passeron's research focused entirely on the university, they pointed out, but Althusser and his students knew that primary and secondary education were just as important for understanding the ways education reproduces capitalism.

Schools was to be a sociological and theoretical examination of French primary and secondary schooling, using national educational statistics. The events of May 1968 disrupted the project but enough work had been completed for a manuscript. Roger Establet (an original co-author of *Reading Capital*) and Christian Baudelot (a sociology student in Althusser's orbit) wrote up the findings in a book called *L'ecole capitalist en France*, published in 1973. In *L'ecole* we find students of Althusser analyzing data, tracing policy histories and organizational structure, and generally trying to understand schoolings' place in the larger balance of social forces of their moment using an Althusserian framework. The text is a mixture of Althusserian ideological analysis backed up by statistics and history. It was never translated into English.

The book takes on two illusions of schooling (Baudelot and Establet 1973: 4). The first is that school is unified in a single, linear path from elementary school to graduate school. In this illusion of the school, the school system is constituted as a whole and organized into a single plan and whose goal is to educate (5). This ideology of schooling is that the system forms "a profound *continuity*" (5). This unity of school appears in two images: the *line of degrees* and the *scholastic pyramid*. (6)

Words and practices perpetuating this ideology say that degrees line up with one another (primary diploma, secondary diploma, etc.), that any student can ascend the pyramid of levels. These are effective images, but are limited to the *"level of words"* uttered in institutional contexts (7). The unity of school is therefore an imagined relation to real conditions, with material practices underlying it. Talking about courses, grades, and graduation all advance the illusion. Yet the authors use data to show the uneven realities (4) underlying this ideology of unity. They look at dropout rates in particular: "One must admit, all children do not complete this entire unique 'course' of scholastic study. It is a *fact*: the majority of French children stop going to school after finishing the "compulsory" amount of schooling" (8).

According to census data, in 1968 France, while 86.6 percent of the population reported having at most a primary school degree, only 6 percent had something equal to a university diploma. Attainment fell along class lines (19). Enrollment rates demonstrate that "a little more than a quarter of 18 year olds were still in school" according to 1968 data. Establet and Baudelot cross reference these findings with breakdowns of student degree completion by age group and find that 67.6 percent of seventeen year olds stayed in school for only the compulsory amount required (22). Yet students did not fall out of the system when they left. Rather, they continued onto different paths that led to vocational degrees of various kinds. Establet and Baudelot speak about this divided reality of the allegedly unified school as an apparatus and dropout rates as a practice composing that apparatus. Indeed, this partitioned school is made to seem like a united one (26), but the unified school is a "vast optical illusion" where "the scholastic apparatus—its smallest fraction—occludes its most significant part: that which most concerns three-fourths of people in school" (8).

They want to demonstrate "a brutal *fact*: the division of schoolchildren into two large masses corresponding to two types of schooling (75%–25%)" (33). There are accordingly two "*networks of schooling*" in France that are "totally separate" (33). The authors call the networks superior-secondary and primary-professional respectively. They are impermeable, heterogeneous in the kinds of content taught within them, and lead to antagonistic social positions where some students end up working against others. Each network of schooling recruits students in massive, general ways.

> These two networks constitute, by the relations that define them, the capitalist scholastic apparatus. This apparatus is an *ideological* apparatus of the capitalist State. As such this apparatus *contributes, for its proper part, to the reproduction* of the relations of capitalist production, which is to say, ultimately, the division of society into classes, to the benefit of the dominant class. The division of society into antagonistic classes explains, in the last instance, not only the *existence* of the two networks, but further (what defines them as such) the *mechanisms* of their functioning, their causes and effects. (Baudelot and Establet 1973: 34)

If there was a question about how reproduction of the relations of production works, or what it looks like, Establet and Baudelot give a very specific answer: the division of school paths through bifurcated networks that lead the majority of students to proletarianized places in the social structure. Furthermore, an ideology of unity papers over the inherently divided pathways that students take through the French school "system." The authors are careful to say that the phrase school system itself is a product of the ideology. There is no school system. Rather, there are two school systems divided by class struggle. In this case, one can see the schools as a condensation of class relations mediating contradictions in economic struggle, reproducing dominant relations of production amidst contradictions on an uneven terrain.

This section examined developments of Althusser's theory of structure in education, drawing from Johnson's concept of reproduction in struggle, Hall's notion of articulation, Poulantzas's structural determination of education, Wolpe's extension thereof into gendered education, Carnoy's concept of mediation in struggle and Baudelot and Establet's arguments regarding the unity of school. This section on structure provides a firm basis for the entire line of advance. Structural education is a class struggle framework whose concept of causality, for example, is asymptotic rather than reflective. In education this means a kind of structural determination that reverses the bourgeois stupidity of the liberal sociology casting inequality as an effect of education rather than the reverse. When schools reproduce relations of production in the class struggle, they do so as condensations of class relations which, to Carnoy, means that they mediate contradictions in the midst of struggle. They are subject to those contradictions but can also soften them. A key example is the false unity of the school system that Establet and Baudelot call out.

These are some examples of insights structural education can contribute as a tradition of left thinking about education. There are clear implications for educational inequality, democracy, grading, the labor market, and public understanding of the school system. A gaping hole in this tradition thus far, however—which is also gaping in Althusser's work—is the question of race, gender, and other identity categories. There are developments on these questions in the line of advance, at least with respect to race and gender. I will start with race and move to gender. Stuart Hall applied his theory of articulation to questions of race and its relationship to class analysis in a famous essay on race and articulation. The contemporary Filipino-American critical pedagogue Zeus Leonardo takes up Hall's claims and applies them to education in the United States.

23

The Structure of Race in Education: From Hall to Leonardo

While some educational theorists have tackled the race/class and education question from a Marxist angle with applications to education in the United Kingdom (Barton and Walker 2011; Cole 2017) and others in the United States have examined the question drawing from multiple traditions as part of a critique of paradigms like critical race theory (Darder and Torres 2004), the structural tradition beginning with Althusser and continuing to Stuart Hall and education researcher Zeus Leonardo is distinctive. Looking at the resonances between these thinkers, scholars can more clearly see some philosophical presumptions underlying accounts like those of Darder and Torres (2004) and Cole (2017). Tracing this tradition of race/class thinking also serves to name the tradition itself, which I call structural education, rather than the more familiar and capacious labels of Marxist or critical education.

The long essay "Race, Articulation and Societies Structured in Dominance" (1996) is Hall's landmark answer to the question of how race relates to class. In it, his goal is to "mark out a set of emergent questions and problems in the study of racially-structured social formations" (305). First, Hall distinguishes between two responses to the question about race/class: an economic response and a sociological response. The economic response is to "take economic relations and structures to have an overwhelmingly determining effect on the social structures ... specifically, those social divisions which assume a distinctively racial or ethnic character can be attributed or explained principally with reference to economic structures and processes" (306). This economic response "gives an over-all determinacy to the economic level" and "imparts a hard centre—a materialist basis—to the otherwise soft-centredness or culturalism of ethnic studies." The economic is hard rather than soft. It is also "mono-causal" because "what is often experienced and analyzed as ethnic or racial conflicts are really manifestations of deeper, economic contradictions" (307). While this is not wrong, it is also not quite right. The economic response "is surely correct when it insists that racial structures cannot be understood adequately outside the framework of quite specific sets of economic relations," but tends to "command all differences and specificities within the framework of a simplifying economic logic" (308).

The sociological response is different. Rather than a hard, mono-causal economic determination, in this case "race is treated as a social category" which prioritizes "the non-reductiveness of race and ethnicity as social features" (306). Race is non-reducible. This tendency is "pluralist in emphasis" and tries to "correct against the tendency of the first towards economic reductionism" by drawing "attention to the actual forms and dynamic of political conflict and social tension in" racially-structured societies. This sociological position where race is treated as a non-reducible category among others insists that there is a "difficulty in subsuming" (307) race and ethnicity into "more classical economic conflicts" and "must be given their due specificity and weight as autonomous factors." Finally, this sociological approach lacks some theorization and tends toward the descriptive. As it looks to "deal with the historical specificity of race in the modern world" the sociological answer tends to "stop short with a set of plural explanations which lack an adequate theorization, and which are descriptive rather than analytic" (308).

With the economic and sociological positions delimited, Hall uses the distinction to raise the question about race/class. Is race reducible to class phenomena, or are race and class equally autonomous from one another? Hall names these two tendencies "economistic monism and sociological pluralism" (336) and then uses the American slave system as an example to illustrate the problem before attempting a response.

When it comes to American slavery, there is "a difficulty of deciding precisely what was the nature of the American slave systems—clearly inaugurated within yet separate from the expanding mercantile capitalist phase" (317). In other words, was American slavery a feature of Atlantic mercantilist capitalism, or was it its own autonomous variation?

Thinking about South African Black and white labor and Latin American relations of dependency in an imperialist context as other cases, Hall's strategy for responding to the race/class question is to look at specific examples like American slavery, and then elaborate how "departures" from "orthodox Marxism" (read: economic monism) have emerged that "rectify some of the weaknesses correctly pinpointed by the critics of reductionism" (317). The "troublesome case of plantation slavery in the New World" leads some to argue that "plantation slavery was a form of capitalism" (319) or a profitable form of capitalist agriculture (320), while others "constitute [it] as its own distinctive 'mode'" (319). The case is opaque because "whereas under capitalism the worker owns his own labour power which he sells as a commodity to the capitalist, slaveholders owned both the labour power and the slave" (320). Is such slavery reducible to capitalism, or is it a self-standing racial relation? (This debate has come alive again recently with the launch of the 1619 Project.) Rather than pick a side, Hall lays out a theory of racial articulation as a third option, distinct from monist economic reductionism and relativistic sociological pluralism. He does this by going into more detail about South Africa and Latin America.

Starting with South Africa, Hall looks at John Rex's 1973 study of the "significant historical fact of *difference*," such as those in "'colonial' formations, where conquest and colonization have been central features" and it is "not simply the class struggle engendered by capitalist development, but the 'race war' engendered by colonial conquest" that matters just as much. In such cases racial hierarchy meets class exploitation. To Rex, the exploitation is necessary but insufficient for the society: "Economic relations are thus the necessary, but not the sufficient condition of the racial structure of the South

African social formation" (310). Thus, Hall writes that Rex's concern is "with the specificity of the *forms* of economic relations." Doing so "enables him to bring forward what Marx in another context called 'differentia specifica'—the basis, as he put it, of an adequate historically-specific abstraction: 'just those things which determine their development, i.e., the elements which are not general and common, must be separated out ... so that in their unity ... their essential difference is not forgotten'" (311).

Hall thereby uses the case of South Africa to illustrate areas in Marx's work that describe situations where exploitation is a necessary but insufficient condition of the social formation. There are differentia specifica in each class struggle that we must take into consideration when making adequate historical analyses. These elements are not general and common and their particularity must not be lost, yet neither are they self-standing autonomous social realities.

Hall is interested in how Rex points to a "specific kind of class struggle" (1996: 311) where race relations "are not ascribable within the 'social relations of production'" including "distinctions at the level of culture and values" (312). To understand the South African social formation, Rex thinks "all of these aspects need to be kept in mind when we speak of a colonial system of social stratification (Rex 1973: 30)" (312). Hall then applies the distinction between monism and relativism. It cannot be true for South Africa that "all the various instances of conflict are subsumable within and dominated by the class struggle" (312), in other words that "groups competing in the struggle over prestige or status may not be the same as groups competing over the power over scarce resources" (313). Economic monism, which calls for this easy bringing-together of racial difference in the class struggle, is not enough. Hall writes that

> simplistic political recipes based on the call for "black" and "white" labour to sink their differences in a common and general class struggle against capital—the famous call to "unite and fight"—are abstract political demands, based on theoretically unsound foundations, since they do not adequately grasp the structurally different relations in which "white" and "black" labour stand in relation to capital. (Hall 1996: 316)

But a relativistic, sociological explanation also does not capture the situation either. Hall agrees with Rex that "the racial fractioning of the South African working classes has a real and substantial basis, with pertinent effects at the economic, as well as the political and ideological level" (317). The question about race/class is clear here: how should Marxists understand the relationship between the racial hierarchy and the capitalist exploitation active in South Africa? Neither monism nor relativism work.

Latin America is another case. Pointing to the United Nations Economic Commission for Latin America as a "school" with its own unique paradigm of dependency theory, Hall summarizes dependency theory as treating "development and underdevelopment ... within the single framework of a world economic system." This framework draws from a broadly Marxist, anti-imperial perspective to understand "general relations of dependency" (318). The dependency theorist Frank, taking an economic approach, commented, however, that dependency "was no recent phenomenon in the region" but rather "the latest form of the long-standing 'satellitization' of the Latin-American economies within the framework of imperialist economic relations" (Hall 1996: 318). Such satellites are distinguished from the metropolis, which "extends the capitalist link between the capitalist world" and its regional dependents. Hall notes the "lack of historical specificity" in this account, rendering "exploitative situations as different as the Chilean *inquilinos*, the Ecuadorian *huasipungeros*, West Indian plantation slaves and Manchester textile workers, for all practical purposes, subsumed into a single relation, declared 'capitalist'" (319). Again, economic monism does not work when thinking about the class struggle in Latin American colonialism. Like in the South African case, there are differences within the social formation falling along racial lines for which simple class struggle cannot account.

Rather than seeing capitalism as some ultimate determining factor making all cases subsumable to the class struggle (like grey cows in the night) or seeing race as a standalone set of relations with its own autonomous force, Hall understands the complex unevenness in these societies, casting them as idiosyncratic sets of relations. Hall's purpose—and ours in examining his arguments—is to answer the race/class question. In Hall's words, we must "by difficult effort of theoretical clarification, through the Scylla of a reductionism which must deny almost everything in order to explain something, and the Charybdis of a pluralism which is so mesmerized by 'everything' that it cannot explain anything" (343).

The theory of articulation is Hall's path through the Scylla and Charybdis of reductionism and pluralism. Looking at American slavery, Hall returns to a distinction in Marx (citing Ernesto Laclau as having noticed it first). While an economistic analysis says plantations are just another place for commodity production, Marx actually qualifies this insight. Hall points out that Marx "describes the plantation as 'commercial speculations, centres of production for the world market' ... proof that Marx regarded them, too, as 'capitalist,'" but Hall notes that "Laclau reminds us that Marx, pertinently, added 'if only in a formal way'" (320).

The last clause is important. Slavery is capitalist but in a formal way. The distinction between the designations—capitalist and capitalist in a formal way—lets Hall interject an Althusserian insight. He says that Marx, in this analysis of the plantation, was picking up on the fact that slavery is "an articulation between two modes of production, the one 'capitalist' in the true sense, the other only 'formally' so: the two combined through an articulating principle, mechanism, or set of relations" (320). The Marxist explanation of these situations has to include a concept that permits what Hall elsewhere describes as differentia specifica, or what in the previous section I noted as unities in difference. Althusser's theory of social formations structured in dominance is one such theory: "the object of inquiry must be treated as a complex articulated structure which is, itself, 'structured in dominance.'" Slave plantation owners thus participated in a general movement of the world capitalist system: but on "the basis of an internal mode of production" (320).

Economic monism swallows the details of the situation to explain the phenomenon in terms of capitalism and class struggle. A relativistic framework just describes the myriad differences present in the phenomenon without establishing the various effectivities of social forces present, perhaps only focusing on racial oppression rather than the connection between oppression and exploitation. Hall's argument is that, in a capitalist social formation with a racial hierarchy, there is an "articulation between different modes of production, structured in some relation of dominance" (320).

He calls this theory of articulation "a revolutionary proposition" (320). The proposition is to adequately theorize differentia specifica by saying that there are two modes of production articulated together in dominance, an "articulated combination of modes" that "inserts economic agents drawn from different ethnic groups into sets of economic relations." Seeing the situation this way gets us past the impasse of monism and relativism. When the society is seen as "articulated into a complex unity, [it] need not be conceptualized as either necessarily the same [as in relativism] or inevitably destined to become [economic relations, as in monism]" (321).

The revolutionary proposition, Hall's theory of articulation applied to race, gives new meaning to "two cardinal premises of Marx's 'method'" of historical materialism, carving out a concept that captures differentia specifica, or unity in the diverse (322). The articulation thesis is that the Marxist method requires looking both at the material conditions of a society's existence and its historical specificity. Historical detail is necessary but insufficient. Materialist theory is necessary but insufficient. (The reading resonates with Richard Johnson's synthesis of the culture/structure debate in the previous chapter.) Althusser's theory is one of complexity that accounts for similarities and differences in society through the combinations and articulations of idiosyncratic parts, not through homology, correspondence, or random association. The same contradiction can exert different effectivities under different conditions. Hall applies this theory to race.

Recalling his reading of Rex and South Africa, Hall uses the logical language of necessity and sufficiency. In this case, the economic is necessary but insufficient for explaining other parts of society. A feature of this method or science of articulation is observing "these 'combinations' as historically specific, rather than specified *a priori*" which means that we must recognize "'laws of tendency'—which can be countermanded by 'counteracting tendencies'" (330). Social formations are shot through with such counteracting, countermanding tendencies. This means reading "Marx's laws of development and motion as laws of tendency (and countertendency) rather than *a priori* laws of necessity" (331). Consistent with Althusser's critique of fustian thinking, the science of articulation is a "dialectic of distincts," a "unity of opposites" that introduces "the criterion of distinction into the structure" (333).

How does this concept of articulation and complex structure, with its implications of cross-cutting, counter-acting modes of production "deliver certain pertinent theoretical effects for an analysis of racism"? By "posing it in its correct, necessarily complex form" (322), Hall bids us understand "race" and its relationship to "class" in a new way. His revolutionary proposition of articulation, which comes out of his reading of Althusser, "constitutes the most generative new theoretical development in the field, affecting the analysis of racially-structured social formations" (321). Hall is so excited about the development because he thinks "there is as yet no adequate theory of racism which is capable of dealing with both the economic and the superstructural features of such societies" (336).

Other inadequate accounts dominate the field. The problem requires walking that razor's edge between reduction and plurality: "one cannot explain racism in abstraction from other social relations—even if, alternatively, one cannot explain it by reducing it to those relations." Hall walks this line and puts forward a general theory of racial articulation. The historical insertions of racial and ethnic groups into capitalist relations of production makes them uneven, fractured, and fractioned (resonating with Poulantzas's insights about the ruling class). These fractures and fractions divide up the class internally, diversifying the relations of production, not just as residuals from previous social structures but contemporary manifestations in the formation. Racial categories cannot capture this complexity, nor can simplified economic categories. Each constitute relations of production that articulate together in capitalism under certain circumstances (337).

In the theory of racial articulation, "the relations of capitalism can be thought of articulating classes in distinct ways at each of the levels or instances of the social formation" where there is a "necessary displacement of relative autonomy operating between them." The displacements within the relations of production, and their relative autonomy when it comes to race, means that "race is intrinsic to the manner in which the black labouring classes are completely constituted at each of these levels" and therefore we should appreciate "the way black labour, male and female, is distributed as economic agents at the level of economic practices, and the class struggles which result from it" (340).

It is in this passage of the essay that Hall writes one of his best-known formulations on the race/class question, arguing that race is the "modality in which class is 'lived,' the medium through which class relations are experienced, the form in which it is appropriated and 'fought through'" (341). This formulation understands race/class distinctly from the reductionist and pluralist tendencies he outlined at the start. Class, understood only as economic relations, remains a necessary but insufficient element when considering Black labor in a white supremacist society. Neither can race stand on its own among a series of social stuff in an indecisive plurality, nor can we take race as an epiphenomenon of capital. Rather, Hall weaves the two together such that neither are necessary and sufficient, on their own, for an explanation of race from a Marxist point of view.

What is more, the explanation is not limited to Black communities, but "has consequences for the whole class" because other racial fractions occur within the working class along such lines. The articulation theory of race pushes the concept of race beyond Blackness, non-whiteness, and minoritization. He writes that "white fractions of the class come to 'live' their relations to other fractions" (341). In Hall's articulation theory, race relations and economic relations are now relatively autonomous parts of the complex unity of a social formation's relations of production, rather than autonomous variations alongside one another (pluralism) or reducible to one another (economism/race essentialism). The theory of racial articulation is a clear application and advance of Althusserian theory of structure.

The theory has strategic implications, specifically with regard to organizing for class unity and education. Hall spells out the former. If we assume that race is a modality through which people live, experience, and resist class relations then it is easier to understand exactly how the working class is divided according to racial difference, but also how it can come together (341). Organizers and researchers must know how "racial ideologies have been constructed and made operative under different historical conditions" and thus make them "thoroughly reworked" (342). This is exactly what Zeus Leonardo has accomplished in his research on whiteness and education.

Leonardo, a contemporary critical pedagogue, applies Hall's race/class analysis of education (2003, 2005, 2009, 2013), using examples of contemporary educational policies and practices as well as phrasings specific to teachers and students. While Leonardo's framework is mixed with other influences like poststructuralism, critical race theory, and discourse analysis rather than strictly following Hall's or Althusser's theory, the connection to Hall is clear, particularly in his 2009 book *Race, Whiteness, and Education*. Leonardo has also written extensively on Althusser and claims him as a central influence.

Leonardo (2009) sets out his project in *Whiteness* in terms of Hall's monism and relativism. Leonardo points to how Marxism economizes "the concept of race and the specific issues found within themes of racial identity, development, and representation." In this reductionist lens all issues "become subsumed in modes of production" (45). Leonardo uses Hall's concept of subsumption here, citing "conceptual monism" (47) when describing Marxism, taking up the project to "maintain the conceptual integrity of both Marxist and race discourses, through a synthesis of their strengths." Finally, Leonardo's formulation of the synthesis recalls Hall. On the one hand, Leonardo promises "a material, objective analysis" and on the other "an analysis of subjectivity, or how the historical conditions of class are lived" (46), citing Hall (1996) explicitly to say that "race is a mode of how class is lived" (49). He calls this framework a "progressive union between Marxist concepts and race analysis" (57).

Like Hall, Leonardo is looking for adequate explanations for racially structured capitalist social formations. Marxism without the lived-through thesis can be "color-blind" and lack "the conceptual apparatus to explain who exactly will fill the 'empty places' of the economy" (49). Unlike Hall, however, Leonardo applies this union directly to education, seeking formulations that can account for experiences in schools. What he calls "orthodox Marxism" tends to "pay respect to race as an important 'distinction', but not a decisive one ... that would otherwise help students make sense of their racialized class experiences" (48). Noting a clear case of fustian thinking in education he writes that "students of color, like many scholars of color, find it unconvincing that they are experiencing only class relations" (49). These insights about students and education are implied in Hall, but Leonardo points them out explicitly. Take parental involvement, for example. Integrating the "race concept into class" can "provide an analysis of parental involvement ... that asks the extent to which parents of color feel intimidated by white teachers or feel tentative during parent-teacher conferences and Open House night" (52). We should understand this intimidation as a complex working-through of racialized class struggle. The teacher's and parent's races are modalities through which they live their class positions. The intimidation parents of color feel cannot be solved merely through worker-controlled means of production, for example, but must be understood as a unity-in-difference, a specific articulation of associations between identity and resources. Neither can we silo the racial experience from the class experience in a dizzying delimitation of differences, as Hall would caution in his critique of sociological relativism.

In addition to noting the structural character of parent-teacher interaction, students' racialized experiences, and understanding the racial division of labor, Leonardo points to applications of the lived-through thesis in multicultural education.

> When multicultural education does not pay critical attention to the commodification of culture via racist signification, it robs students of the liberating aspects of cultural training. A materialist outlook on culture and race understands that too much *pluribus* and not enough *unum* takes for granted differences that only lately walked onto the scene. That is, although a multiculturalist should surely fight against what Memmi calls "heterophobia," or fear of difference, he or she should surely also reject differences that were constructed in order to create differences, rather than merely to observe them. (Leonardo 2009: 59)

We can see Hall's articulation thesis clearly in this passage, Leonardo providing a profound application to multicultural education. The latter can, in this view, take at least two approaches when thinking about race, falling in line roughly with sociological relativism and economic monism. In Leonardo's turn of phrase, the former focuses on plurality (*pluribus*) and the other on unity (*unum*). The plurality approach fights against heterophobia and emphasizes the distribution of differences. Yet this pluralism misses structural features that unite and cut across those differences. The framework can even create differences rather than observe them. Multicultural education, Leonardo notes, takes a sociological-relativistic approach.

In some cases, Leonardo claims that multicultural education takes these differences for granted, refusing to properly historicize them, treating them as though they "only lately walked onto the scene" (59). In this case, there is a lack of understanding about a unifying feature of racial difference, which is its structural history as a difference "constructed in order to create differences." An economic monist approach would reduce these differences to capitalist exploitation and ignore so much complexity to explain something. This would be too much unum. But a relativistic approach becomes so fascinated with differences that it explains nothing. This is too much pluribus. Multicultural education should not just observe these differences, but should include insights about their structural features in terms of class. Leonardo suggests an approach between this Scylla and Charibdis, one that seeks the unities in difference, or, to use the American tagline, *e pluribus unum*.

Schools are key sites of racial interpellation for Leonardo. He goes so far as to call them "a racial state apparatus (RSA)" because "the school is a material institution where race takes place, where racial identity is bureaucratized and modernized, where people are hailed as racialized subjects of the state." He likens racial interpellations at school to taking attendance: "teachers take the roll as they hail students in the homeroom as much as teachers hail them to answer when their race is called" (42). Like calling a student's name, teachers call students' races through their practices. A structural view of race in schools understands it as coming from particular material practices, or "how racial ideology actually functions or works on a daily basis" (43) through "tracking practices, to resource disparities, to different rates of achievement" (42).

As much as these practices hail students to racial subjectivity and reproduce dominant structures, Hall's emphasis on countertendency shows up in Leonardo's thinking as well, particularly in reference to race and the curriculum. Not everything in schools is top-down, dominating, and deterministic. Leonardo explicitly references Hall's racial articulation thesis to make the point.

> To the extent that racial supremacy is taught to white students, it is pedagogical. Insofar as it is pedagogical, there is the possibility of critically reflecting on its flows in order to disrupt them. The hidden curriculum of whiteness saturates everyday school life and one of the first steps to articulating its features is coming to terms with its specific modes of discourse. In an interview with Grossberg Stuart Hall defines "articulation" as "the connection that *can* make a unity of two different elements, under certain conditions. It is a linkage which is not necessary, determined, absolute, and essential for all time." (Leonardo 2009: 83)

This passage is notable for at least two reasons. First, it is precisely because a social force like racial supremacy is pedagogical that "there is the possibility of critically reflecting on its flows in order to disrupt them." Part of that process of disrupting racial supremacy is articulating its specific modes. Here Leonardo cites Hall's theory of articulation. The second notable feature of the passage is that the concept of articulation, elaborated by Hall, makes its way into Leonardo's thinking to justify the disruption of racial supremacy in schooling, specifically the possibility of countering racial supremacy in curriculum. Leonardo's concept of school as a racial state apparatus includes the possibility of agency and resistance against racism's social force because it is a theory of articulation (and not despite it).

This agentic feature of the theory of articulation shows up again in Leonardo's thinking about whiteness and pedagogy. Later in *Whiteness* he takes up the project of searching "for a rearticulated form of whiteness that reclaims its identity for racial justice" (93). In pedagogical terms:

> The rearticulation of whiteness is part of an overall emancipatory project that implicates a host of institutions from economic to educational. Discursive interventions in education to transform whiteness attempt to explain the whiteness of pedagogy as they encourage a pedagogy of whiteness. That is, shifting the white racial project from one of dominance to one of justice requires a pedagogical process of unlearning the codes of what it currently means to be white and rescuing its redeeming aspects. (Leonardo 2009: 94)

Rearticulating whiteness is a pedagogical process of unlearning and rescuing whiteness. Whiteness in this view is contingent and malleable. Keeping class in mind is part of the rearticulation, "just as Lenin once remarked that whereas the proletariat must merely be educated and the bourgeoisie must be revolutionized (see Althusser, 1976), so must whites be transformed" (96). Leonardo also bids us examine the unevenness of whiteness itself: "Whiteness represents a constellation of differences articulated to appear as a 'lump-sum' category … when in fact there are many ways to be White"

(96). The theory of articulation, a structural approach, imbues race with contingency rather than determinism. Leonardo thus emphasizes the "range of possibilities for white students to relate to one another" (97), which, he hopes, "may find its way into education as a pedagogical principle" (99). This principle of rearticulated whiteness in education, following David Roediger's elaboration of W. E. B. Du Bois's concept of the wages of whiteness, "requires that we transform 'reverse racism' into an injunction (Reverse racism!)" (105). The structural approach can help shift reverse racism into reversing racism.

But social forces in the scholastic apparatus are arrayed against this rearticulation project. Leonardo focuses a later chapter of *Whiteness* on the No Child Left Behind Act of 2002 (NCLB), specifically calling out how the law is "an 'act of whiteness' and perpetuates the innocence of whiteness as a system of privilege" (127). Leonardo applies the Hallian-Althusserian framework of articulation to George W. Bush's signature education policy, specifically how it "creates U.S. nationhood through the educational construction of whiteness." The law both "assists in creating the nation" and recreating whiteness, since the latter "is recreated through the historical process of expansion or restriction" (128). Rather than see this whiteness as a "transcendental essence," Leonardo's structural view of race and education takes it as a "*white formation*" that is "malleable according to social conditions and the state of white hegemony" (129).

Leonardo's view of NCLB is structural rather than experiential. Thinking about race as attitudinal or prejudicial "fails to account for the material consequences of institutional racism, behaviors that produce unequal outcomes despite the transformation of racial attitudes, and the creation of policies, such as NCLB, which refuse to acknowledge the causal link between academic achievement and the racial organization of society" (132). For example, the law does not target any of the structural causes of inequality that prevent educational success. "NCLB does not make visible the structural obstacles that children of color and their families face, such as health disparities, labor market discrimination, and the like" (136). Unequal school outcomes do not cause social inequality. Rather, social inequalities like health disparities and labor market discrimination cause unequal school outcomes.

Leonardo is careful to note that this structural education approach is not reductionist. Focusing on material consequences of structural practices, independent of experience, does not mean "subsuming racial oppression under the general framework of class exploitation." Recalling his use of Hall's synthesis, he reiterates that his theory of race is one of "race structures," which entails "a well-informed race analysis" (134). Such analysis "is arguably richer (no pun intended) with class analysis" but it cannot be color-blind. Leonardo thus finds Hall's happy medium between monism and relativism, applying his structural and well-informed race analysis to education, by pointing to how the mutual recreation of whiteness and nationality happens through educational practices.

For another example, when "educators face punishments resulting from inadequate yearly progress, they are policed by an unspoken whiteness (as well as a certain bourgeois worldview …)" (130). He cites scholars who claim that "NCLB comes with a 'diversity penalty' by punishing schools with higher populations of students of color." Leonardo pushes on this logic. If there is such a thing as a diversity penalty, "then the opposite must also be true insofar as NCLB comes with *whiteness reward* for mostly white schools" (138). Tying school funding directly to student performance on standardized tests creates a racialized distribution of school funding and other resources, a kind of white funding benefit or educational wage of whiteness.

After pointing to NCLB's diversity penalty and white reward, Leonardo argues that these penalties and rewards are articulated with the US repressive state apparatus. Indeed, "part of nation building" includes "what Althusser called Ideological State Apparatuses." Schools, for example, "have always been part of the military project" by "inculcating militaristic values." He goes so far as to claim that "NCLB is the educational cognate of the Patriot Act" because it is "consistent with the discourse of the War on Terror, if there are any failing schools in the USA, NCLB will smoke 'em out" (135). Whether or not we believe Leonardo's claim here, we can clearly see the Althusserian influence in his thinking about how schools, as ISAs, articulate with both material distributions and repressive institutions, like government and military. They are a state project.

Echoing Hall's reading of Marx on race, specifically Laclau's point about formality, Leonardo notes that "despite my sympathies with Marxism, the root of racial disparity is not *economic in nature* since an analysis of the inner workings of capitalism alone cannot explain it. Rather, racial oppression takes an economic form without necessarily being economic in nature" (138). Just as Marx said the slave plantations are commodity production "only in a formal way," Leonardo qualifies his own claims about race/class in education. He navigates between the Scylla and Charidbis again. Saying race is economic in nature is reductionist because it implies that an account of the inner workings of capitalism alone would be able to explain the root of racial disparity. Saying race is just another social category alongside class is too relativistic. Yet there is another possibility. It could be that race is economic in form but not in nature. Leonardo opts for the second position, drawing from Hall's racial articulation thesis.

In sum, Leonardo's work is an application of Hall's synthesis to education. He brings the racial articulation thesis to bear on tracking, taking attendance, and the No Child Left Behind act. His is a structural account of race in education.

24

The Structure of Gender in Education: Wolpe, Barrett, Arnot, Deem, and Valli

A South African radical in the 1960s, AnnMarie Wolpe belonged to the African National Congress, Nelson Mandela's political party. She married fellow organizer Harold Wolpe during their political work but Harold was arrested along with Mandela and many others in the struggle against apartheid. AnnMarie helped Harold and other organizers plan an escape from the infamous Marshall Square police blockade. She was allowed to visit Harold, do his laundry, and bring him food. In the course of their visits, they wrote to one another in secret code beneath Harold's shirt collars, and she brought him tools baked in loaves of bread and even a roast chicken. Harold and other comrades successfully made their escape using these tools. AnnMarie was arrested and questioned regarding the escape but police did not detain her long. The Wolpes fled South Africa and ended up in England, where AnnMarie began a career as a path-breaking researcher, focusing at first on Yugoslavian politics and then moving on to become one of the founders of the *Feminist Review* in 1979. She returned to South Africa in 1991 and worked in education policy. She died in 2018 in Cape Town (Wolpe, Chamaille, and Green 2018).

Wolpe drew from and advanced Althusser's theory of education in important ways, applying it both to girls' education and South African education more broadly. In her contribution to the collection *Feminism and Materialism* (1978), she starts by pointing out how the division of labor is flexible, contradictory, and constantly changing. Marx's writings on absolute surplus value (the amount of extra value produced by workers during the working day) and relative surplus value (the amount of extra value produced by workers that corresponds to alterations in the means of production) imply "not only different labour processes but also, as a necessary concomitant of this, different divisions of labour, and furthermore the transformation of the labour process with the tendency towards relative surplus value implying a continuous transformation of the division of labour" (Wolpe 1978: 309). The division of labor is not fixed. Rather, because the means of production change, each kind of surplus value "coexist[s] within the capitalist mode of production, but in unequal degrees and in an asymmetrical and contradictory relationship" (309). She calls this relationship "uneven" (309) and makes it clear that this changing dynamic in the division of labor "applies also to a considerable extent to the sphere of 'unproductive' labour" like in families and schools, particularly as the means of production change. She elaborates:

> The continuously present and yet changing multiplicity of requirements for varying quantities and differing types of labour power is expressed in contradictory demands on all types of labour producing institutions and organizations—schools, colleges of further education, universities, polytechnics, and so on. The attempt to mold educational and training policies to suit particular types of demands thus becomes the site of political and ideological struggles which have consequences for the system of education. (Wolpe 1978: 311)

Thinking back to Poulantzas's counterfactual regarding the relationship between education and the economy, it is clear that when business changes, education has to respond. This dynamic becomes a site of struggle since training programs and curricula must consider shifting. If computers become important in a society's dominant mode of production, then schools have to consider getting computers. Wolpe is pointing this out, but also emphasizing that such changes are not simple and easy. These are sites of struggle. Which schools get computers, for instance? How many computers? What can they use them for? Do parents want the computers in the schools? The same could be true for any technological, political, or economic change. The point is that structure is always a struggle, and so are educational policies and pedagogies (312). Wolpe develops this structure-is-struggle position further in the essay, thinking specifically about reproduction, the division of labor, and girls' education.

The struggles of the education system to keep up with the economy, and the contradictions therein, means that there is a "necessary disjunction between the 'requirements' of the economy and the range of skills the educational system can produce" (314). There is never a one-to-one correspondence between the economy and the school system because one is catching up with, digesting—or, as Carnoy would put it, mediating—what is happening in the other. The meanings of the words skills and training shift from context to context and overtime. In other words, what counts as skill or training is ideological: "the way in which the demand for skills becomes translated in the educational system is to an overwhelming extent at the level of the school in the form of more or less general training which is itself ideologically overdetermined" (314). This insight is not only a clear rejection of the idea that structuralism is a reflection theory, but Wolpe uses this unevenness and overdetermination to analyze the particularities of girls' education.

In a nod to Baudelot and Establet, Wolpe looks at dropout rates of female students in England, where "just over half of all British girl school leavers in 1974 had no 'graded result' in public examinations." Wolpe confirms their finding but shows that dropout rates are gendered. When it comes to full-time education "there were approximately nine percent who continued formal education" (315). She mentions, for instance, how girls are overrepresented in courses on catering, nursing, or secretarial work (315), an example of how the reproduction of agents and places is articulated with patriarchy. Applying the distinction between places (positions in a structure) and agents (people who hold those positions), Wolpe observes that "agents may be classified according to wide differences in terms of the jobs they perform, the status they are accorded, the incomes they earn, their ethnic and sexual membership" (320).

Wolpe is particularly interested in gender differences in the division of labor, and as such she extends the analysis to include the family unit (321), which has its own differential history with respect to capitalism. "The relatively unchanging nature of the sexual division of labour within the family is an important element in the legitimation process for the specific condition of women in the labour force" (321). She claims there is a "wife-mother image" (323) that comes to bear on women's lives in capitalist society. Particularly since "it is seen as the women's major role to care for and maintain the family, a wide range of 'reasons' can be called upon to justify the low wages women earn, the relatively unskilled nature of their jobs and the preference given to employing men rather than women in certain areas" (321). While Wolpe does not use the term, Hall might call this connection between the labor force and familial patriarchy as an articulation of two distinct modes of production. (Barrett will use the term explicitly as I show later in this chapter.)

The articulation to which Wolpe points has consequences for the education system, since, when educating girls, schools can "contribute to the reinforcement of the ideal wife-mother image" (323) and selectively impress upon girls "a dedication ... to roles which are exclusive of a technological commitment" (323). Schools can reinforce the articulation between the patriarchal, familial, and capitalist modes of production in their curricula and pedagogy. She gives an example: women in science. Rather than attributing low rates of women in the field to individual motivation and aspiration (325), Wolpe says we should consider "the structural constraints at work in the education specifically related to girls which need to be taken into account" (323). One structural constraint is the presence of women in science professions, or generally "the way in which the educational system mediates between girls and their allocation to their future roles" (326). For example:

> Even if girls and young women were able to get the necessary qualifications which would give them access to a wider range of occupations, this would in no way guarantee their entry into those occupations. Factors which relate not only to the availability of jobs through employment opportunities but also to the struggle within fractions of the working class need to be considered. (326)

In general, Wolpe provides a key contribution in specifying these examples. But her explanation of her approach in the line of advance succinctly describes structural education as a framework. She writes that the whole process of school policy implementation is "overdetermined by the operation of class struggle" (312).

> It does not follow, however, that education policies advanced by even the hegemonic fraction of the dominant classes will actually be carried into effect within the system of education. The reason for this is that the educational system does not immediately and directly reflect the "necessities" of the economy. That is to say, the educational system is not functional for production in the sense that the "functional" requirements of production can be met through the operation of educational institutions. The point is that the educational sector is itself the site of struggles not only within the structure of the educational system but also in so far

as, for example, "interests" within the system resist or support "external" demands made on it from different sectors of the economy. These struggles are fought out in terms of educational ideologies and within structures—forms of administration, class-room, curricula, and so on—which define the specificity of the educational system. Despite its ambiguity, it can be said that these "factors" place the educational system in a position of relative autonomy with regard to the economy: that is, the struggles which occur both within and outside educational institutions tend to result in "compromises" in the operation of the system, and these "compromises" constitute the form and content of the struggle which is itself in part structured by the ideological and organizational conditions of education. (312)

In this long but important passage, Wolpe here expresses, with greater clarity than Althusser, an Althusserian theory of education. She says the "educational system as a structure" is one where the system "has a relative autonomy viz. the capitalist mode of production and which is the site of the operation of that mode," understanding education "in its historical specificity" (313). These terms are hallmarks of the theory laid out in Part I and Wolpe uses them to understand girls' education as well as the struggle-laden relationship between economy and education in the Althusserian tradition.

She later applied this framework to gender and South African educational reform (1995). This later essay is a clear rejection of the line of critique, applying Althusser's thinking to the South African context and defending it from critics. Indeed, she writes that "far from Althusser's concepts being mechanistic, they open up the way to consider the complexities of the education system. His insights provide the basis for examining the relationship between schools, the gendered division of labor, and the role of the family" (Wolpe 1995: 301).

After discussing examples of Black pupils resisting their schools' inferiority in apartheid during the Sowetan uprising of 1976, Wolpe points to the weakness of simple cultural explanations of it and the strength of the Althusserian approach. While she acknowledges that the "Willis argument" analyzing the rebellion "drew attention to the actions of pupils as active agents rather than as passive recipients," she explicitly states that "resistance in schools does not of itself negate the Althusserian thesis." She continues:

Indeed, Althusser acknowledged the existence of resistance within ISAs and the difficulties this created for the maintenance of power and control over ISAs. He allowed for a plurality and diversity of ideologies that compete with and contradict each other. It follows therefore that the diversity and plurality of competing and contradictory ideologies does not preclude the counter-cultural ideologies from being accommodated to the dominant ruling ideology. Furthermore, there is no way of determining whether and to what extent oppositional groups internalize, unconsciously, the ruling ideology while simultaneously practicing their own oppositional culture. If these ideologies are profoundly unconscious, as Althusser pointed out, then there is every reason to believe they can be acquired notwithstanding oppositional practices. (Wolpe 1995: 305)

Moving to further demonstrate the Althusserian structural framework's worthiness in understanding the complexity of education and class struggle structurally, she uses it to analyze gendered divisions within education that resonate with Stuart Hall's developments of the theory, stating that schooling "can be understood only as the outcome of an interrelated set of processes in which what is important is the *articulation* between, among other things, disciplinary order, aspects of sexuality of both pupils and teachers, and the curriculum" (Wolpe 1995: 309). With the Althusserian theory of education:

> It becomes possible to analyze the behavior of teachers and pupils, including resistance by pupils, the background against which learning takes place, and the form of gender differentiation ... This provides the setting in which subcultural formations may be discussed and analyzed. Thus, the concept of resistance takes on a different dimension when located within this particular context. It cannot be seen as operating outside a number of existing structures. (310)

Wolpe gives one detailed example to reject "conventional feminist wisdom" that places such importance on teachers' and boys' behavior in relation to girls' level of attainment and regards "girls as victims of various patriarchal relations." Not only does she point out that students rebel against their own educations, she also says that "girls can and do act violently and aggressively. They are not passive victims." She also points out that girls' rejection of dominant school culture will differ markedly from that of boys (310).

Throughout the chapter, Wolpe juxtaposes forms of disciplinary control in school with other instances where such control is exerted throughout South African society, along with many other related themes. She analyzes workers' training for labor in South African gold mines, trends in educational attainment before and after the Bantu Education Act, related trends in per pupil funding in the 1990s, as well as the development of a People's Education Movement in opposition to ruling-class educational practices to achieve these victories (317–19). This movement, she notes, without proper and ongoing support from government, led to chaotic outcomes in both teachers' lackadaisical pedagogical methods and violent student behaviors (320). The text was written and submitted before the ANC "became the controlling force in a government of National Unity." Wolpe adds in a footnote that "the Minister of Education is struggling to implement the ANC's education policy" (320).

Wolpe's chapter is remarkable in a number of aspects, including its fine-grained analysis of the South African education apparatus in its economic context, its historical awareness of student resistance throughout apartheid, and the recognition of the ANC's goal to implement education policies that would support students and teachers. The chapter both uses the Althusserian framework to understand these tendencies and counter-tendencies and, in so doing, advocates for its usage across educational struggles internationally. Wolpe concludes that the "viability of employing aspects of Althusser's analysis is not in doubt. But what is needed is an extension of his ideas and an adaptation to the specific social conditions" (319). Other Marxist feminist researchers in England and the United States would do just that.

In *Women's Oppression Today: The Marxist/Feminist Encounter*, leading Marxist feminist theorist Michèle Barrett (2014) wrote that "developments in Marxist feminist theory are indebted to the Althusserian and post-Althusserian shift in the theory of ideology" (32). Barrett has largely focused on literature, making key materialist contributions to Virginia Woolf studies, but has also been a leading light in Marxist feminism, particularly as a member of the Marxist-Feminism Literary Collective in the 1970s. *Women's Oppression Today* is a seminal work in the field that has been widely translated and republished.

Barrett is insistent in the first publication, republication, and afterward to the 2014 reissue of *Women's Oppression*, that "there are a number of serious problems to [Althusserian theory's] use" (19) and that the Marxist feminist trend of following Althusser constituted a likely "widespread misreading" of Althusser's thinking about reproduction (269). Yet Barrett is equally clear that "the work of Louis Althusser has been crucial" (30) and disagrees with Thompson and the line of critique to say that Althusser's theory of ideology is in fact one of lived experience and furthermore this theory has been invaluable to Marxist feminism (31). Barrett's concern in the book generally is "the object of Marxist feminism," and to "identify the operation of gender relations as and where they may be distinct from, or connected with, the processes of production and reproduction" (9). Akin to Hall's theory of articulation (Barrett would dedicate a 1991 book on ideology to Hall) and Wolpe's work in this area, she and others in her milieu examined the ways "the specific oppression of women in capitalist relations of production ... must be seen in the light of gender divisions which preceded the transition to capitalism and which, as far as we can tell, a socialist revolution would not itself abolish" (9).

Education is an important feature of the inquiry. Indeed, the fourth chapter of *Women's Oppression Today* is called "The Educational System: Gender and Class." In it Barrett advances her own thinking about the distinctions and connections between gender and class relations via the concept of articulation, specifically in her understanding of relative autonomy. She states explicitly that the term relative autonomy "does not mean 'somewhat autonomous' but indicates autonomy *in relation to* something else—hence the usage in these contexts of the notion of 'articulation', where x and y may be autonomous but nevertheless operate in some respects in relation to each other" (121). After engaging with some of Wolpe's thinking on the subject, she claims that "analysis of gender division in education would benefit from the analytic separation of two elements: the relations of the educational system to the state ... and the relations of gender division to the state" (121). This separation-through-articulation defines Barrett's unique approach to analyzing patriarchy, capitalism, and education.

While she admits that "we can endorse Althusser's conceptualization of the educational system as an institution which functions to reproduce a divided workforce" (122), as Barrett noted earlier, this is not an unproblematic move. Reductionism is a real threat to the argument (115). It is this difficulty of transposing gender and class relations that Barrett examines. First, she points out that the relationship to the state is more uneven than Althusser lets on. Repression could be more than just a secondary consideration, for example. At the time she is writing, Barrett points to enforced compulsory education where parents face child services for not sending their children to school and students are threatened by police and prison for resisting school policy (122). Unlike in the economy, students can go to prison for misbehaving and parents can face dire consequences for resisting state education requirements.

Second, and more importantly for the line of advance and Barrett's stated goal, there are complications in understanding gendered divisions in schools as being somehow related to gendered divisions in the modes of production. In this she agrees with Wolpe but pushes the point further. "To argue, from an Althusserian point of view, that gender division in the education system may be understood in terms of the reproduction of the sexual division of labor and relations of dominance and subordinancy between men and women, would beg some fundamental questions" (124). The problem is how class relations should or should not be "transposed" on "the question of gender" (124). Barrett takes on this larger question of transposition before responding to the more particular case of that transposition in education.

The parallels with Hall's thinking continue, as Barrett sketches two past approaches to the question of gender and class relations in Marxism. Whereas Hall used the term subsumption to describe a reductionist account of race and class, Barrett writes the word absorption. Such a view is that "gender is not a separable element of class relations, but is completely absorbed within them" (124). On the other hand, somewhat like Hall's pluralism, others say that "gender division constitutes a system of oppression which is utterly independent of class division" (125). Barrett then proposes compromises between these two positions. One option, she says, is to measure observable phenomena and show how gender and class relations mix, like in the persistence of gender pay gaps (she cites Bowles and Gintis 2011 here) (128). Another option, following Lucy Bland, Charlotte Brunsdon, Dorothy Hobson, and Janice Winship, is to show how gender relations are "'outside' these economic relations, and historically prior to their emergence ... which capital has 'taken over'" (Barrett 2014: 133). In this case, gender relations are non-capitalist residual relations articulated with capitalist relations from which capital benefits (despite their not being explicitly capitalist).

This residual approach imbues both sets of relations with a relative autonomy, permitting Barrett to chart out what she calls an historical approach to the question. Like Hall's lived-through thesis to race/class, this approach shows how "the general relations of production by which capitalism is defined in Marxism constitute the historical context in which gender relations are now played out" (137). For the historical approach, we have to tell a story about how the sexual division of labor as we now understand it "was a product of an ideology of gender division that was incorporated into the capitalist division of labor rather than spontaneously generated by it" (138). Gender relations as they exist now, in this view, are a residual of previous social formations that the current formation incorporated into itself, despite changes elsewhere. This historical thesis means that the sexual division of labor is "*historically constituted*" rather than "a *logically pre-given* element of the class structure" (138). This is important for education because, if gender relations are not logically pre-given in the current class structure, then it is not at all clear that those gender relations "would *automatically* be reproduced by the reproduction of this class structure" in places like schools (138).

In terms of education, Barrett's historical thesis looks for examples of how such a pattern is too simple. Take the following, which both provides examples of this unevenness—or, in Barrett's terms, the dual relation—between the reproduction of gender and class relations, and displays Barrett's theory of education (139). First, the general theorization. Barrett claims that women have a "*dual* relationship to the class structure." This does not mean she advocates the utter independence of gender and class relations. Her historical approach is to neither absorb gender relations into class relations nor to think of them as utterly independent. Her concept of duality is that of articulated duality, unevenness between two sets of relations that manifests differently through different practices at different times. Here she makes the turn to school. We cannot say that school reproduces gender relations just as it reproduces class relations, she claims. Nor can we say that gender relations are utterly independent of class. Rather, Barrett says that school reproduces women's dual relationship to the class structure; an articulated duality between the relations that is historically specific.

Now for the examples. Barrett's theory would have us expect that working-class women's education will reproduce a different dual relationship than bourgeois women's education, each of which are distinct from a working-class boy's education (140). A bourgeois woman who goes to an independent school would be equipped to occupy a place in the division of labor above a working-class boy. However, that place she occupies will be gendered. She may end up in a place where she simultaneously owns but does not control capital. Meanwhile, working-class women may neither own nor control capital. If a working-class woman works for money and participates in the traditional patriarchal family, she may be both directly and indirectly exploited. The direct exploitation is traditional wage exploitation. The indirect exploitation means reliance on a male breadwinner and the performance of housework, uncompensated. In each case, gender relations articulate with class relations (140).

Furthermore, Barrett points out that gendered practices in schools might not be directly related to the division of labor writ large, but rather divisions of gendered work in schools themselves or reproductions of gendered work in families (142). Certainly "during roll-call, when children are sent out for milk or into dinners, the distinction between boys and girls presents itself as an obvious organizational aid" (142). But practices themselves differ and the ideologies they reproduce differ. Consider the gender dynamics in school leadership where in "many schools at the secondary level there is a headmaster, with whom executive and disciplinary powers reside, and a senior mistress, whose role is conceived of as primarily 'pastoral'" (142). Barrett says this "pattern clearly mirrors the norm of the nuclear family" (142). She points to the different distributions of male and female teachers across primary, secondary, and higher education (142); differences in the gendered quality of certain subjects, like English versus science (143); tracking girls into curricula of domestic labor while boys take subjects like woodwork or metalwork (144); the amounts of training girls receive compared to boys (146); as well as the gendered quality of what counts as legitimate academic knowledge (148).

Barrett's contribution is largely theoretical. She lays out a series of possible positions when it comes to gender and class relations: absorption, utter independence, empirical observation, and articulated duality. Barrett also distinguishes between transposition and historical approaches. While she attributes an absorptive-transpositional approach to Althusser, and provides ample evidence for that interpretation in her 2014 afterword, the theory of articulation between relatively autonomous variations underwrites her account of duality as a historical approach to gender and class relations. Rife with examples from schools, she applies the framework to education as an ideological state apparatus that reproduces gendered relations of production, giving clear examples like those above of how that uneven duality articulates in different contexts and between apparatuses like the family and the school.

We can use Barrett's concept of articulated duality to read other Marxist feminist educational researchers in her milieu. Each makes their own distinct contributions to understanding gender and class relations as articulated dualities, examining how schools reproduce both gendered and classed relations of production (and drawing directly from Althusser to do so).

Madeleine Arnot studied with British linguistic sociologist of education Basil Bernstein at the Open University, focusing her initial research on class codes and pedagogy. She participated in Bernstein's research group on schooling and society, the group to which Bernstein invited Michael Apple and inaugurated the latter's exposure to British cultural theory and left thinking about education. But Arnot did not simply follow Bernstein's framework. Rather she took from other social reproduction theories to develop a uniquely Marxist feminist framework for education. One of those theories was Althusser's.

In the early 1980s, Arnot (1982) took up a reproduction-in-struggle account of women's education using a non-culturalist concept of hegemony (citing Johnson 2018) in "Male Hegemony, Social Class, and Women's Education." She wrote generally that the aim of Marxist feminist research in education is to "develop a political economy of women's education which moves out and away from the limitations of a purely cultural theory of gender" (70). She begins with Althusser rather than the culturalists. Contrary to the line of critique, her understanding of Althusser's theory leads her to emphasize "the *active* nature of the learning process, the existence of dialectic relations, power struggles, and points of conflict, the range of alternative practices which may exist inside, or exist outside and be brought into the school" (66). Althusser's theory helps capture this dialectical interplay.

Arnot insists that "the power of dominant interests is never total nor secure" (66), and calls for more "concern for the *origins* and the conditions of school processes or the *sources* of potential conflict and contradiction within gender socialization" (69). She calls her perspective on women's education one that can reveal the "*diversity* of class experience and the nature of *class hegemony* in education" (69). Recalling Hall's differentia specifica and Wolpe's highlighting of plurality in Althusser's theory, Arnot aims for her political economy of women's education to account for "the unity *and* the diversity of the educational lives of women" (85).

Arnot has an eye for finding the points where gender and class relations articulate in education (Lussier and Backer 2020). For example, a more cultural or liberal perspective on gendered education, she says, would emphasize the docility and submissiveness of femininity, assuming that "masculinity means being aggressive, independent, competitive and superior" (Arnot 1982: 77). Yet through a social reproduction theory perspective like that of Althusser's, Arnot points out that the liberal theory would tell us to expect docility from girls' education and aggression from boys' education. But the political economy of women's education shows that docility is a trait taught to all genders of working-class children (78).

Arnot's political economy of gendered education, because it takes class contradictions into account as it examines gendered difference, understands docility as both gendered and classed for working-class children in school. Contrary to frameworks that see gender and class as utterly different, separating gendered subjects without any unifying experiences, new things become clear to the political economy of gendered education. For instance, given this insight about docility the Marxist feminist framework would tell us to expect that "working class boys and girls do actually share some experiences in school such as alienation from the school values of discipline and conformity, estrangement from school culture, and skepticism as to the validity of an ideology which stresses the possibility of social mobility" (69).

Like Barrett, Arnot is aware of, and to some degree convinced by, the line of critique against Althusser and social reproduction theory. She says Althusser suffers from functionalism and a lack of emphasis on struggle (74). She writes insightfully that such theories "conflate educational conditions with educational outcomes, giving the appearance that the rationales and rhetoric of state policy successfully determine the products of the educational system" (74). This conflation of conditions with outcomes, like Connell's critique from promiscuity, is one of the more substantive critiques though it takes place in a text advancing Althusser's thinking. Arnot finds Basil Bernstein's concept of class codes just as helpful, if not more so, than Althusser's theory. Yet her political economy of women's education advances Althusser's theory nonetheless. Like with Leonardo, her application of Althusser's work comes with a critique that helps clarify the weak points of the theory rather than merely dropping a devastating hot take aimed at revoking the theory altogether.

While Arnot's is a contemporary look at articulated dualities in gendered relations of production, Rosemary Deem uses a more historical approach to examining such articulations in British education. In *Women and Schooling*, Deem argues that "sexual divisions, in the process of bringing up children within the family, and more especially in the formal education of children carried out by schools, are of crucial importance both to an understanding of the position of women in capitalist society, and to a comprehension of how the division of labour between the sexes is maintained" (1978: 2). She cites Althusser: "Althusser has argued that societies involved in the production of goods must, in order to continue that production, reproduce both the forces of production ... and the existing relationships of production" (2) and summarizes Althusser's arguments about competence as knowhow and submission (3). Deem uses the framework to examine the articulated unity of gender and class relations in women's schooling in the United Kingdom from the nineteenth century through the 1970s. She looks at both policy and practices, focusing on how schooling reproduced both gendered and classed relations of production.

The 1870 Education Act made provisions for elementary education, which some saw as major progressive advances. But Deem notes that for working-class girls then, the 1870 Act did not provide them with any solutions to their problems of being confined to low status work and domestic labour within the family, but indeed ensured that the structure of capitalist society which located men without capital in the labour market, and women without capital in domestic drudgery, continued to be reproduced. (1978: 11)

Rather than progress toward equality, girls' schooling was "to the benefit of society, to capitalist production and to family life, rather than being seen to benefit girls themselves." Domestic economy was a core subject, including cookery and laundry work for working-class girls (11). Their education prepared them for a dual life of varying degrees of exploitation and oppression. Many practices anchored and reproduced this dually gendered and classed imagined relation to real conditions, all against the backdrop of the Suffragette Movements.

Compulsory education was enacted in 1880 in England and enforcement was difficult due to competing interests in children working to support the family (10). While boys may have been truant because they worked for wages, girls were truant also, but less often, because of their domestic duties in relation to men's waged labor (10). The trend for working-class girls to learn housework and care work continued to the twentieth century. "By the 1930s some secondary schools even had special housecraft flats built in to their domestic science rooms, so that even at school girls could not escape being inextricably linked with the home and domestic work" (17).

Middle-class girls' education had the same dual character as both gendered and classed, but there were obvious class differences, like a lack of science education and—when present—a focus of science education on domestic work like cooking (18). Middle-class girls' education dulled whatever class privilege they had, since they "were taught arithmetic in relation to household budgeting, and spent more time engaged in music, singing, and dancing lessons, riding, embroidery and foreign conversation" (13). The focus was on what a husband would want. Testing is another example. In higher education, in 1870, girls could take the exams that would qualify them for Oxford or Cambridge. Middle-class girls could sit for exams to get into university, but, absurdly, those exams were assessed differently than boys' exams (12) and while they could gain admittance to a university, the university would not give them a degree (13).

Deem concludes that while girls "entered education in large numbers during the late nineteenth and early twentieth centuries ... on the whole, what they got out of that education was a confirmation of the position of women in the social relations of capitalism" (19). As a 1904 Introduction to the School Code ambiguously reported, elementary schooling was to assist "both girls and boys, according to their different needs, to fit themselves practically as well as intellectually, for the work of life" (16). Deem comments that it "goes almost without saying that the 'work of life' assumed for girls was still that of being housewives and mothers, and domestic subjects" (16).

Being a domestic subject is an articulated duality between gender relations and class relations. Girls' schooling, across class differences, confirmed a gendered division of labor suited to the moment. Deem would do the same kind of examination with a history of British state educational policy between 1944 and 1980, following Miriam

E. David's (1978) work using Althusser's concept of the family-school couple to analyze the British state's influence on family in the school system.

The practices Deem talks about did not end with the onset of the twentieth century. Linda Valli's (1986) *Becoming Clerical Workers* adds to this project of tracking class and gender relations in education, but through an ethnographic look at a Midwestern High School's job training program in the United States. Like Arnot, Barrett, and Deem, her framework contains a mixture of theories and is far from a strictly Althusserian account. Yet Althusser's thinking was nonetheless influential. She writes that the

> basic theoretical perspective underlying the study is one of social and cultural reproduction, one in which people actively engage their institutional and cultural surroundings to make and create meaning and ultimately shape their everyday lives. These surroundings are envisioned as Althusser's structured totality, in which various domains are in relative autonomy to one another and in which reciprocal action is possible. (Valli 1986: 2)

Part II of her book is called "Reproducing the Division of Labour" and talks about how the job placement program at the high school maintains a gendered division of labor by focusing on girls' appearance when training them to become typists and secretaries. Valli calls this a selection process, displaying the intersection of gender and middle-class reproduction in schools. She focuses on a teacher named Mrs. Lewis, who teaches a course on job placement and finds girls positions at firms in the town.

In one anecdote, Mrs. Lewis tells the class about a situation where a bank employer complained that she was "not sending him very pretty girls" (63). The school in this case is responding to pressures from firms in the economy to send women that look a certain way to fill certain positions. This connection between physical appearance and skill is one example of how to think about the articulated duality of gender and class relations, resonating with Wolpe's structural insights into girls' education. In this case, instruction for girls means submitting to dominant ideologies about their bodies in the workplace. One anecdote involving two students, Dorothy and Maureen, is particularly telling.

> Maureen, for instance, was placed as the receptionist in a major city department which daily received a heavy flow of both city employees and the general public. She was, in fact, located down the hall from the mayor's office and on occasion was asked to fill in for his receptionist. In explaining the placement process at the beginning of the year, Mrs. Lewis said she sent Maureen to the interview with the city because they need good typists. As it turned out, Maureen was not a good typist. She had only a year of typing as a sophomore and often commented that she needed to improve her skills. When a typing assignment was given out in class, several students (including Dorothy) would finish the work more accurately and swiftly than she ... At the beginning of the year Mrs. Lewis described Maureen as "very outgoing and attractive ... the type of person an office likes to have around ..." About Dorothy, however, Mrs. Lewis had said the reason she was not placing her very fast was because her business background was so slim, her GPA was

not very high and she did not have good skills. Only later in the conversation did she add "and her appearance is poor" ... [O]nly the last comment seemed to be an accurate description of Dorothy. Yet this factor apparently overshadowed Dorothy's job skills and prevented them from being noticed. Not until well into the semester did Mrs. Lewis become aware of how skilled and conscientious a worker Dorothy was. (Valli 1986: 64)

This passage describes a set of practices that vividly illustrates how schools reproduce the social division of labor, specifically articulating gender relations and class relations. In principle (or in the technical division of labor), what it means to be a good typist is to have good typing skills, good business sense, and general office management skills. According to that rubric, Dorothy is clearly the best choice for the mayor's office job. Yet there is clearly a social division of labor layered into that technical division, and, at least in 1970s Midwestern United States, that division of labor was highly gendered—articulated with specific forms of patriarchy—and selects for women considered attractive by male employers.

Mrs. Lewis, pressured by contacts in the firms where she is attempting to place her students, has been interpellated by these gendered relations of production and reproduces them when choosing female students that look a certain way for such positions, rather than girls who have a tested set of skills. To be a good typist, for Mrs. Lewis, is therefore to be "very attractive, outgoing ... the type of person an office likes to have around." Valli is describing a social formation, a structured totality, where gender relations articulate with class relations such that the resulting relations of production set "good-looking" girls into certain kinds of clerical positions.

In general, the advances in Marxist feminism flowing downstream from Althusserian theory were largely of the kind evident in Valli: a focus on the sexual division of labor and how schools reproduce both class and gender relations. From Wolpe's careful expression of structural education in her examination of girls' education and her insistence on the Althusserian framework's usefulness despite the line of critique; to Barrett's historical concept of reproducing articulated dualities of patriarchal and exploitative relations; to the group of Marxist feminist researchers looking at examples of such articulated dualities like docility (Arnot), curricular history (Deem), and job training (Valli), there is an historical record of advances in Marxist feminism using Althusser's theory as a touchstone.

Contributions to the line of advance thus include both clarifications, applications, and critiques of Althusser's theory of education such as Arnot's from outcomes. These contributions unpack structural education as a framework. Furthermore, in the bravery and power of AnnMarie Wolpe's activism in South Africa is a clear example that Althusser's theory need not be associated with stasis, domination, one-way determination, reductionism, or a lack of agency. Wolpe's life and work are a testament to the theory's appeal to organizers and social movement.

These developments also show aspects of the line's weakness. While there are clear precedents for structural theory of race (Hall's articulation) and gender (Barrett's duality), I did not find accounts in the line of advance—except perhaps Wolpe's (1995), implicitly—taking an intersectional view. Black Marxist feminists produced important research and organizing during this period, notably Davis's (2011) chapter on Black women's liberation and education in *Women, Race, and Class* among others. Yet these works do not cite Althusser. I take up this and related critiques in the conclusion.

Finally, we can see in Valli's work another way the contributions apply Althusserian thinking: examples of interpellation. The case of Mrs. Lewis, Maureen, and Dorothy is not just an example of how articulated gender and class relations are reproduced but, by extension, it is also an example of gendered and classed interpellations. Deem's historical work presents a kind of history of gendered and classed interpellations in the British education system. Barrett's concept of articulated duality clarifies how two kinds of relations can ride the same interpellation as an articulated duality. Wolpe's account shows how such interpellations are predictable in a structurally determined education system, and also notes resistance both by students against the educational apparatus and by girls within the patriarchal relations that apparatus attempts to reproduce in school. Part of the power of interpellation as a concept is rendering structure individual, to show how individuals and groups immanently bear social structure in such a way as to accentuate the contradictory and struggle-laden quality of that structure.

Like the rest of Althusser's theory, the concept of interpellation was not static. Other scholars took up the concept of interpellation and applied, augmented, and extended it in new and interesting directions that have direct implications for educational research and structural education. Like so much of the line of advance, this story starts with Stuart Hall.

25

Ideology in Struggle: Advances in Interpellation

Consistent with his theory of articulation as unity-in-difference, Hall took Althusser's theory of ideology—specifically interpellation—to be a contingent, material, and struggle-laden process. He brought the two theories together in the essay "Signification, Representation, and Ideology: Althusser and the Post-Structuralist Debates." Hall rehashes articulation here, but adds in considerations about ideologies, specifically how "political practices of different kinds are *condensed*" (Hall 1985: 93). Given the relatively autonomous relationship between elements in an articulated social formation, following his rejection of simple correspondence between base and superstructure, Hall offers one of his most famous theses about ideology: "There is no law which guarantees that ideology of a class is already and unequivocally given in or corresponds to the position which that class holds in the economic relations of capitalist production" (94). This is the "claim of 'no guarantee'—which breaks with teleology" because "there is no guarantee that, under all circumstances, ideology and class can never be articulated together in any way or produce a social force" (95).

Against the idea that interpellations are always fixed on behalf of the ruling classes, the claim of no guarantees emphasizes "the possibility of the articulations between social groups, political practices and ideological formations which *could* create, as a result, those historical breaks or shifts" (96). In line with his theory of articulations, Hall can talk about the struggle-laden quality of structure and ideology's role in it:

> Structures exhibit tendencies—lines of force, openings and closures which constrain, shape, channel and in that sense "determine." But they cannot determine in the harder sense of fix absolutely, guarantee. People are not irrevocably and indelibly inscribed with the ideas that they *ought* to think; the politics they *ought* to have are not, as it were, already imprinted in their sociological genes. (Hall 1985: 96)

Near the end of this essay, Hall breaks into an autobiographical mode similar to the style Althusser uses at the end of the chapter on ideology in *OTRC*. He uses the autobiographical style to illustrate the idea that there are no guarantees in ideology, and how interpellations get caught up in the guarantee-less struggle of social structure.

> In Jamaica, where I spent my youth and adolescence, I was constantly hailed as "coloured." The way that term was articulated with other terms in the syntaxes of race and ethnicity was such as to produce the meaning, in effect: "not black." The "blacks" were the rest—the vast majority of the people, the ordinary folk. To be "coloured" was to belong to the "mixed" ranks of the brown middle class, a cut above the rest—in aspiration if not in reality. My family attached great weight to these finely-graded classificatory distinctions ... You can imagine how mortified they were to discover that, when I came to England, I was hailed as "coloured" by the natives there precisely because, as far as they could see, I *was* "black" for all practical purposes! (108)

The Jamaican and British social formations had different articulations, levels, and balances of forces. Hall goes on to do a structural analysis of this personal dissonance in his own subject formation. Social formations in the Caribbean articulate differently than in imperial centers (108). Each of them entail bitter struggle, but the struggle takes place on different terrains. In the imperial center, when it comes to racial subjection, there are binaries between white and non-white. Yet in peripheral formations like Jamaica, Hall notes there is a bitter struggle over place and position among multiple categories in a different scale. In the end, what it means to be "Black" differs dramatically, "coloured" referring to middle class while "black" refers to working class. The lesson here is that there is no guarantee an interpellation will have the same intended effect or be received similarly across contexts, or even within contexts. Hall experienced a kind of cognitive dissonance when he moved to England and was read as "black." The upshot is that subjectivity is rife with uneven complexity because of interpellations, not in spite of them.

> As a concrete lived individual, am I indeed any of these interpellations? Does any one of the exhaust me? In fact, I "am" not one or another of these ways of representing me, though I have been all of them at different times and still am some of them to some degree. But there is no essential, unitary "I"—only the fragmentary, contradictory subject I become. (109)

Here, Hall provides a precise application of Althusser's theory. The unevenness of the subject matches the unevenness of the social formation out of which it emerges, yet subjects are never essentially one way or another. There are only fragmentary and contradictory subjects interpellated by different practices in different contexts across different formations over time. While interpellation hails individuals, and ideology composes subjectivity, the hailing and subsequent composition are contingent processes. There is no guarantee how you or I become subjects, what our subjectivities are like, because the interpellations coming at us differ dramatically across and within contexts.

Contingency and unevenness go all the way down in social structure. Hall's (2001) claims about encoding and decoding further demonstrates, and clarifies, how guarantee-less ideology is when delivered by media. In "Encoding/Decoding," an essay addressing issues in media and culture, Hall uses the articulation theory to understand how media state apparatuses attempt to translate discourse into action through moments, forms, and flows (Hall 2001: 164). He claims that effective production depends on a successful passage of messages from ideological state apparatuses to the population. When an event happens, the media will encode it in a certain way that encourages a certain kind of action that benefits ruling class blocs. Yet these moments and their codes, with their specific modalities and conditions, are articulated with one another under specific conditions, which means that nothing is guaranteed.

Codes might not be decoded properly, for instance, where "the degrees of 'understanding' and 'misunderstanding' in the communicative exchange—depend on the degrees of symmetry/asymmetry (relations of equivalence) established" (166). Indeed, misunderstandings "arise precisely from the *lack of equivalence*" between the two sides, which "defines the 'relative autonomy' and 'determinativeness', of the entry and exit" (166) of interpellations. In general, "decodings do not follow inevitably from encodings" and "they are not identical," which "reinforces the argument [that there is] no necessary correspondence" (171).

Rather than an identity, or correspondence between sent and received messages, Hall insists that people negotiate ideologies. Hall claims it is rare for ruling class interpellations to land unproblematically. Interpellations are always *attempts* by ruling classes to get that message across. That means it is much more likely that, rather than downloaded in their original versions like robots, there is actually a "*negotiated version*" of the interpellation that "contains a mixture of adaptive and oppositional elements" which "acknowledges the legitimacy of the hegemonic definitions to make the grand significations (abstract), while, at a more restricted situational (situated) level, it makes its own ground rules—it operates with exceptions to the rule" (172). While the receiver of a negotiated code sees the dominance in an interpellation, they can also make their own ground rules for this reception under the circumstances.

Hall takes the insight one step further. Beyond negotiated codes that recognize the legitimacy of certain hegemonic constraints, it is also possible to "decode the message in a *globally* contrary way" (172). In this case, the receiver "detotalizes the message in the preferred code in order to retotalize the message within some alternative framework of reference" (173). Where a subject decodes a message by detotalizing it and retotalizing it an alternative framework, they create "what we must call an *oppositional code*" (Hall 2001: 173). Thus with Hall's thinking we get crucial insight into interpellations' mutability. Interpellations are always coded messages that can be decoded in multiple, uneven ways. There can be misunderstanding. There can be negotiation. There can even be opposition.

Yet the language here is still somewhat clumsy. Should we really call every attempt at hailing, every attempt to reproduce ideology on any side of any struggle, an interpellation, or can we specify different forms of interpellation depending on the moment, purpose, or position? Further, how can we think through these insights in terms of education? Hall provides the conceptual grounding for ideology's contingency in Althusser's theory. There are no guarantees when it comes to subjection. Messages get encoded and decoded idiosyncratically, unevenly, and in sometimes reversed or detotalized ways from their original intention. A cohort of thinkers took these premises and generated more precise language classifying the kinds of uneven attempts at reproducing imagined relations to real conditions. Counter-interpellation is one such example.

Jean-Jacques Lecercle (2006) proposes the term counter-interpellation in a Marxist analysis of language. In Lecercle's theory, linguistic meaning is composed of sedimented ideological constraints, established over time in the balance of forces via layers of interpellations occurring throughout multiple apparatuses. Speaking, in this theory, is a perpetual fixing of subject positions. Yet the ideological constraints which compose linguistic meaning, and thus the constant flow of interpellations, are always "subject to creative exploitation" (208). The fixed subject position can be unfixed; in fact, it is always in a constant state of struggle over its composition in the balance of forces.

Lecercle's argument for why the fixed subject position is always subject to unfixing comes from an insight about idiosyncratic speech. We must learn to speak a language which preexists us and within which we must form our sense of self, but we also speak the language in undeniably unique ways. Poetry, innuendo, paradox, neologism, philosophy, and puns all happen within and against the prefabricated linguistic structures speakers must speak. Lecercle's extends this insight about language to ideology and generates the notion of counter-interpellation.

> As I speak, I counter-interpellate the language that interpellates me to my place as a speaker, which makes me what I am. I exploit the potentialities of meaning that it provides me with, I play tricks with and on it, I accept or reject the names with which it assigns me a place in the community of speakers or excludes me from it … the speaker acts on and in language by using it. (2006: 208)

What "makes me what I am" is not the one-way interpellation of the subject by state power, but rather the two-way negotiation between the interpellation and the interpellateds' tricks, rejections, and exploitations of that interpellation. He writes that "the insult that wounds me and seeks to fix me in an interlocutory, subjective position which I do not want to occupy can not only be returned, but taken up, taken on, and revalued" (115).

Counter-interpellation is therefore an insult to the insult of interpellation, a linguistic-ideological negation of the negation by negotiation. This negotiation happens in speech acts, the things we say to one another every day, but has ideological and political ramifications. Rather than large-scale dialectical movements these are minute dialect moments: the conversations, chats, and back-and-forth of everyday life which can constitute, deconstitute, and reconstitute our relations of production. These interactions can fix individuals in subjective positions through successful insults, insofar as the interpellation reproduces, through the speech act, an exploitative, debasing, marginalizing, alienating relation of production. A successful interpellation requires the message be encoded by the apparatuses of ruling classes properly and decoded properly by subject. But the background of struggle within which that interpellation has fixed the subject, the social formation and its balance of forces, implies the equal and opposite possibility for that subject's unfixing. The interpellation can be returned, taken up, taken on, and revalued through creative exploitation.

> The speaker is therefore interpellated to her place by language, but, in so far as she makes the language her language, she counter-interpellates it: she plays with it, pushes it to its limits, accepts its constraints in order to subvert them ... Hence the interpellated one counter-interpellates the ideology that interpellates her. (Lecercle 2006: 164)

Thus there is a kind of free and creative expression possible within the play, push, and subversion of interpellations. This free creativity is sponsored by the conditions of the interpellation itself: struggle. There would be no interpellations unless there was a struggle where groups have an interest in recruiting. Interpellations only make sense in the context of struggle. Furthermore, this arena of struggle does not disappear after the interpellation hits its mark. Rather, society itself is a social formation where forces constantly struggle. The counter-interpellation where speakers speak in their own right is part of struggle, an answer to the interpellations issued by ruling classes. The concept honors the ways working classes wage successful battles in the ISAs, using ideology as a weapon against the ruling classes. Lecercle clarifies as well that not just any refusal, rejection, or reaction would count as a counter-interpellation. Only those responses and speech acts which take on, take up, and return the interpellation: that is the counter-interpellation.

Examples abound in education. Take the case of Joe Szwaja and his students in Celia Oyler's *Actions Speak Louder than Words: Community Activism as Curriculum* (2012). In 1996, at the protests against the World Trade Organization in Seattle, Mr. Szwaja incorporated the protests into his social studies class focusing on globalization. Oyler reports that

> they planned a street theater piece with large Bread and Puppet style puppets ... According to a student named Amber, they had about 500 people watching the street theater at one point in time. Then, after the protests were over, the class created a quiz for the media to take related to facts about globalization because they were dismayed that the coverage was about the small incidents of violence [at the protests] rather than about the major issues. They sent out the quiz as a press release and invited journalists to come to their class. (2012: 26)

Planning for this project and executing it were clearly counter-interpellative. Students quizzing the news media is a particularly creative exploitation of the balance of forces at that moment: students are typically the ones who are quizzed about their knowledge of history and social studies, but in this case the students decided to quiz society about its knowledge of free trade. They even invited the media to their class to learn something about globalization. To complete this project, Szwaja assigned essays on the history of the WTO, as well as the General Agreement on Tariffs and Trade Act (GATT). In addition, "students wrote a play about sweatshop labor around the world, including alternatives to such practices" (Oyler 2012: 21). Amber, the student mentioned above, reported that "we made huge puppets. We used cardboard and newspaper and rags. We made masks too" (31). Further, students being present at the protests had firsthand experiential knowledge of social studies and history in action. Oyler reflects that Szwaja "gave his students the opportunity to engage in a curriculum of public protest" (38).

By way of contrast, Tyson Lewis (2017) distinguishes counter-interpellation from disinterpellation. A disinterpellation is neither a reproduction of existing relations of production nor a creative expropriation of that interpellation. Rather, recalling terms from Althusser's later work on aleatory materialism, disinterpellation is the productive non-production of a nonstate. Disinterpellative study, for Lewis, preserves the weak power of impotentiality by suspending the interpellation or counter-interpellation of anything. Interpellation is an insult. Counter-interpellation insults the insult. Disinterpellation is neither an insult nor an insult to the insult, but rather the suspension of any insult.

Lewis goes on to identify disinterpellation as educational, properly speaking. The disinterpellation clears a space "outside any ideologically bound territories" in an encounter between "nameless atoms, [in] a field of force relations rather than knowing relations" (Lewis 2017: 313). It is this force emerging from the encounter that provides the educational experience, since it is not a "subjective disposition or even a desire but rather a *force* that emerges from a clash and pileup of atoms" (315). The subject dissolves in this clash-force, an "unpredictable eruption wherein ... no one controls it, no one has particular rights over interpreting it, and no one can predict its outcomes" (314). The subjectless moment of force in this clash is therefore "an education through desubjectification" and "is part of a larger Marxist agenda because it is only in the abrupt collapse of the ... subject that one can touch a communist horizon" (315).

The conclusion here is a significant one, as it yields a model for critical educational practice: "Marxist education is a practice in which ... the product is a subject without a subject (a subject estranged from itself, a desubjectivized subject)" (314). Disinterpellation is the definition of Marxist education because it "destabilizes and suspends any and every interpellative process in order to open the subject to that which is beyond subjectivity" (316). The seminar, for Lewis, is a pedagogy for disinterpellation since

> students, materials ... and the teacher enter into a constellation of forces that destabilize and thus open up a space and a time wherein a new kind of educational life beyond the subject temporarily forms ... that does not have a proper name or destination. (2017: 316)

During seminars, "the very conditions for a different world open up" and thereby set the "preconditions for a different kind of world" (316).

In Lewis' account, a counter-interpellation sets a counter-constraint. This counter-restraint recruits individuals to positions in the balance of forces. Education, for Lewis, hangs in the balance: since a counter-ideology is still an ideology, and a counter-interpellation still fixes a subject position, neither can be properly educational. Rather, they are political activism. Only the disinterpellation, which is neither interpellation nor counter-interpellation, can be called educational. I respond to this claim by noting the educational quality of counter-interpellations. Allison G. Dover (2009) provides useful case studies. Dover studied teachers who incorporate social justice into their public-school classrooms, specifically under constraints of state-mandated curricula and tests. Dover describes a literature teacher named Karen who, along with her students, counter-interpellated against their dilapidated school infrastructure.

> [Karen] described her unit as one that uses "literature to facilitate" wider conversations regarding race, class, and inequality; in her case, *Macbeth* leads to a wider examination of pressing social issues. After teaching the play, the students evaluated how the poor physical condition of their school affected their ability to perform theater. Students completed a thorough analysis of resource shortages and physical deficiencies at their school, developed a wish list of materials that would facilitate informal theater production, created formal proposals for renovations, and wrote letters to local businesses requesting donations to support their efforts. (2009: 524)

The school and its infrastructure prevented these students from learning and performing *Macbeth*, the productive and repressive social forces acting on the school made it under-resourced in this way. The purpose of this unit, according to Karen, was to give students the opportunity to "write to change their environment" (Dover 2019: 524). Like Szwaja's curriculum of public protest, this opportunity for students to write to change their environment is a counter-interpellative pedagogy. Students took up and took on the interpellation of their school building, juxtaposed with their curricular requirements for reading *Macbeth* and writing, to change the balance of forces in their part of the social formation. Karen attempted to teach her students to intervene in that prohibitive political terrain, to struggle within and against the ideological constraints of their curriculum and facilities. Dover does not report the consequences of the letter-writing campaign, but we imagine the class exerted a force of some impact: perhaps a newspaper article, a response from City Hall, or even funds from local businesses.

Clearly both are educational. Yet both accounts miss a third kind of interpellation: misinterpellation. James Martel (2017) opens *The Misinterpellated Subject* with Franz Kafka's retelling of the Biblical story of Abraham sacrificing his son Isaac, with a twist: there were also other Abrahams who responded to God's call, but they were not the right Abraham. One Abraham that is not the correct Abraham hears the call anyway, comes "unsummoned" (Martel 2017: 2) to perform the sacrifice in a different way than God intended. In this case, the other Abraham "is not called (not interpellated), yet he responds nonetheless. He is the one who gets the interpellation wrong; he turns a call by authority into farce, or perhaps—considering who is doing the calling—something far more subversive than farce" (2). The wrong Abraham answering God's call "is a challenge to and interruption of the intended narrative" (2). Martel's idea is that there is a form of ideological reproduction that is sometimes unintentional and sometimes a *"purposive misunderstanding"* (63) that "has the potential to cause an unprecedented kind of mayhem" where "all the schemes of the mighty and the powerful could—and just as easily could not—be unmade or undone by this unexpected arrival" (3).

Misinterpellation is therefore when "people respond to perceived calls (calls to freedom, calls to sacrifice, calls to justice, calls to participation, calls to identity) that are not meant for them, and how the fact that they show up anyway can cause politically radical forms of subversion" (4). It is a "mismatch" from "deep within the maw of established forms of power" (5) that "capitalism has no way of guarding against" because "the threats come out of its own phantasms" (5). While the mistakes of misinterpellation "come and go all the time without taking root, without producing radical responses" it can happen that "they produce effects that are so dramatic that nothing is ever the same again" (5).

Interestingly, Kafka elaborates misinterpellation using a classroom example: "It is as if, at the end of the year, when the best student was solemnly about to receive a prize, the worst student rose in the expectant stillness and came forward from his dirty desk in the last row because he had made a mistake of hearing, and the whole class burst out laughing" (2). Martel's point is that the mismatch, misunderstanding, and misfiring of interpellation is not only ever-present in social formations, but that such mistakes reveal the delicate and precarious quality in the balance of forces. Just as the class erupts in laughter, a laughter that—while directed at the worst student—painfully reveals the status ranking system inherent in grading, misinterpellations reveal the hierarchies and forces at work in social formations generally. Sometimes to revolutionary ends.

Martel gives two convincing examples of such large-scale mismatched responses, or "misfirings of interpellation" (7) in the history of liberalism that had widespread radical implications: the Haitian Revolution and revolutionary responses to Woodrow Wilson's Fourteen Points speech. In the first case, Martel considers the Haitian slaves of the late 19th century misinterpellated subjects for mishearing the call of Lafayette's Declaration of the Rights of Man and Citizen. There was a "complicated dance between those who penned the document and its recipients in Haiti" because "the rights and freedoms promised by that Declaration were never intended for the ... slave of Haiti. Yet, for all of this, the Haitians responded to this call nonetheless" (63). Yet the slaves "knew—at least to some extent—that the words of the Declaration were not addressed to them" (63) they purposively misunderstood it and thus became misinterpellated subjects.

The second example is President Woodrow Wilson's "Fourteen Points" speech in January 1918, calling for national self-determination. Martel follows historical accounts of this period that claim Wilson "had in mind only people very much like himself; his intentions were focused on European peoples and his call was specifically for the cessation of the power of old empires that had long dominated Europe" (72). Yet subjects of dominated territories, such as "activists and leaders ranging from Ho Chi Minh ... in Vietnam to Wellington Koo in China" (71), Lala Lajpat Rai in India (75), and Filipino resistance movements (77), saw "themselves as being similarly addressed by Wilson's call" (72).

In this case, "the contrast between what the supplicants read in Wilson's call ... and what was intended by Wilson himself became increasingly evident. As the fact of misinterpellation became clearer and clearer to all involved ... the mismatch of interpretations became dramatized, highly legible, in a way that was maximally inflammatory for a politics of resistance" (73). When these mistaken subjects of national self-determination found out the call was not meant for them, popular uprisings emerged throughout their countries (73), and many of them "turned in disgust from Wilson and moved instead toward the orbit of the Soviet Union, which issued a different sort of call" (73). Martel points to Ho Chi Minh in Vietnam as one such example.

In each case, liberal calls from the center of empires got creatively, purposively, and sometimes unintentionally received by people living in peripheries. From the first successful slave revolution in Haiti to movements of self-determination in countries for whom the concept was not necessarily intended, misinterpellations illuminate "the way that Western ideologies can often turn on their wielders, leading to radical, rather than reactionary outcomes" (76). These are cases of "how interpellation can fail, can reveal itself to be—or perhaps hijacked to become—misinterpellation" (78).

Martel argues that the misinterpellated subject, the one who answers a call not intended for them, "is an anarchist one and that misinterpellation is itself an inherently anarchist phenomenon exactly because it decentralizes and opposes those highly regulated and singular selves that interpellation tells us that we are and have always been" (Martel 2017: 6). Misinterpellation emphasizes "being the heteronymous" (6) kind of subject that just exists in a complex social formation, and by extension "the accidental subjects that come out of this process are the very 'agents' who further its effects" (6). There is therefore an anarchist agency within the "randomness and unknowingness at the heart of the interpellative process" (7). For Martel, the state never knows who it is calling and that there is not a "direct and absolute connection between the intentions of the powerful (those who put out of the call) and the subjects that are produced in response to that power" (7). Inside the state's arrangements there is "a source of permanent vulnerability" within which a "radical potential lurks in every one of us at every moment" (7).

In general, Martel claims that "a theory of misinterpellation is . . . largely and mainly consistent with anarchist theory and practice" (29). He continues:

> The very model of call and response that sets up a theory of interpellation is inherently "archic," that is, tied up with ruling and statecraft, with authority asserted from above and beyond. Misinterpellation comes from an anarchist perspective; it comes out of collective patterns of behavior, a form of steady and ongoing resistance to interpellative authority. It pays attention to alternative calls, calls that come from within and beneath and among the communities and individuals in question. These calls form other sources and models of authority that may rival or displace archist forms of interpellation. In this regard, I see misinterpellation as a key aspect of anarchist power, a product of endless ferment and resistance to a system that might seem utterly dominant but that is characterized by numerous and endless forms of vulnerability and dysfunction. (Martel 2017: 29)

Interpellations, while they have a "deadening effect" on rebellion, can always be "ripped asunder by a process like misinterpellation" wherein "the authority rendered by interpellation returns to being the nothing is always has actually been, disappearing seemingly in an instant" (84). Misinterpellations "serve as instructions for how to engage with the substructures of political agency and how, it could be said, to both understand and subvert the ways that power is sustained and produced through the production of authority" (86). Martel's concept relies on the idea that "our life is flooded with conflicting signals, assuagement, despair, anger, and joy" which encourages us to "anarchize the way we think about time and agency" (23).

Developed out of the long tradition of Althusser, Hall, Lecercle, and others, Martel's point is that a social formation is a welter of complex forces, forming complex subjects, where there is hegemony but only in an uneven and staggered way, full of unpredictability. Like the worst student shows us in Kafka's example, interpellations are always attempts that can be misunderstood, negotiated, and opposed. They can be unstuck, where subjects are neither interpellated nor not-interpellated—as in a disinterpellation. They can be taken up and taken to shift the formation in counterinterpellations.

These extensions of the concept of interpellation are part of what I have called the line of advance, forming a tradition of left thinking I call structural education. Distinct from critical education, structural education includes theoretical clarifications, augmentations, illustrations, and syntheses across geographical contexts. Scholars contributing to this tradition augment and build on the Althusserian theory of education. Combined, they furnish resources for a contemporary and properly Althusserian pedagogy.

Conclusion

In this book, I have examined Althusser's theory of education and how it was critiqued and advanced in educational research. In Part I, I reread the ISAs in the context of the book from which it was excerpted, setting out eleven rules of thumb for understanding education as an ideological state apparatus. I include them here in Table 1 with associated theoretical terms and concepts.

Next in Part II, I traced the common sense about Althusser's theory that developed in critical education, namely that the theory is functionalist, leaves no room for agency, and tragically fails. The critique from functionalism claims Althusser's theory aligns with the sociological tradition (orthogonal to Marx) that understands social practices as functions maintaining social equilibrium and cohesion. The critique from agency is that Althusser's theory casts society as wholly determining individuals like teachers and students, rendering them as automatons in the face of overpowering social machinery. The critique from tragedy is that while the theory is important historically, and while its project is a worthy one, it is a failed project. When Michael Apple and Henry Giroux configured critical education as a framework separate from neo-Marxism, by dichotomizing reproduction and resistance for example, they relied on these critiques against Althusser for their arguments.

After reconstructing Apple and Giroux's interpretations I found an inconsistency in their readings, which relied on a distinct line of critique put forward by other theorists. I revisited these critiques and assessed them for their inclusion of arguments and, if present, whether the arguments threatened Althusser's theory of education as I constructed it through the eleven rules in Part I. I found that most of the key texts in the line of critique do not include arguments and, where they do, the arguments are lacking and do not point to weaknesses in the theory. Rancière and Thompson, for example, each admit in their key texts that they are not offering analysis but rather polemic. Erben and Gleeson repeat Rancière's provocations with academic language, leaving major claims unsubstantiated. Hirst and Callinicos's texts include arguments, yet they leave much to be desired and do not pose a threat to the eleven rules. While the politics and personalities at play when these texts were published lent their content a force of legitimacy, there is little evidence that Althusser's theory of education is vulnerable to the critiques from functionalism, agency, and tragedy.

A reader might still be skeptical, however. How could such a longstanding series of critiques be faulty? Let us assume that they are true and look at the research produced by those influenced by Althusser. If the line of critique were true, then we would expect functionalist accounts that do not leave room for agency and fail on their own terms. Yet the opposite is true. There is a series of texts that applied and advanced Althusser's theory of education rooted in the Marxist tradition of class struggle, make room for agency, and succeed in providing useful analyses of education and capitalism. I lay out this line of advance in Part III. Stuart Hall's work on the theory of articulation, race/class, and encoding/decoding is a major thread throughout this line, to which there are many other contributions.

Hall's theory of articulation and its asymptotic concept of determinism clarify Althusser's notion of structural causality which, when applied to education, underwrites findings like Establet and Baudelot's analysis of the false unity of schooling,

Poulantzas's rejoinder to the bourgeois problematic of inequality and education, and Carnoy's theory of mediation. Hall's application of Althusserian theory to race was influential on Zeus Leonardo's thinking about whiteness and education. Leonardo produced interpretations of pedagogy and educational policy through this framework, claiming Althusser as an influence.

I also find resonances of the concept of articulation in Michèle Barrett's theorization of gender and class as articulated duality, and her application of this concept to education. Understood alongside AnnMarie Wolpe's feminist materialism of girls' education, I find Althusserian influences in the work of Madeline Arnot on gendered/classed docility in students; Rosemary Deem's analysis of ideologies of patriarchy and exploitation in the history of British education policy; and Linda Valli's ethnographic research on gender/class articulations in job placement programs in an American high school.

Finally, Hall's thinking on signification and encoding/decoding—that messages can be decoded differently than they are encoded through negotiation, detotalization, and retotalization—resonates with a series of advancements in the theory of interpellation. Lecercle's counter-interpellation, which is a practice that takes up and takes on an interpellation to shift the balance of forces, is one example, as is Lewis's disinterpellation, which is neither an interpellation nor a counter-interpellation but rather desubjectifies the subject in an encounter. Finally, Martel's misinterpellation builds out the space of misunderstanding and negotiation Hall mentions.

While this book has reconstructed Althusser's theory of education and how it was critiqued and applied in educational research, it provides the basis for larger reflections in educational thinking. In its full sweep, it is a reconsideration of Althusser's theory of education and a rehabilitation of a lesser-known framework in left educational thinking that I call structural education. Settling up, there are two kinds of conclusions to put forward. The first regards Althusser's theory of education and the line of critique. I have summarized these findings above, namely that Althusser's is a dynamic, profoundly influential Marxist theory of education in capitalist societies with resources for questions at the largest and smallest scales, from systems of institutions to everyday gestures. The critiques launched against this theory tend to lack clear argumentation and, when they do include arguments, are not convincing when held up next to the theory when it is considered in its fullest form in *On the Reproduction of Capitalism*.

For example, while the critique from functionalism took up many pages of text, it is difficult to robustly make the connection when one does a side-by-side comparison to paradigmatically functionalist educational theories like Talcott Parsons's. The idea that Althusser's theory is somehow closer to Durkheim's than Marx's is capricious and unfounded. Yet Madeline Arnot's remark that Althusser's theory confuses conditions for outcomes is something to ponder. To what extent does the theory of education as an ideological state apparatus mistakenly interpret mere educational stuff for outcomes of a process? To the extent that Althusser's is a Marxist theory, and Marxist theory—at minimum—is a theory of class struggle, then educational stuff will have some significance for class struggle according to the theory. Thus Arnot's question may be one for Marxism generally speaking. Is it possible for a Marxist theory to admit that some educational things do not have significance to class struggle? There is little room in Althusser's theory for this possibility, which may indicate what others in both the lines and critique and advance point to as a functionalist tendency. Yet in this form, the term functionalism loses so much purchase that it threatens to become meaningless, and a debate about its purview, I would suggest, approaches uselessness.

Yet the confusion of outcomes and conditions is useful. While far from Rancière's original critique from functionalism—that Althusser's theory is more in line with arguments about cohesion and the state of nature—it stands nonetheless. Not everything in education must have a significance to class struggle. We should be careful when using the theory and its terms, making a clear case for how and why a certain practice or institution is reproducing a dominant relation of production. Advances in interpellation are helpful in this regard. A practice may be a misinterpellation, disinterpellation, or counter-interpellation rather than an interpellation. There are certain phenomena that may not have any interpellative content whatsoever.

The second point is Thompson's trenchant historical account of the Marxist paradigms at play during the height of the line of critique against Althusser. A generation of voluntarist antifascist Marxists, alienated from the USSR and drawn to struggles like those against Franco in Spain, would find the kind of cold structuralist discourse not to their liking. As Thompson points out there are good historical reasons for this preference. Further, complaints about structuralism's abstraction are another notable discursive preference. While Hirst's argument that Althusser's theory is somehow too abstract does not land, Johnson's point that this abstraction can miss certain details is another helpful warning. Fortunately, Althusser's theory is set up well for this consideration with its focus on immanence. Again, as is the case with Arnot's comment and the critique from functionalism, this issue may be one in Marxism generally rather than Althusser specifically. Thompson is right to point out the competing problematics in Marx's own writing, all but agreeing with Althusser's own reading in *For Marx* that there is a younger and an older Marx each of which are paradigmatically different.

Of course, none of these warnings and historical notes add up to the critique from agency. While Althusser's structuralism focuses on positions, it does not ignore the change over time these positions undergo nor the forces that individuals and groups actively exert on them. Further, the concept of society as a social formation constantly in flux due to struggle applies from subject to structure, as Althusser notes and for which he gives many examples. Choices get made in the uneven and complex din of society. This concept of structural agency in Althusser's theory must be developed further and read alongside accounts of agency in Marxism such as Andersons's and Callinicos's to see whether my rendering of it holds up. I could not do this due to space constraints but I am convinced that there is more than enough room for agency in the theory. One need only consider Wolpe's (1995) account of student uprisings, her own crucial work with the ANC, and her advocacy for Althusser's theory as a counterfactual.

The final point regards the critique from tragedy. While many in the line of critique put this forward without argument, Raewyn Connell's observation that Althusser's structuralism is too promiscuous is something to seriously consider. The promiscuity arises, she says, from the combination of the theory's rigid adherence to concepts like base-superstructure while simultaneously claiming that terms within this theory can be moved around in multiple ways to fit any idiosyncratic situation, thus avoiding essentialism and reductionism. The problem of promiscuity is particularly evident in the last instance thesis, which comes to bear on what is perhaps the key causal question in Marxism. Althusser says the economy is determinant in the last instance, but the last instance never arrives. This is certainly a promiscuous formulation of an equally promiscuous concept. Hall tries to clarify that the relationship between economic and other forces is asymptotic, but the mathematical analogy to a line which only approaches another at infinity—promiscuous in its own way—inspires as many questions as it does answers.

When it comes to education, Carnoy's theory of mediation helps a little, in the sense that it specifies education's contribution to class struggle is to navigate capital's tensions by providing a softening of contradictions, such that schools find ways of working through contradictions that threaten the legitimacy of capitalist production. Yet even Carnoy admits that schools can sometimes not succeed in this and even go against capital's interests in promising democracy, overeducating, and so on. Poulantzas and Establet and Baudelot also help when they apply the theory to discrete issues like the relationship between inequality and schooling and the ideology of school unity. Yet I do not see a clear response to Connell's problem of promiscuity in strictly theoretical terms and thus it requires more consideration.

The clearest response to the problem of promiscuity, as I say in Part III, is to look at the ways the theory has been applied. I claim the line of advance, a tradition of scholars who developed Althusser's theory in education, converges on a tradition of left education thinking called structural education. If the theory were too promiscuous, such a thing would likely not be possible as the theory could not hold together well enough to make interesting and useful conclusions about education. But the opposite is true. After the reconsideration of Althusser's theory of education in light of its critics, this distinct tradition is the second major finding of the book.

To repeat, structural education says society is a formation of forces. These forces emerge from relations between people and groups of people. The relations show up in practices: the ways the people have their hands on things, how they treat each other, how they understand and enact their positions in society. People come in and out of these positions, but the positions themselves change and stay the same at a different pace. There is thus a key difference between people and their positions, and the different ways positions impact people and vice versa. The basic insight comes from the early nineteenth-century linguist Ferdinand de Saussure. In his landmark book *Course in General Linguistics*, Saussure says that languages change, but not because any one speaker by themselves decides to change it through speech. The language rather exists in the collectivity over time. Indeed, by thus separating language (a well-defined object outside the individual that they cannot modify by themselves) from speech (individuals speaking), Saussure states that "language is not a function of the speaker; it is a product that is passively assimilated by the individual" (Saussure 2011: 14).

Structuralists use this distinction to understand society. While the speaker has to learn the language through somewhat passive assimilation, that is not to say that language does not change or cannot be creatively exploited, shifted, and so on (like Lecercle shows). That change happens under certain conditions at a certain pace.

Language is different than speech; position is different than person. Individual speakers have agency but that agency runs up against a more obdurate structure of the language. So it goes with social structures. To use a simple analogy, peoples' experiences run through structures like water through rock. The rock is solid, forceful, and has its own tendencies distinct from the quick flow of water. Each has a power, each impacts one another, but differentially. The structural insight is that we have to understand both these effectivities if we want to change the terrain of social structure. Rock is very solid, directing water. But water changes rock over time. Neither is impervious to the other but their effectivities—the quantity and quality of the force they exert on one another—differ.

When it comes to education, the structural framework is quite distinct from the critical framework. The critical framework understands the social status quo as a system that is oppressive, exploitative, marginalizing, patriarchal, racist, ableist, nationalist, over-rational, colonial, totalitarian, authoritarian, technical-industrial-financial dehumanizing. But also, the critical framework says that society is made up of people and their experiences. These people can rise up and express themselves through critique of the system, raising their own and each other's consciousness, and, acting through creative praxis against that system, resisting it, disrupting it, even prefiguring other ways of being (and not necessarily in that order). Painting in broad strokes the critical education framework has two main principles: a critique of dehumanization that when thoroughly followed can lead to liberation, centering human experience against systems via the agency inherent in cultural practices. This book has traced a history of the second principle of culture, experience, and agency. (I have not dealt with the Frankfurt School's key influence on critical education and the concept of dehumanization.)

Johnson's adjudication between structuralism and culturalism names something important about the critical framework to the extent that it relies on authors such as Thompson: it is founded, at least partially, on a theory of no-theory. This is not to say that the critical education framework has no theory. It is itself a theory. However, some of its basic terms remain under-theorized on purpose, namely the concepts of experience and agency. Influenced by a tradition following Thompson that believed in the poverty of theory, when it comes to its concepts of experience and agency—the two main terms of its second principle—the critical education framework is intentionally lacking a foundation. By the same token, as Johnson points out, structuralism has concepts for its basic terms, though these may contain certain kinds of discursive violence, namely abstraction.

This insight leads to a final question needing response, which perhaps sums everything up quite well: Rancière's question regarding Althusser and the pedagogical relation. Does structural education include within its attendant pedagogy, an Althusserian pedagogy, elements of oppression despite its stated goal of being liberatory? Looking at the line of critique, the critiques from functionalism and agency quickly turn into propositions about the oppressive quality of Althusser's theory. I hope to have treated these issues fully in the pages of this book, specifically the long and generative tradition of anti-oppression research flowing downstream from Althusser. The existence of this tradition, largely hidden in common treatments of Althusser's work in education, provides a reductio ad absurdum argument. If we assume that Rancière and others are correct, then we should see Althusser's thinking inspiring oppressive research. But it would be difficult to characterize the tradition of structural education I have laid out as oppressive, featuring such thinkers as Stuart Hall, AnnMarie Wolpe, Michèle Barrett, Martin Carnoy, and others. These scholars move Althusser's theory forward in their work on ideology, race, gender, and structure.

Overall, while the line of critique may be understandable as an historical phenomenon given the contexts in which it was launched and cited, I find that it does not hold up under scrutiny now. When we reread Althusser's thinking about education as an ISA and test these critiques against it, the latter leaves much to be desired. Looking at how Althusser's theory of education was built upon by others, we can also see how Althusser's thinking is not what we would expect given what these critiques say. Examining these interpretations and their historical context, as well as research his work in education inspired in the form of the structural tradition, reveals not only a new understanding of Althusser's theory of education but also a reassessment of critical education as a field and paradigm.

Epilogue

While researching and writing this book, I drew from the structural framework in my teacher education courses, research, and political organizing. This structural perspective benefitted me in ways relevant to the project, perhaps providing the most convincing evidence for me personally of the theory's benefits, the limitations of the critiques launched against it, and a glimpse of Althusserian pedagogy in action. While these experiences are anecdotal and not featured in the main text of the book, they form a crucial background for how I came to my interpretation of Althusser.

A return to structure was in the air during the period between 2015 and 2021 in the American left. A new generation of activists became interested in confronting state power electorally with a socialist vision. This strategy was a distinct break from the more anarchist-influenced Occupy Wall Street movement. Following Kshama Sawant's election to Seattle's City Council as a member of Socialist Alternative, Bernie Sanders made a surprisingly successful run for president in the Democratic primary as an open socialist. With Donald Trump's shocking victory against Hillary Clinton in 2016, socialist groups saw their numbers swell. Most notably, the Democratic Socialists of America's (DSA) membership increased from six thousand to twenty-five thousand within a matter of months. The DSA's membership continued to grow and has now surpassed a hundred thousand.

I was part of this wave and saw it flow in real-time. Having been active in Occupy, I was interested in the shift taking place with Sanders's campaign. At that time, I was reading more of Althusser's oeuvre trying to understand how the claim about ISAs fit in the broader scope of his earlier and later theory. I was also looking for a new movement to join in the summer of 2016. I joined the Brooklyn chapter of Democratic Socialists of America in May. I knocked doors for Debbie Medina's failed state representative race in Brooklyn, stuffed envelopes at the main office in Manhattan, and attended Brooklyn DSA's meetings. There were about twenty people at my first meeting, the group adopting a single page of new bylaws by hand vote. I participated in *Jacobin* reading groups, became a subscriber, and through connections to the magazine's editorial board, I published an essay there on social reproduction theory and education for a general audience.

By that time, I had found that the Althusser I knew was not the Althusser talked about in my field. To critical education, his theory was part of a cohort of misguided but historically important theories that were too functionalist and deterministic, and supposedly did not lend themselves to activism. For me it was the reverse. I was very involved in organizing and Althusser was helping me understand education as an active part of capitalist social structure as well as the organizing I was doing to change it. I accepted a job outside of Philadelphia at the uniquely leftist department at West Chester University.

I joined the Philadelphia chapter of DSA, becoming the chair of the outreach committee as the organization experienced an unprecedented surge in membership after Donald Trump was elected. We went from twenty-five people regularly attending meetings to a hundred in a matter of weeks. (I heard the Brooklyn chapter had gone from twenty to two hundred to one thousand.) Being in a majority non-white city, and with my nascent Althusserian understanding of race in the United States via Stuart Hall, I was adamant that socialists should work in coalition with organizations committed to racial justice to seek unity-in-difference, even if their mission was not explicitly socialist. My comrades did not see things the same way. They were students of Adolph Reed, Jr. at the University of Pennsylvania. As a delegate to the national DSA convention in 2017, I saw the differences between us as the Momentum and Praxis slates diverged into warring caucuses, in some part due to Philadelphia members' influence.

I had formed a different ideology resulting from different interpellations, from working in South America to organizing in Occupy, and my theoretical perspective was largely rooted in Althusser rather than Reed. Despite these differences, there was an open agreement among all involved that it was DSA's moment to advance a socialist agenda in the United States for the first time in a hundred years. But things got tense. I was one of the first coordinators of the Local Initiative/ Local Action Committee (LILAC) in Philly DSA, which was structured by member-led working groups who sought to join coalitions, though this was prohibited by the Steering Committee. I became embroiled in an internal factional dispute in our chapter that got national attention when I helped organize a reading group of Asad Haider's book *Mistaken Identity: Race and Class in the Age of Trump* that was not sanctioned by the Political Education Committee and Steering Committee. The Philly DSA Steering Committee also refused to recognize a socialist feminist working group that had emerged. I was active there as well, helping push for a childcare committee in the chapter and being part of the organizing team behind the socialist feminist convergence in Philly. By this time, I was active in my faculty union and getting involved in multiple struggles across the city and state through LILAC, including getting arrested for civil disobedience in Harrisburg with the Poor People's Campaign in 2018.

All the while, I was reading Althusser. The theory of social formations influenced my thinking about LILAC's strategy. Throughout this moment I was getting deeper into secondary literatures on Althusser and education, putting the pieces of the story together that eventually became this book. The theory was a touchstone for me in my activism. LILAC eventually split off from the local Philly DSA chapter to avoid further internal disputes that sapped energy away from more productive organizing. Before and during that process, LILAC was a player in local actions that pushed Philly's mayor not to renew an information-sharing contract with federal immigration enforcement under the Trump administration. We were also a key organization in the coalition that elected socialist city councilwoman Kendra Brooks and were involved in housing, abolition, labor, and educational struggles. The social feminist working group also split off from DSA and became an effective fundraiser for left causes in Philly including sex worker organizers, striking teachers, and Brooks. My socialist organizing spilled over into other realms. Becoming a state delegate for my union's legislative assembly, I helped write and advocate resolutions that directed union money to Black Lives Matter organizing across Pennsylvania, create advocacy programs for survivors of workplace violence, and push the union to become more involved in the fight for public higher education nationally.

Althusser's theory helped me make sense of what I was doing strategically throughout this period. It helped me communicate the basics of Marxist theory and history to younger socialists. It helped me anticipate changes in various social formations, whether it was my organization or city. It helped me see the complex and uneven articulations between different structures, and helped me strategize about where to put energy, how much, and how to evaluate whether the energy was effective. It was not the only theory or influence on my thinking, but it was a primary one. I wrote *The Gold and the Dross: Althusser for Educators* during this period as a way to make Althusser's thinking more accessible to a wider audience of organizers and teachers.

During this time, I was also teaching teachers at West Chester. The theory was helpful in that regard as well. I built many of my courses at West Chester around an immanent structural approach to ideology. The concept of interpellation is particularly helpful when teaching teachers about school's influence on society and vice versa. My master's level course in American School as a Social Narrative examined everyday practices that reproduce and counter dominant ideologies in schools. I taught the concepts of interpellation and counter-interpellation side by side, citing local examples of teacher and student organizing in response to oppressive practices in their schools. I had teachers keep journals recording the events of their day to track interpellations and counter-interpellations. I also taught Marxist feminism, race, and intersectionality to give teachers an appreciation of the unevenness and complexity of material ideologies in their schools.

Students found fascinating interpellations and counter-interpellations in their schools, from curricular changes to disciplinary measures to interactions with colleagues and management. One student emailed me a year after completing the course, asking if a story at her alma mater included a counter-interpellation. The example is illustrative. Sister Barbara Buckley, the principal of the elite private Catholic Merion Mercy high school in Merion, Pennsylvania abruptly resigned in 2018. A 64-year-old nun, she said the school year had been a "challenging one," and that after twenty-five years and some "prayerful considering," it was "time for [her] to step down."

Days earlier, a senior name Zenia Nasevich had posted a letter online saying she had reached her "breaking point." Several politically charged events had happened at the school, to which the administration, Nasevich said, had no response. First, there was a physical fight between two students after the 2016 presidential election that was never addressed publicly. Next, it was a "racially charged" video that "went viral" at the school without comments from the administration.

But it was what happened with Maggie Winters that pushed Nasevich over the edge. Winters had been a religious director at a nearby Mercy school, Waldron Mercy. Winters was fired from Waldron in 2015 when some parents found out that she had been in a same-sex marriage since 2007, setting off an uproar that cast national attention on the small private school. Fast forward to April 2018. Students at Merion Mercy were working on a project researching homelessness and invited Winters to come speak with them about the issue. Then, Nasevich wrote in her letter, Winters was "'escorted out of the building' despite having a visitor pass and permission from the chair of the theology department" at Merion. Nasevich continued, "The project had nothing to do with [Winters's] sexuality, and the harshness with which she was treated is not what one would expect from an accredited Mercy school." Two months later Nasevich posted her letter, which came with a petition demanding "sincere honest discourse" at the school about these events. The petition had nearly 1,200 signatures. Sister Buckley then resigned. I agreed with my student: this indeed was a counter-interpellation.

I used this same framework in classes on higher education policy and student affairs, applying the interpellation lens to universities with students studying to become college staff and administration. Students found examples of the university interpellating its community. In one vivid example, a student brought in an image the university sent out in a welcome email to new students. The image featured the letters of the university in large font filled with photos of students. The students in these photos were all white. My student wrote to university officials, and a day later another image—this time with nonwhite faces included—was sent as part of a second welcome email. The example was instructive of how practice produces ideologies.

My doctoral courses in educational policy, law, and politics draw from Althusser's theory of base-superstructure to understand school law as well, as it is helpful for pointing out how school fits into the larger formation of social forces and what this means for teachers, administrators, and staff. I teach Carnoy in this context, emphasizing mediation and repression in school law. This approach to policy and law led me to publish two essays, one on Althusser's theory of school law (Backer 2020) and another on school funding inequality.

In the last two years of working on this book, my research shifted entirely to focusing on school funding. After achieving some clarity about the differences between critical and structural education, and as my own framework shifted to the latter, I noticed that very little left thinking in education examined what is perhaps the most concrete touchpoint between capitalism and schooling: funding. The financing of education is an obvious site of schools' contribution to the larger class struggle, particularly given school districts' relationship to property taxation and bond markets. While powerful structures exerting repressive and economic force act on schools in this situation (housing policy, segregation, municipal markets), students, teachers, and community members organize to take up and take on these practices through unions, activism, and research. The question of school funding is inherently a question about the structure of schooling in capitalism, one that has received little attention in the critical education literature. My focus on school funding has changed my research production as well. I am now advising socialist candidates and elected officials, for example, I wrote Nikil Saval's school funding proposal for his successful state senate race in Pennsylvania in 2020 and I have advised Jamaal Bowman's office on related issues.

In addition, I recently engaged in organizing a policy effort to help poor school districts apply for Federal Reserve bond purchases through the pathbreaking Municipal Liquidity Facility, created during the Fed's response to the pandemic. I see this project as the next step after my work with Althusser. I attribute this next step to my understanding of education from a structural perspective in Althusser's sense. Thus, at least using this anecdotal evidence, structural education can yield interesting insights in teaching, educational research, and organizing. This framework is underwritten by Althusser's theory of education and how it was advanced in educational thinking.

When it comes to the theory's critics, I can say from personal experience that it is not anathema to resistance, agency, or organizing. Indeed, having used the theory in teacher education, I have seen that it can provide a rigorous framework for teachers to understand and wield their power in society rather than come to functionalist or deterministic conclusions. I found something in Althusser's writing and how it was advanced by others that helped me become a more effective teacher and organizer. The theory and its concepts deepened and broadened my understanding of education and politics, leading me to new research and organizing projects. The theory and its development both clarified and directed me toward crucial aspects of class struggle, which resulted ultimately in the interpretation of the theory set forth in this book.

References

Agamben, Giorgio. (2009). *"What Is an Apparatus?" and Other Essays*. Palo Alto: Stanford University Press.
Alloggio, S. (2012). "The Reproduction of Control: Notes on Althusser's Notion of Ideological State Apparatuses (ISAs) and the Use of Machiavelli," *African Yearbook of Rhetoric*, 3 (1): 79–88.
Althusser, Louis. ([1964] 2011). "Student Problems," *Radical Philosophy*, 170: 11.
Althusser, Louis. (1970). "Ideology and Ideological State Apparatuses: Notes towards an Investigation." *Marxists*. Available online: https://www.marxists.org/reference/archive/althusser/1970/ideology.htm (accessed April 12, 2020).
Althusser, Louis. (1971). "Ideology and Ideological State Apparatuses: Notes towards an Investigation." In *Lenin and Philosophy and Other Essays*, trans. Ben Brewster, 127–89. New York: Monthly Review Press.
Althusser, Louis. (1976). *Essays in Self-Criticism*. London: New Left Books.
Althusser, Louis. (1995). *Sur La Reproduction*. Paris: Presses Universitaires de France—PUF.
Althusser, Louis. (1996). *Writings on Psychoanalysis: Freud and Lacan*. Columbia: University Press.
Althusser, Louis. (2003). *The Humanist Controversy and Other Writings (1966–67)*. London: Verso.
Althusser, Louis. (2005). "Contradiction and Determination," *For Marx*, 87–129. London: Verso.
Althusser, Louis. (2006). *Philosophy of the Encounter: Later Writings, 1978–87*. London: Verso.
Althusser, Louis. (2014). *On the Reproduction of Capitalism: Ideology and Ideological State Apparatuses*. London: Verso.
Althusser, Louis. (2016). *Reading Capital: The Complete Edition*. London: Verso Books.
Althusser, Louis. (2017). *Philosophy for Non-Philosophers*. London: Bloomsbury.
Althusser, Louis. (2019a). *History and Imperialism: Writings, 1963–1986*, ed. and trans. G. M. Goshgarian. London: Polity.
Althusser, Louis. (2019b). *Lessons on Rousseau*. London: Verso.
Althusser, Louis. (2020). "What the Honest Capitalist Will Say," *London Review of Books*. Available online: https://www.nybooks.com/daily/2020/02/21/what-the-honest-capitalist-will-say/.
Althusser, Louis, Olivier Corpet, and Yann Moulier Boutang. (1993). *The Future Lasts Forever: A Memoir*. New York: New Press.
Anyon, Jean. (1981). "Social Class and School Knowledge," *Curriculum Inquiry*, 11 (1): 3–42.
Apple, Michael W. (1978). "Ideology, Reproduction, and Educational Reform," *Comparative Education Review*, 22 (3): 367–87.
Apple, Michael W. (1982). *Cultural and Economic Reproduction in Education: Essays on Class, Ideology and the State*. London: Routledge.

Apple, Michael W. (1985). *Education and Power*. London: Routledge.
Apple, Michael W. (2012). *Can Education Change Society?* New York: Routledge.
Apple, Michael W. (2015). "Reframing the Question of whether Education Can Change Society," *Educational Theory*, 65 (3): 299–315.
Arnot, Madeleine. (1982). "Male Hegemony, Social Class and Women's Education," *Journal of Education*, 164 (1): 4–89.
Aronowitz, Stanley. (2016). *The Crisis in Historical Materialism: Class, Politics and Culture in Marxist Theory*. New York: Springer.
Backer, David I. (2017). "The Politics of Recitation: Ideology, Interpellation, and Hegemony," *Harvard Educational Review*, 87 (3): 357–79.
Backer, David I. (2018). "The Distortion of Discussion," *Issues in Teacher Education*, 27 (1): 3–16.
Backer, David I. (2019). *The Gold and the Dross: Althusser for Educators*. Netherlands: Brill.
Backer, David I. (2020). "Althusser on School Law," *Legal Form*. Available online: https://legalform.blog/2020/02/13/backer-althusser-school-law/ (accessed May 13, 2020).
Backer, David I., and Tyson E. Lewis. (2015). "The Studious University: A Marxist-Psychoanalytic Groundwork," *Cultural Politics*, 11 (3): 329–45.
Bargu, Banu. (2015). "Althusser's Materialist Theater: Ideology and Its Aporias," *Differences*, 26 (3): 81–106.
Barker, Jason, ed. (2016). "Marginal Thinking," *Los Angeles Review of Books*. Available online: https://lareviewofbooks.org/feature/marginal-thinking-forum-louis-althusser/.
Barrett, Michéle. (1991). *The Politics of Truth: From Marx to Foucault*. Cambridge: Polity Press.
Barrett, Michele. (2014). *Women's Oppression Today: The Marxist/Feminist Encounter*. London: Verso.
Barton, Len, and Stephen. A. Walker, eds. (2011). *Race, Class and Education*. Vol. 162. London: Routledge.
Baudelot, Christian, and Roger Establet. (1973). *L'école capitaliste en France*. Paris: Maspero.
Beetz, J., and V. Schwab. (2018). "Conditions and Relations of (Re)production in Marxist and Discourse Studies," *Marx and Discourse*, 15 (4): 338–50.
Benadé, Leon W. (1984). "Is the Althusserian Notion of Education Adequate?" *Educational Philosophy and Theory*, 16 (1): 43–51.
Benston, Margaret. (1969). "The Political Economy of Women's Liberation," *Monthly Review*, 41 (7): 31–44.
Benton, Ted. (1984). *The Rise and Fall of Structural Marxism: Louis Althusser and His Influence*. New York: Macmillan International Higher Education.
Bhattacharya, Tithi, ed. (2017). *Social Reproduction Theory: Remapping Class, Recentering Oppression*. London: Pluto Press.
Bourdieu, Pierre, and Jean Claude Passeron. (1979). *The Inheritors: French Students and Their Relation to Culture*. Chicago: University of Chicago Press.
Bourdieu, Pierre, and Jean-Claude Passeron. (1990). *Reproduction in Education, Society and Culture*. Vol. 4. New York: Sage.
Bowles, Samuel, and Herbert Gintis. (2011). *Schooling in Capitalist America: Educational Reform and the Contradictions of Economic Life*. Chicago: Haymarket Books.
Callinicos, Alex. (1976). *Althusser's Marxism*. New York: Pluto Press.
Carnoy, Martin. (1974). *Education as Cultural Imperialism*. New York: Longman.

Carnoy, Martin. (1982). "Education, Economy and the State." In *Cultural and Economic Reproduction in Education*, ed. Michael W. Apple, 79–126. London: Routledge.

Carnoy, Martin. (1999). "Globalization and Educational Reform: What Planners Need to Know. UNESCO, International Institute for Educational Planning." Essay on Educational Change (2002). Available online: http://unesco.amu.edu.pl/pdf/Carnoy.pdf (accessed March 10, 2022).

Carnoy, Martin. (2014). *Education and Social Transition in the Third World*. Princeton: Princeton University Press.

Carnoy, Martin, and Henry Levin. (1985). *Schooling and Work in the Democratic State*. Palo Alto: Stanford University Press.

Carnoy, Martin, and J. Marshall. (2005). "Cuba's Academic Performance in Comparative Perspective," *Comparative Education Review*, 49 (2), 230–61.

Carnoy, Martin, Amber K. Gove, and Jeffery H. Marshall. (2007). *Cuba's Academic Advantage: Why Students in Cuba Do Better in School*. Palo Alto: Stanford University Press.

Caws, Peter. (1997). *Structuralism: A Philosophy for the Human Sciences*. New York: Humanities Press.

Clarke, Simon. (1980). *One-Dimensional Marxism: Althusser and the Politics of Culture*. London: Allison & Bisby.

Cleaver, Kathleen, and George Katsiaficas. (2018). *Global Imagination of 1968: Revolution and Counterrevolution*. Chicago: PM Press.

Cohen, Gerald Allan. (2000). *Karl Marx's Theory of History: A Defence*. Oxford: Clarendon Press.

Cole, M. (2017). *Critical Race Theory and Education: A Marxist Response*. New York: Springer.

Connell, R. W. (1979). "A Critique of the Althusserian Approach to Class," *Theory and Society*, 8 (3): 303–45.

Connell, R. W., D. J. Ashenden, S. Kessler, and G. W. Dowsett. (2020). *Making the Difference: Schools, Families and Social Division*. London: Routledge.

Corrigan, Philip, and Derek Sayer. (1978). "Hindess and Hirst: A Critical Review," *Socialist Register*, 15 (15): 194–214.

Cross, Michael. (1986). "A Historical Review of Education in South Africa: Towards an Assessment," *Comparative Education*, 22 (3): 185–200.

Dalla Costa, Mariarosa, and Selma James. (1975). *The Power of Women and the Subversion of the Community*. Bristol: Falling Wall Press.

Darder, Antonia., and Rodolfo. D Torres. (2004). *After Race: Racism after Multiculturalism*. New York: New York University Press.

Davis, Angela Y. (2011). *Women, Race, & Class*. New York: Vintage.

Deem, Rosemary. (2012). *Women & Schooling*. London: Routledge.

Delphy, C
hristine. (2016). *Close to Home: A Materialist Analysis of Women's Oppression*. New York: Verso.

De Saussure, F. (2011). *Course in General Linguistics*. New York: Columbia University Press.

De Sutter, Laurent. (2013). *Althusser and Law*. London: Routledge.

Diefenbach, Katja, Sara R. Farris, Gal Kirn, and Peter Thomas. (2013). *Encountering Althusser: Politics and Materialism in Contemporary Radical Thought*. New York: Bloomsbury.

DiTomaso, N. (1982). "'Sociological Reductionism' From Parsons to Althusser: Linking Action and Structure in Social Theory," *American Sociological Review*, 47 (1): 14–28.
Dover, Alison. G. (2009). "Teaching for Social Justice and K-12 Student Outcomes: A Conceptual Framework and Research Review," *Equity & Excellence in Education*, 42 (4): 506–24.
Durkheim, Emile. (2005). *Suicide*. New York: Routledge.
Dworkin, Dennis L. (1997). *Cultural Marxism in Postwar Britain: History, the New Left, and the Origins of Cultural Studies*. Chapel Hill: Duke University Press.
Eagleton, Terry. (2014). *Ideology*. London: Routledge.
Edwards, J. (2007). "The Ideological Interpellation of Individuals as Combatants: An Encounter between Reinhart Kosselleck and Michel Foucault," *Journal of Political Ideologies*, 12 (1), 49–66.
Elliott, Gregory. (2006). *Althusser: The Detour of Theory*. Netherlands: Brill.
Erben, Michael, and Denis Gleeson. (1975). "Reproduction and Social Structure: Comments on Louis Althusser's Sociology of Education," *Educational Studies*, 1 (2): 121–7.
Evans, Martin, and Emmanuel Godin. (2014). *France since 1815*. New York: Routledge.
Farahmandpur, Ramin. (2004). "Essay Review: A Marxist Critique of Michael Apple's Neo-Marxist Approach to Educational Reform," *Journal of Critical Education Policy Studies*, 2(1): 95–138.
Federici, Silvia. (1975). *Wages against Housework*. Bristol: Falling Wall Press.
Fraser, Nancy. (1995). "From Redistribution to Recognition? Dilemmas of Justice in a 'Post-Socialist' Age," *New Left Review*, 212 (1): 68–149.
Freire, Paulo. (1970). "The Adult Literacy Process as Cultural Action for Freedom," *Harvard Educational Review*, 40 (2): 205–25.
Fritsch, Kelly, Clare O'connor, and Andrew Kieran Thompson, eds. (2016). *Keywords for Radicals: The Contested Vocabulary of Late-Capitalist Struggle*. New York: AK Press.
Gallas, A. (2017). "Revisiting Conjunctural Marxism: Althusser and Poulantzas on the State," *Rethinking Marxism*, 29 (2): 256–80.
Gilcher-Holtey, Ingrid. (2008). "The Dynamic of Protest: May 1968 in France," *Critique*, 36 (2): 201–18.
Giroux, Henry A. (1976). "Schooling as a Process: The Role of Dialogue in Education," *Clearing House*, 50 (1): 20–3.
Giroux, Henry A. (1980a). "Beyond the Correspondence Theory: Notes on the Dynamics of Educational Reproduction and Transformation," *Curriculum Inquiry*, 10 (3): 225–47.
Giroux, Henry A. (1980b). "Teacher Education and the Ideology of Social Control," *Journal of Education*, 162 (1): 5–27.
Giroux, Henry A. (1984). *Ideology, Culture, and the Process of Schooling*. Philadelphia: Temple University Press.
Giroux, Henry A. (2001). *Theory and Resistance in Education: Towards a Pedagogy for the Opposition*. Bergen County: Greenwood Publishing.
Glucksmann, Miriam. (2014). *Structuralist Analysis in Contemporary Social Thought (RLE Social Theory): A Comparison of the Theories of Claude Lévi-Strauss and Louis Althusser*. London: Routledge.
Gottesman, Isaac. (2016). *The Critical Turn in Education: From Marxist Critique to Poststructuralist Feminism to Critical Theories of Race*. New York: Routledge.
Grace, Gerald. (1978). *Teachers, Ideology and Control*. London: Routledge.
Gramsci, Antonio. (1971). *Selections from the Prison Notebooks*, trans. Quintin Hoare and Geoffrey Smith. London: Lawrence and Wishart.

Haider, Asad. (2020). "Are We Not Always in an Exceptional Situation?" *Casualties of History Podcast*. Available online: https://podcasts.apple.com/us/podcast/casualties-history-are-we-not-always-in-exceptional/id791564318?i=1000474637154 (accessed March 6, 2022).

Hall, Stuart. (1977). "'Rethinking the Base-and-Superstructure' Metaphor." In *Papers on Class, Hegemony and Party*, ed. Jon Bloomfield, 43–72. London: Lawrence & Wishart.

Hall, Stuart. (1985). "Signification, Representation, Ideology: Althusser and the Post-Structuralist Debates," *Critical Studies in Media Communication*, 2 (2): 91–114.

Hall, Stuart. (1996). "Race, Articulation, and Societies Structured in Dominance." In *Black British Cultural Studies: A Reader*, ed. H. A. Baker, M. Diawara, and R. H. Lindeborg. Chicago: University of Chicago Press.

Hall, Stuart. (2001). "Encoding/Decoding." In *Media and Cultural Studies: Keyworks*, ed. Meenakshi Gigi Durham and Douglas M. Kellner. New York: John Wiley.

Hamilton, Scott. (2013). *The Crisis of Theory: EP Thompson, the New Left and Postwar British Politics*. Manchester, UK: Manchester University Press.

Hill, Dave. (2001). "State Theory and the Neo-Liberal Reconstruction of Schooling and Teacher Education: A Structuralist Neo-Marxist Critique of Postmodernist, Quasi-Postmodernist, and Culturalist Neo-Marxist Theory," *British Journal of Sociology of Education*, 22 (1): 135–55.

Harvey, David. (2013). *A Companion to Marx's Capital: Volume 2*. New York: Verso.

Hattam, Robert, and John Smyth. (2014). "Thinking Past Educational Disadvantage, and Theories of Reproduction." *Sociology*, 49: 270–86.

Hegel, Georg Wilhelm Frederich. (2018). *The Phenomenology of Spirit*. Oxford: Oxford University Press.

Hindness, Barry, and Paul Q. Hirst. (1975). *Pre-Capitalist Modes of Production*. London: Routledge.

Hindness, Barry. (1977). *Philosophy and Methodology in the Social Sciences*. Netherlands: Humanities Press.

Hirst, Paul. (1976). *Problems and Advances in the Theory of Ideology*. Cambridge: Communist Party Pamphlet.

Howard, Michael C., and John Edward King. (1989). "The Rational Choice Marxism of John Roemer: A Critique," *Review of Social Economy*, 47 (4): 392–413.

Hudson-Miles, R. (2021). "Is It Simple to Be a Marxist in Pedagogy? Book Review of: 'The Gold and the Dross: Althusser for Educators' by David Backer". *Pedagogy, Culture & Society*, 29 (4), 669–76.

Hussain, Althar. (1976). "The Economy and the Educational System in Capitalistic Societies," *Science and Society*, 5 (4): 413–34.

Johnson, Richard. (2018). "Histories of Culture/Theories of Ideology: Notes on an Impasse." In *Routledge Revivals: Ideology and Cultural Production (1979)*, ed. Michèle Barrett, Philip Corrigan, Annette Kuhn, and Janet Wolff, 9–77. London: Routledge.

Jones, Gareth. (2009). "Polish Philosopher and Author Kolakowski Dies at 81," *Reuters*, July 17. Available online: https://www.reuters.com/article/us-poland-kolakowski/polish-philosopher-and-author-kolakowski-dead-at-81-idUSTRE56G67Q20090717 (accessed June 3, 2020).

Kafka, Franz. (1919). "In the Penal Colony," trans. Ian Johnston, *Kafka*, Available online: https://www.kafka-online.info/in-the-penal-colony.html (accessed April 30, 2020).

Kelsh, Deb., and D. Hill. (2006). "The Culturalization of Class and the Occluding of Class Consciousness: The Knowledge Industry in/of Education," *Journal for Critical*

Education Policy Studies, 4 (1). Retrieved from: http://www.jceps.com/archives/513 (accessed March 10, 2022).

King, Donna Lee. (1994). "Captain Planet and the Planeteers: Kids, Environmental Crisis, and Competing Narratives of the New World Order," *Sociological Quarterly*, 35 (1): 103–20.

Kirkpatrick, Ellen. (2020). "Identity in the Age of COVID-19: The Myth of 'Togetherness,'" Masters diss., Macquarie University, Sydney.

Kolakowski, L. (1971). "Althusser's Marx," *Socialist Register*, 8: 111–28.

Koppel, Niko. (2010). "Peter Keefe, Creator of Cartoon Voltron Dies at 57," *New York Times*, July 11. Available online: https://www.nytimes.com/2010/06/11/arts/design/11keefe.html (accessed April 23, 2020).

Krupskaya, Nadezhda Konstantinovna, and G. P. Ivanov-Mumjiev. (1957). *NK Krupskaya on Education: Selected Articles and Speeches*, Moscow: Foreign Languages Publishing House.

Kukla, R. (2018). "Slurs, Interpellation, and Ideology," *Southern Journal of Philosophy*, 56: 7–32.

Kulish, N. (2019). "Leszek Kolakowski, Polish Philosopher, Dies at 81" *New York Times*, March 6, 2022. Available online: https://www.nytimes.com/2009/07/21/world/europe/21kolakowski.html.

Lampert, M. (2014). "Theoreticism and Ideology: A Critical Reappraisal of the Althusser-Rancière Split," Doctoral diss., The New School, New York.

Lecercle, Jean-Jacques. (2006). *A Marxist Philosophy of Language*. Netherlands: Brill.

Lefebvre, Henri. (1976). *The Survival of Capitalism*. London: Allison and Busby.

Lenin, Vladimir. (1965). "The Trade Unions, the Present Situation and Trotsky's Mistakes," *Collected Works*. Vol. 32. Moscow: Progress Publishers.

Leonardo, Zeus. (2003). *Ideology, Discourse, and School Reform*. New York: Praeger Publishers.

Leonardo, Zeus. (2005). "Through the Multicultural Glass: Althusser, Ideology and Race Relations in Post-Civil Rights America," *Policy Futures in Education*, 3 (4): 400–12.

Leonardo, Zeus. (2009). *Race, Whiteness, and Education*, New York: Routledge.

Leonardo, Zeus. (2013). *Race Frameworks: A Multidimensional Theory of Racism and Education*. New York: Teachers College Press.

"Leszek Kolakowski," (2009). *Telegraph*. June 10. Available online: https://www.telegraph.co.uk/news/obituaries/culture-obituaries/books-obituaries/5873129/Leszek-Kolakowski.html (accessed June 3, 2020).

Lewis, Tyson E. (2017). "A Marxist Education of the Encounter: Althusser, Interpellation, and the Seminar," *Rethinking Marxism*, 29 (2): 303–17.

Lewis, William S. (2019). "But Didn't He Kill His Wife?" *Verso Blog*, May 29. Available online: https://www.versobooks.com/blogs/4336-but-didn-t-he-kill-his-wife (accessed April 14, 2020).

Lussier, Jessica, and David I. Backer. (2020). "Recovering the Marxist Feminist Eye," *Philosophy of Education Archive*, 1: 205–17.

Macherey, P. (2012). "Figures of Interpellation in Althusser and Fanon," *Radical Philosophy*, 173: 9–20.

Malott, C. S. (2011). "Pseudo-Marxism and the Reformist retreat from Revolution: A Critical Essay Review of Marx and Education," *Journal for Critical Education Policy Studies*, 9 (1): 2–17.

Martel, James R. (2017). *The Misinterpellated Subject*. Chapel Hill: Duke University Press.

Marx, Karl. (1956). *Capital: Volume Two*. Moscow: Progress Publishers.

Marx, Karl. (2008). *The 18th Brumaire of Louis Bonaparte*. New York: International Publishers.
Marx, Karl. (2019). *Capital: Volume One*. Mineola: Dover Publications.
"May 68: The Student Movement in France and the World," (2008). *International Communist Current*, April 6. Available online: https://en.internationalism.org/wr/313/may-68 (accessed April 19, 2020).
Merton, Robert C. (1968). *Social Theory and Social Structure*. New York: Simon and Schuster.
McGrew, Ken. (2011). "A Review of Class-Based Theories of Student Resistance in Education: Mapping the Origins and Influence of Learning to Labor by Paul Willis," *Review of Educational Research*, 81 (2): 234–66.
McInerney, David. (2005). "Althusser's Underground Railroad: From Dialectical Materialism to the Non-Philosophy of the Non-State," *Borderlands*, 4 (2): 2–12.
McIntosh, Mary. (1982). "The Family in Socialist-Feminist Politics." In *Feminism, Culture and Politics*, ed. Rosalind Brunt and Caroline Rowan, 109–29. London: Lawrence and Wishart.
McLaren, P. L. (1988). "On Ideology and Education: Critical Pedagogy and the Politics of Empowerment," *Social Text*, 19 (20): 153–85.
Miliband, Ralph. (1994). "Thirty Years of the Socialist Register," *Socialist Register*, 30 (30): 1–19.
Montag, Warren. (2002). *Louis Althusser*. New York: Macmillan International Higher Education.
Montag, Warren. (2013). *Althusser and His Contemporaries: Philosophy's Perpetual War*. Chapel Hill: Duke University Press.
Montag, Warren. (2018). "Althusser: Structuralist or Anti-Structuralist?" In *A Companion to Literary Theory*, ed. D. H. Richrer, 229–38. Hoboken: Wiley.
Morrow, Raymond Allen. (2014), "Reproduction Theories." In *Encyclopedia of Educational Philosophy and Theory*, ed. D. C. Phillips, 706–11, Thousand Oaks: Russell Sage.
Morrow, Raymond Allen, and Carlos Alberto Torres. (1995). *Social Theory and Education: A Critique of Theories of Social and Cultural Reproduction*, Binghamton: SUNY Press.
Mouffe, C. (1979). *Gramsci and Marxist Theory*. London: Routledge & Kegan Paul.
Munro, Kirstin. (2019). "'Social Reproduction Theory' Social Reproduction, and Household Production," *Science & Society*, 83 (4): 451–68.
Nesbitt, Nick, ed. (2017). *The Concept in Crisis: Reading Capital Today*. Durham: Duke University Press.
O'Neill, J. (1972). *Sociology as a Skin Trade: Essays Towards a Reflexive Sociology*. New York: Harper & Row.
Oyler, C. (2012). *Actions Speak Louder than Words: Community Activism as Curriculum*. New York: Routledge.
Park, Peter. (1967). "Measurement of the Pattern Variables," *Sociometry*, 30 (2): 187–98.
Parsons, Talcott. (2017). "The School Class as a Social System: Some of Its Functions in American Society." In *Exploring Education*, ed. Alan R. Sadovnik, Peter W. Cookson, Susan F. Semel, and Ryan W. Coughlan, 151–64. London: Routledge.
Parsons, Talcott, and Edward A. Shills. (1962). *Toward a General Theory of Action*, Cambridge, MA: Harvard University Press.
Pfeifer, Geoff. (2015). *The New Materialism: Althusser, Badiou, Zizek*. London: Routledge.

Pimlott, Ben. (2003). "Paul Hirst," *The Guardian*, June 20. Available online: https://www.theguardian.com/news/2003/jun/20/guardianobituaries.highereducation (accessed June 16, 2020).
Poulantzas, Nicos. (1973). *Political Power and Social Classes*. London: NLB.
Poulantzas, Nicos. (1978). *Classes in Contemporary Capitalism*. London: Schocken.
Rancière, Jacques. (2011). *Althusser's Lesson*. Bloomsbury Publishing.
Rehmann, Jan. (2013). *Theories of Ideology: The Powers of Alienation and Subjection*. Netherlands: Brill.
Resch, Robert Paul. (1992). *Althusser and the Renewal of Marxist Social Theory*. Berkeley: University of California Press.
Rex, John. (1973). *Race, Colonialism and the City*. London: Routledge.
Rikowski, Glenn. (2006). "In Retro Glide," *Journal for Critical Education Policy Studies*, 4 (2). Available online: http://www.jceps.com/archives/532 (accessed March 10, 2022).
Ronen, Shelly, and David I. Backer. (2018). "The Key to the Key: A Socialist-Feminist Rank-and-File Strategy," *Democratif Left*, December 8. Available online: https://www.dsausa.org/democratic-left/the-key-to-the-key-a-socialist-feminist-rank-and-file-strategy/ (accessed April 22, 2020).
Sakellaropoulos, S. (2019). "The Althusser-Poulantzas Discussion of the State," *International Critical Thought*, 9 (11), 128–41.
Schelling, F. W. J. (1988). *Ideas for a Philosophy of Nature*, Cambridge: Cambridge University Press.
Schnapp, Alain, and Pierre Vidal-Naquet. (1971). *The French Student Uprising, November 1967–June 1968: An Analytical Record*, Boston: Beacon Press.
Sotiris, P. (2014). "Rethinking Structure and Conjuncture in Althusser," *Historical Materialism*, 22 (3/4): 5–51.
Stalin, Joseph. (1938). *Dialectical and Historical Materialism*. Moscow: Foreign Languages Publishing House.
Thompson, E. P. (1978). *The Poverty of Theory*. New York: New York University Press, p. 55.
Thompson, E. P. (1991). *The Making of the English Working Class*. New York: Penguin.
Therborn, G. (1985). *Science, Class & Society: On the Formation of Sociology and Historical Materialism*. London: Verso.
Uljens, M., and R. M. Ylimaki, eds. (2017). *Bridging Educational Leadership, Curriculum Theory and Didaktik: Non-Affirmative Theory of Education (Vol. 5)*. New York: Springer Open.
Valli, Linda. (1986). *Becoming Clerical Workers*. London: Routledge.
Vasconi, Tomás Amadeo. (1974). *Ideología, lucha de clases y aparatos educativos en el desarrollo de América Latina*. Buenos Aires: Laboratorio Educativo.
Vogel, Lise. (2013). *Marxism and the Oppression of Women: Toward a Unitary Theory*. Netherlands: Brill.
Walker, Stephen, and Len Barton. (2013). *Gender, Class and Education (Routledge Revivals)*. London: Routledge.
Willis, Paul. (1981a). "Cultural Production Is Different from Cultural Reproduction Is Different from Social Reproduction Is Different from Reproduction," *Interchange*, 12 (2–3): 48–67.
Willis, Paul. (1981b). *Learning to Labor: How Working Class Kids Get Working Class Jobs*. New York: Columbia University Press.

Wolf, Frieder Otto. (2008). "Reproduktion und Ideologie bei Louis Althusser. Eine aktualisierende Annäherung." In *Welt ist Arbeit. Im Kampf um die neue Ordnung*, ed. Frieder O. Wolf and Gerd Peter, 41–54, Münster: Westfälisches Dampfboot.

Wolf, Frieder Otto. (2013). "The Problem of Reproduction: Probing the Lacunae of Althusser's Theoretical Investigations into Ideology and Ideological State Apparatuses." In *Encountering Althusser: Politics and Materialism in Contemporary Radical Thought*, ed. Katja Diefenbach, Sara R. Farris, Gal Kirn, and Peter Thomas, 247–61. New York: Bloomsbury.

Wolpe, AnnMarie. (1978). *Feminism and Materialism*. London: Routledge.

Wolpe, AnnMarie. (1995). "Schooling as an ISA: Race and Gender in South Africa and Education Reform." In *Postmodern Materialism and the Future of Marxist Theory: Essays in the Althusserian Tradition*, ed. Antonio Callari and David F. Ruccio, 300–35. New England: Weslyan University Press.

Wolpe, Peta, Alicia Chamaille, and Pipa Green. (2018). "AnnMarie Wolpe Was a Pioneer in Gender Education," *GroundUp*, February 19. Available online: https://www.groundup.org.za/article/annmarie-wolpe-widow-rivonia-trialist-was-pioneer-gender-and-education/ (accessed August 18, 2020).

Index

absorption of gender divisions in class relations 161–3
African National Congress (ANC) 155, 159, 182
agency 1, 5, 179–80
  Apple's critique from 82, 86–8
  Callinicos's critique from 124
  centering human experience via 8, 64–5, 74
  Erben and Gleeson's critique from 101–2
  Freire's line of advance in 6, 127
  Giroux's critique from 79–80, 84–7
  go rule and 73–4
  Hirst's critique from 107
  Marxist vocabulary of 118–19
  McLaren's critique from 125
  Morrow's critique from 73–4
  Rancière's critique from 98–100
  in relations of production 23, 28
  resistance-reproduction dichotomy and 74
  in theory of articulation 151
  in theory of interpellation 63–5, 69
  Thompson on 113–15, 123
  Wolpe's line of advance in 182
  of working class in ISAs 49, 51, 182
Althusser, Louis 1
  common sense on 4, 74–5, 88–9, 121, 123–5, 179, 185
  creative mistranslation of Marx 17
  critical turn in education theory and 79–81
  Hall's theory of articulation and 147
  illness and mental health 14–15, 96
  interpellations forming 63
  May 1968 student protests and 14–15, 57–8, 95–8, 102, 140
  personal life 8–9
  political practice of 39, 111, 112, 120
  Poulantzas and 133
  on *Poverty of Theory* 113, 117
  Rancière and 13, 95–100
  revolutionary interests of 28
  Stalinism and 111–12, 115, 120, 124
  style of 8
Althusser, Louis, works by
  Contradiction and Overdetermination 46
  Essays in Self-Criticism 111
  Lenin and Philosophy and Other Essays 39
  For Marx 73, 112, 182
  Reading Capital 2
  "Student Problems" 27, 50, 96–7, 140
  See also "Ideology and the Ideological State Apparatuses: Notes towards an Investigation"; *On the Reproduction of Capitalism*
American Express, Parisian students' bombing of (1968) 13, 44
anarchism 177
anchors and anchor rule 3t, 42, 62, 68, 180t
Anderson, Perry 91, 92, 107, 113, 119
Anyon, Jean 29
apparatuses
  ideological vs. repressive 3–4, 3t, 35–6
  ideology in 61
  Marxist context for 33–4, 37, 103–4
  from relations of production 129
  toe rule in functioning of 41–2, 73, 139
  See also ideological state apparatuses; repression
Apple, Michael 1
  Aronowitz and 121
  background and critical context 5, 75, 77, 89, 92–3, 107
  Carnoy and Levin on 136–7
  common sense on Althusser from 88–9, 91, 124, 125, 179
  Cultural and Economic Reproduction in Education (ed.) 79–80

Education and Power 4, 86–8
"Ideology, Reproduction and Educational Reform" 78
resistance-reproduction dichotomy in 81, 82, 86–7
Thompson and 113, 114
Arnot, Madeleine
    critiques of Althusser 181, 182
    on gender divisions in schools 7, 163–4, 181
    line of advance in 127
    "Male Hegemony, Social Class, and Women's Education" 163–4
Aronowitz, Stanley 77, 82
    Apple and 121
    The Crisis of Historical Materialism 83
    Giroux and 121
    Kolakowski and 92
    Thompson's influence on 121
articulation
    Althusser's theory of ideology and 169
    Arnot on gender and 163–4
    Barrett on gender and 160, 162, 163, 168, 181
    Hall's concept of 127, 131–4, 140, 142, 146–7, 151–2, 159, 160
    line of advance through 180
associative ideological state apparatuses 39, 40, 50

Balibar, Étienne
    on Althusser and May 1968 protests 14–15, 95
    gender and 19
    on ISA terminology 33
    in *Reading Capital* 18, 24, 98
    on relations of production 109
Barrett, Michèle 18
    Arnot and 164
    on gender division in schools 160–3
    Wolpe and 160
    Women's Oppression Today 7, 127, 160
Barton, Len 77
base-superstructure models 3*t*, 180*t*
    autonomy of superstructures in 3–4, 35, 38, 73
    education as mediation in 129, 137–40
    Hall on 129, 131–3, 169
    ISAs in context of 33–8, 54

Johnson on 131
Marx on 2
rule of special thirds in 33–8
Baudelot, Christian. *See* Establet, Roger and Christian Baudelot
Benston, Margaret 18, 19
Bernstein, Basil 77, 121, 163, 164
Bhattacharya, Tithi 19
Bland, Lucy 161
Bourdieu, Pierre and Jean-Claude Passeron 13, 18–19, 77, 121, 140
Bowles, Samuel 77, 78, 121, 136, 140
Brewster, Ben 62
Brunsdon, Charlotte 161
Bush, George W. 152

Callinicos, Alex
    Althusser's Marxism 83, 111
    critiques of Althusser 5, 75, 111–12, 121, 123–4, 179
    Kolakowski and 92
    Thompson and 120, 122
Cambridge University Communist Party 107
capitalism
    American slavery and 144, 146
    gender divisions in 7, 160, 161
    Hirst on 108
    ISAs under 41
    political ISAs in 55
    racial articulation on 148, 149
    relations of production under 17, 21–2, 169
    repressive functions under 36–7
    scholastic ISA dominant in 55–6
    schools mediating 138
    schools reproducing 15, 18–19, 27–8, 56–7
    State Ideology of 39
care work 19, 165
    See also childcare; gender
Carnoy, Martin
    critical context 77
    mediation concept of 6–7, 127, 129, 137–40
    Schooling and Work in the Democratic State 136
    Wolpe and 137
Catholic Church 64

causality and causality rule 43–8, 68
  condensation concept of 134
  go rule of ideology and 60, 66
  in Hall's base-superstructure model 129
  Poulantzas on 136
  promiscuity challenges to 183
  as rejection of Stalinism 112, 120
  schools and class struggle 44–8, 50, 73
  schools and inequality 6, 135
  structural vs. linear understanding of 3t, 4, 86
  Wolpe on 136
charter schools 41
childcare and childcare facilities 18, 19, 40, 56–7, 68, 164
  See also students
China
  Chinese Cultural Revolution 111
  relations of production in 108–9
churches
  as ISA 15, 33, 39, 53–5, 61–2
  Poulantzas on 135
  Rancière on 99
  repressive function of 36
  reproductive rights and 64
  scholastic ISAs compared to 52–7
class struggle. *See* struggle
Cohen, G. A. 21–2, 34–7
Cold War 118, 123
Combahee River Collective 135
communism
  relations of production under 21–2
  trade unions and 37
competencies and competency rule 3t, 25–31, 40, 67, 68, 82, 164, 180t
Comte, Auguste 100, 102, 123
condensation of class relations 129, 136–7, 139, 141
Connell, Raewyn 5
  "A Critique of the Althusserian Approach to Class" 122
  Kolakowski and 92
  Making a Difference 81, 122
  promiscuity critique of Althusser 5, 75, 122, 124, 125, 164, 182–3
  Thompson's influence on 121, 122, 124
contraception and reproductive rights 64, 65
correspondence principle 30

Costa, Mariarosa Dalla 18
counter-interpellation 7, 128, 172–5, 181, 182
courts and justice system 33, 36, 161
critical education 4
  common sense on Althusser in 4, 74–5, 88–9, 121, 123–5, 179, 185
  disinterpellation and 174–5
  division of labor and 29
  influence of "Ideology and the Ideological State Apparatuses" in 15, 79–81
  principles of 8
  structural education vs. 8, 184–5
  Westhill Conferences groundwork for 77
  See also specific scholars
cultural apparatuses 39, 42, 80
culturalism
  Arnot on 163
  Gramsci's hegemony in 131
  Hall on 132
  Johnson on 129–31, 184
  See also practices
curricula
  Althusser on 44–5, 96
  causality rule on 68
  gender and 162, 165
  May 1968 student movements and 44–5, 96–7
  race and 151
  schools' mediation of 138, 156

David, Miriam E. 166
decoding. *See* encoding/decoding
Deem, Rosemary 127
  on gender divisions in schools 164–6, 181
  Women and Schooling 7, 164–5
Delphy, Christine 18
democracy, schools' mediation of 138, 139, 183
Democratic Party (United States) 40
dependency theory 145–6
determinism. *See* economy and economic determinism; fustian thinking; overdetermination
differentia specifica 145, 146, 163
discipline 36, 139, 152, 159, 164
disinterpellation 7, 128, 174, 182

DiTomaso, N. 17, 104
division of labor
    Baudelot and Establet on 141
    competency rule and 25–31, 67
    in functionalist critiques 79, 85, 108–9
    Hirst on 123
    struggle in 51
    Valli on gender and 166–8
    Wolpe on gender and 155–7
Dover, Allison G. 175
dropout rates 141, 156
dual relationship of women to class 7, 162, 163, 168, 181
Durkheim, Emile 2, 17, 19, 77, 100, 102, 181
Dutschke, Rudi 122
Dworkin, Dennis L. 113, 117

economy and economic determinism
    Apple's critique from 80–2
    as capitalist value 39
    Carnoy on 136
    competencies external to 27–8
    Giroux's critique from 73
    Hall on asymptotic last instance of 129, 132–3, 136, 142, 180–1, 183
    ISAs vs. 1, 130
    Johnson on 130
    racial social divisions and 143–6, 153
    schools responding to 156
    Stalinism and 111
    See also base-superstructure models; functionalism
education
    autonomy from class struggle in 181–2
    Barrett on gender in 160–2
    competencies through 27–8
    division of labor and 26
    Leonardo on race in 149–53
    Lewis on disinterpellation in 174–5
    multiculturalism in 150
    Poulantzas on structural determination of 127, 129, 142, 181, 183
    revolution and 47
    theory of mediation on 6–7
    unions' role in 37
    See also critical education; ideological state apparatuses; schools; social structures; structural education

Education Act (1870, United Kingdom) 164–5
Educational Studies 101
effectivities. *See* indices of effectivity
eleven rules of thumb 3*t*, 180*t*
    See also ideological state apparatuses; specific rules
Elliott, Gregory 14, 96
    The Detour of Theory 120
encoding/decoding 6, 7, 170–2, 180, 181
Encyclopedia of Educational Theory and Philosophy 1, 73
Engels, Friedrich 6, 34, 117
Les Enragés 13–14
Erben, Michael and Denis Gleeson 4–5
    critiques of Althusser 75, 101–5, 121, 123, 124, 179
    Giroux influenced by 79, 84
    Hirst compared to 107–8
    Kolakowski and 92
    Rancière's influence on 96, 101–5, 123
    Thompson and 114, 122
eristic dialogue 98
Establet, Roger and Christian Baudelot, *The Capitalist School in France* 6, 56, 127, 129, 140–1, 180, 183
experience
    Barrett on 160
    culturalism grounded in 130
    structuralist vs. critical framework for 184
    Thompson's theory of 115–17, 119, 160
exploitation
    in division of labor 25–6
    gender and 162, 164
    Giroux on 108
    ideology and 30, 60
    ISAs as venue for 41
    proper language and 29–30
    school systems and 27, 28, 55–6
    in state apparatuses 36–7
    See also ruling classes

families
    domestic subjects in 165–6
    gendered dynamics of labor in 155–7, 162
    as ISA 33, 39, 40, 64
    reproduction of gendered places and 136
    social reproduction through 15

fascism 49–50, 63, 64, 118, 182
Federici, Silvia 18
feminism 7, 9
  Althusser's theory in 155, 158–61, 163–4, 166–8
  Arnot on 163–4
  Barrett on 160
  line of advance through 127, 160
  social reproduction and 18–19
  Wolpe on 159
Feminist Review 155
feudalism 53–4
Foucault, Michel 124
Fouchet Plan 13, 140
France
  demographics of schooling in 141
  Fouchet Plan for universities in 13, 97, 140
Franco, Carlos 49–50
freedom. *See* agency; resistance
Freire, Paulo 6, 82
  "Adult Literacy Process as Cultural Action" 127
  Pedagogy of the Oppressed 127
French Communist Party (PCF)
  August 1978 electoral defeats 114
  Callinicos on 111, 112
  influence on schools 99
  Parist student protests (1968) and 14, 96
functionalism 1, 5, 17, 179–82
  Apple's critique from 80–3
  Arnot's critique from 164
  Connell's critique from 122
  Erben and Gleeson's critique from 101–5
  Giroux's critique from 85–6
  Hirst's critique from 107–9, 124
  Johnson's critique from 130
  Rancière's critique from 98–100, 123
  Thompson's critique from 114, 123
fustian thinking 45–6, 68, 147, 149

gender 7
  Barrett on schools and 160–3
  in French universities 13
  interpellation into 62
  Poulantzas on 135
  in relations of production 160–1
  social reproduction and 18–19
  Valli on divisions of labor and 166–8, 181

Wolpe on education and 129, 135–6, 142, 155–61, 181
General Agreement on Tariffs and Trade Act (GATT) 173
Gintis, Herbert 77, 78, 121, 136, 140
Giroux, Henry A. 1
  Aronowitz and 121
  background and critical context 75, 77, 89, 92–3, 95, 100, 104, 107, 121
  "Beyond the Correspondence Theory" 79
  Carnoy and Levin on 136–7
  common sense on Althusser from 88–9, 91, 124, 125, 179
  critiques of Althusser 4–5, 83–6, 88, 121
  Ideology, Culture, and the Process of Schooling 79
  on ideology 85
  McLaren and 124
  on relations of production 108
  "Teacher Education and the Ideology of Social Control" 78
  Theory and Resistance in Education 4, 82–3
  Thompson's influence on 114
  Willis's influence on 121
Gleeson, Denis. *See* Erben, Michael and Denis Gleeson
Glucksmann, Miriam 23
  Structuralist Analysis in Contemporary Social Thought 78
Goffman, Erving 102
go rule 3t, 59–66, 69, 73, 120, 180t
Gottesman, Isaac 75, 88
Grace, Gerald 78
Gramsci, Antonio
  Althusser compared to 82
  Carnoy and 6, 137
  Johnson on 129–31
  theory of hegemony 37, 130–1
Grimaud, Maurice 14, 36

Haddad, Samir 8
Haider, Asad 113
Haitian Revolution 8, 176, 177
Hall, Stuart 6, 7
  articulation concept of 127, 131–4, 140, 142, 146–7, 151–2, 159, 160

on base-superstructure
    models 129, 131–2
Carnoy and 137
on culturalism 132
on ideologies 7, 132–3, 169
on interpellation 131–2, 169–70
Leonardo and 127, 142, 149, 151–2
on race and racism 144–9, 180–1
racial articulation theory of 144–9
Thompson and 117, 129–31
Hall, Stuart, works by
    "Encoding/Decoding" 171
    "Race, Articulation and Societies Structured in Dominance" 143
    "Rethinking the 'Base and Superstructure' Metaphor" 131–2
    "Signification, Representation, and Ideology: Althusser and the Post-Structuralist Debates" 169–70
Hamilton, Scott 113
hands. *See* rule of hands
Harvey, David 17
Hattam, Robert 74
Hegel, Georg Wilhelm Friedrich 45, 92
Hindness, Barry 82, 107
Hirst, Paul Q 5, 75
    critiques of Althusser 82, 107–9, 121, 123, 179, 182
    Erben and Gleeson compared to 107–8
    Kolakowski and 92
    On Law and Ideology 107
    Pre-Capitalist Modes of Production (with Hindness) 107
    Rancière and 107
    Thompson and 122
History Workshop (Ruskin College) 113
Hobbes, Thomas 100, 102, 123
Hobson, Dorothy 161
Ho Chi Minh 177
Hudson-Miles, R. 100
humanism 39
Hussain, Althar 109

identity correspondence position 132
ideological state apparatuses (ISAs) 1, 2, 3*t*, 180*t*
    anchor rule of 42, 68
    Apple's critique of 80–1, 87
    Barrett on 163

base-superstructure model as context for 33–8
    Baudelot and Establet on 141
    causality rule of 46–8
    Connell's critique of 122
    defined 33, 40, 42
    Erben and Gleeson on 101–4
    Giroux's critique of 85
    go rule of 60–6
    Hirst's critique of 109
    Leonardo on 153
    May 1968 student protests and 14–15
    pattern variables compared to 104–5
    Rancière on 95–100, 123
    relations of production reproduced in 41, 42, 47–8, 109
    repressive state apparatuses vs. 36–8, 46–9, 73
    school rule of 52–8, 68–9
    struggle in 3*t*, 4, 6, 49–52, 61, 69, 134
    systems rule of 3–4, 3*t*, 40–2
    Thompson on 114
    toe rule of 41–2, 68
    types of 39–40
    See also education; schools
ideology 2, 3*t*
    anchor rule of 42, 62
    in base-superstructure models 35–8
    causality rule of 45–8
    counter-interpellation and 172–3
    defined 59–60
    Giroux's critique from 85
    go rule on 59–66, 73–4
    Hall on 7, 132–3, 169
    institutional practices realizing 4, 43–8
    instruction in submission to 28–31, 36, 55–6
    Johnson on 130
    McLaren on 124–5
    misinterpellation and 175–6
    primary and secondary 43–4
    Rancière's influence on Althusser 96, 98
    structural education and 127–8, 178
    from struggle 169–71
    unions and 37
"Ideology and the Ideological State Apparatuses: Notes towards an Investigation" (Althusser) 1, 2
    critical reception of 59

on dominance of scholastic ISAs 55–56
Paris student protests (1968) and 14–15
Poulantzas and 133
publication and intention 67
relations of production in 21, 23–4
on repressive state apparatuses 36, 39
social reproduction in 19
Thompson on 114
Willis on 121
See also *On the Reproduction of Capitalism*
indices of effectivity
in base-superstructure models 33–6, 68, 73, 133
of different ISAs 51, 52
go rule and 73
rule of special thirds and 38
inequality
No Child Left Behind Act and 152
Poulantzas on 6, 134–6, 181
schools reproducing 78, 134–6
stratification theories on 6, 135–6, 139, 142
in structural education framework 142, 183
structuralist vs. idealist view of 134–5
between student and teacher 97
See also gender; race and racism
institutions
Carnoy on 138–9
causality rule and 46–8
Hirst on 109
practice preceding ideology in 43–4, 48, 73
Rancière on 95, 98
systems and ISAs vs. 40–1
toeing the line in 42, 73
International Socialists 111, 112
interpellation 4, 7–8, 181, 182
agency in theory of 63–5, 69
Althusser's concept of 4, 7, 59, 62–5
counter-interpellation and 172–3, 181
defined 62
encoding and decoding of 171
Hall on 131–2, 169–70
line of advance through 127–8, 131–2
misinterpellation and 177–8
Rancière preceding theory of 98

recruitment to ideologies through 62–3, 69
schools as sites of racial 151–2
Thompson on 119
Valli and 168
intersectionality 81, 135, 166–8

James, Selma 18
Johnson, Richard 6
Carnoy and 137
critiques of Althusser 182
"Histories of Culture/Theories of Ideology" 130
"Notes on an Impasse" 81
on reproduction as struggle 129–30, 133, 142
Thompson and 129–30

Kaepernick, Colin 41
Kafka, Franz 175, 176, 178
Karsz, Saul 96
Katz, Michael B. 77
Kennedy, Robert 129, 136
keys. *See* rule of keys
knowledge
Callinicos on 123–4
developing new ISAs 47
division of labor and 25–6, 67
proper speech and 29–30
in social being vs. social consciousness 115–16
students and 101
teachers' ideological resistance and 50, 56, 97
Kolakowski, Leszek 91–5
"Althusser's Marx" 91–2
Main Currents in Marxism 92
Thompson and 122
Krupskaya, Nadezdha 28, 47, 49

Lampert, M. 95
language
relations of exploitation in 29–30
speech vs. 22–3, 184
Latin America, Hall on race in 144–6
law
in base-superstructure models 35
categorizing ISAs and 40–1
interpellation and 62

schools compared to 47–8, 152
subject position under 61
See also repression and repressive state apparatus
Lecercle, Jean-Jacques 7, 172–3, 181
Lefebvre, Henri 127
legal institutions and organizations. *See* institutions; law
Lenin, Vladimir
 base-superstructure models and 132
 Carnoy and 6
 educational policy of 28, 46–9, 68
 on trade unions 37
Leonardo, Zeus 6
 Althusser and 149, 181
 Hall's articulation concept and 127, 142, 149, 151–2
 Race, Whiteness, and Education 149, 151
 on race/class in education 149–53
Levin, Henry 77, 136
Levi-Strauss, Claude 78
Lewis, Tyson 7–8, 174
liberalism 39, 78, 163–4

Mandela, Nelson 155
Maoism 112
Martel, James, *The Misinterpellated Subject* 8, 175–8, 181
Marx, Karl
 on apparatuses 33, 103–4
 Bernstein and 77
 Capital 118, 131–2
 The 18th Brumaire of Louis Bonaparte 33
 The German Ideology 131–2
 Grundrisse 118
 Hall on 145, 146
 on preservation of workers 18, 19
 on social reproduction 17–18
 on state as superstructure 2
 on surplus value 155
 Thompson on structuralism of 118, 119, 123
Marxism
 base-superstructure models in 33–8, 67–8
 Callinicos on 111, 112
 Erben and Gleeson's critique from 102–3
 functionalism vs. 5
 Hall on 131, 132, 145
 "Ideology and the Ideological State Apparatuses" and 15
 ISAs in theory of 39, 41
 Kolakowski on 91–5
 Leonardo on 149, 153
 Lewis on 174
 Rancière's critique from 97–9
 relations of production in 21, 24
 schools in 56, 78
 social reproduction in 2, 17–19
 theory of mediation and 6–7
 Thompson and 113–16
 worker resistance in 49–50
 See also feminism; neo-Marxism
Marxist-Feminism Literary Collective 160
materialism and material practices 3*t*
 causality rule and 43–8
 disinterpellation and 174
 in ideology 61–2
 racial social divisions and 143
 Thompson on 115, 116
May 1968 student protests 13–14, 44
 Althusser and 14–15, 51, 57–8, 95–8, 101, 140
 Erben and Gleeson on 101
 Rancière and 95–8, 100
 schools warning ruling class 51–2, 57–8, 68
McCarthyism 77
McIntosh, Mary 17
McLaren, Peter, "Ideology and Education: Critical Pedagogy and the Politics of Empowerment" 124–5
means of production
 division of labor and 26
 relations to 21–4
 worker competencies and 28
 See also modes of production; relations of production; rule of hands
mediation
 Carnoy's theory of 6–7, 127, 129, 137–40, 181, 183
 schools' role in 129, 137–40, 142, 183
 youth culture and 139
misinterpellation 8, 128, 175–8, 181, 182
modes of production 21–2
 in base-superstructure models 34, 35
 division of labor and 26

families and 157
gender in 161
ideologies as condition for 130
schools serving 28
slavery in 146
Morrow, Raymond A.
critical context of 5
critiques of Althusser 1–2, 4, 73–5, 125
Social Theory and Education: A Critique of Social and Cultural Theories of Reproduction 1
Movement of March 22 (M22) 13–14
multiculturalism 150

Nanterre campus student protests (1968) 13–14
See also May 1968 student protests
nationalism 39
Nazi occupation of France 63, 64
neo-Marxism 4, 77, 123, 179
New Left Review (NLR) 91, 92, 107, 131
No Child Left Behind Act (2002) 152–3

October Revolution (1917) 37, 118
O'Neill, John 102
On the Reproduction of Capitalism (Althusser) 1–2, 4
anchor rule from 42
autobiographical style in 169–70
Balibar's preface to 96
base-superstructure models in 33–5
causality in 45
on class struggle over state apparatuses 49–50
communist political practice and 39
competencies in 27–8
division of labor in 26
dual tone of 15
on ideology (go rule) 59–66
on interpellation 4, 7, 59, 62–5
on ISA terminology 33, 39–40, 42
May 1968 student protests and 14–15, 51
practice preceding ideology in 43–8
Rancière's influence on 96, 99
relations of production in 21, 23–4
on repressive state apparatus 36
on schools as dominant ISA 52–8
on struggle over state apparatuses 37, 87
translation of 69

opioid epidemic 139
organizing
Althusser's theory as framework for 78
developing new ISAs 47
in struggle internal to ISAs 50–1
theory subordinate to 39
Wolpe and 167
Other and otherness 97
overdetermination
causality rule and 120
Freire on 6, 127
McLaren on 125
of school practices 46, 48
Wolpe on 157–8
over-education 137–8, 183
Oyler, Celia, *Actions Speak Louder than Words: Community Activism as Curriculum* 173–4

parent associations and parents 44–6, 149–50
See also families
Paris University, Les Enragés occupation of 13–14, 44
See also May 1968 student protests
Park, Peter 103
Parsons, Talcott 102–4, 123, 181
Parti Communiste Français (PCF). *See* French Communist Party
Pascal, Blaise 61
Passeron, Jean-Claude. *See* Bourdieu, Pierre and Jean-Claude Passeron
patriarchy 7, 9, 156–7, 181
See also feminism
pattern variables 103–5, 123
pedagogy
base-superstructure model and 33
divisions of labor and 27
interpellations and 8
May 1968 student protests and 96
Rancière on 100
structural education and 6, 128
See also education; schools
police
in base-superstructure models 34
ideology compared to 59–60
as ISA 36
political economy 7, 117–19, 163–4

political ideological state
  apparatuses 49, 50
  effectivity of 51, 53
  scholastic ISAs compared to 54–5
  social reproduction through 15
  struggle in 50
postmodernism 124
Poulantzas, Nicos 6, 7, 82
  Apple on 82
  Carnoy and 137
  Classes in Contemporary Capitalism 133–4
  Political Power and Social Classes 133
  structural determination of education 127, 129, 142, 181, 183
  Wolpe and 136
practices
  agency in 8
  anchor rule and 42, 68
  causality rule and 43–5, 68, 73
  class emerging from 134
  competency rule and 26
  in culturalism 130
  cultural mediation of 83–4, 88
  effectivity of 38
  go rule and 59–65
  ideologies from 60–5, 98
  irreducibility to ideology 42, 80, 81
  overdetermination of 46–8
  repressive functions of 57–8, 74
  reproduction as condition for 108
  rule of hands and 23
  social formations composed of 132–3
  struggle in 49
  theory following 39
  toeing the line 3
preservation of workers 18, 19, 67
prisons. *See* courts and justice system
private vs. public sector 40–1
production. *See* means of production; modes of production; relations of production; social reproduction
proletarians. *See* workers
promiscuity critique 5, 122, 124, 125, 164, 182–3

qualification 28–30, 40
  See also competencies; division of labor

race and racism
  Hall on class and 144–9, 180–1
  interpellation and 151–2, 170
  Leonardo on class and 149–53
racial state apparatuses 150
Rancière, Jacques 4, 13
  Althusser's Lesson 75, 79, 95–7, 100, 107, 114
  critiques of Althusser 95–100, 121, 123, 124, 179, 185
  Erben and Gleeson influenced by 96, 101–5, 123
  Hirst and 107
  The Ignorant Schoolmaster 97
  Kolakowski and 92
  May 1968 student protests and 95–8, 100
  "On the Theory of Ideology: Althusser's Politics" 96–9
  Reading Capital (co-author) 95, 98
  Thompson and 114, 122
Reading Capital (Althusser and students)
  immanent social structure in 22, 24
  Rancière and 98
  translation of 2
  views of social reproduction in 18
recitation pedagogy 131, 138
relations of production 3t
  Barrett on 162
  critiques of Althusser from 84
  division of labor and 25–6, 123
  Hall on 132–3, 169
  Hirst on 107–9, 123
  ideology and 61, 65
  ISAs reproducing 41, 42, 47–8, 109
  race in 145, 148
  rule of hands and 3t, 21–4, 61, 109
  schools reproducing 4, 15, 21, 24, 28, 31, 56–7, 78, 129
  structural determination and 134
  struggle and 17, 23–4, 129, 133, 135, 163
  submission to ideology and 30–1
  Valli on 167
  worker distinct from labor in 23
relative autonomy
  in Althusser's base-superstructure models 4, 35, 38
  Barrett on 160–1
  economism vs. 73

functionalist critiques vs. 81–3, 88
  in Hall's theory of articulation 133, 148
  of interpellations 171
  rule of special thirds on 86
  Wolpe on 158
religious ideological state apparatuses. *See* churches
repression and repressive state apparatuses (RSAs)
  Barrett on 160–1
  in base-superstructure model 35–7
  Erben and Gleeson on 103–4
  ideology and 60
  ISAs compared to 36–8, 46–9, 73
  No Child Left Behind Act and 153
  Poulantzas on 133
  by supervisors 25
  toe the line rule and 41
  unions vs. 37
reproduction. *See* social reproduction
reproductive rights 64, 65
Republican Party (United States) 40
resistance
  Apple's critique from absence of 87
  Erben and Gleeson's critique from absence of 101
  Giroux's critique from absence of 85
  reproduction vs. 74, 82–3, 86–7, 124–5, 137, 163, 179
  Thompson on 119–20
  Wolpe on 158–9
revolution 28
  Althusser on conditions of 51–2
  capitalist focus on schools in 55
  gender and 160
  ideology and 66
  pre-capitalist Church and 53–4
  theorizing political practice and 39
Rex, John 144–5, 147
Roediger, David 152
Ronen, Shelly 19
rule of competence 3*t*, 25–31, 40, 67, 68, 180*t*
rule of hands 3*t*, 21–4, 61, 109, 180*t*
rule of keys 17–19, 67, 180*t*
rule of special thirds 33–8, 50, 54, 68, 73, 86, 180*t*
ruling classes
  competency rule and 25
  curricular influence of 44
  interpellation and 169, 171
  ISAs and struggle with 49–52
  political ISAs and 54–5
  schools and struggle with 52–4
  state apparatuses and 37
  toe rule and 41–2
Russian Revolution (1917) 37, 118
Rytmann, Hélène 9

Saussure, Ferdinand de, *Course in General Linguistics* 22–3, 183
Schelling 45
school rule 3*t*, 52–8, 68–9, 180*t*
schools
  agency in 5, 52, 84, 88
  anchor rule of 42
  competencies from 27–31
  democracy mediated in 138, 139, 183
  as dominant ISA 52–8, 69
  as force in base-superstructure models 34
  gender divisions in 155–68
  ideology from practices of 43, 46–8, 62–6
  illusions of unity in 140–2
  as ISA 3*t*, 15, 28, 39–41, 44, 52–8, 137
  knowledge and division of labor 26–7, 157
  as mediators of struggle 7, 137–40, 156
  racial divisions in 149–53, 158
  relations of production reproduced in 4, 15, 21, 24, 28, 31, 56–7, 78, 129
  repressive function of 36, 55–6
  social reproduction in 19, 24, 31, 47–8, 56, 133, 136, 137
  structural determination and 134–6
  struggle in 4, 6–7, 44–6, 50–2
  toeing the line in 3–4, 41–2, 51, 57
  unions as 37
  value of labor in 155–6
  See also education
Schools (project by Althusser's students) 140
science
  of articulation 147
  competence vs. 29
  gender and 157, 165
  Rancière compared to Althusser on 97

selection 36, 166
Shills, Edward A. 103
1619 project 144
slavery
  in America 144, 146
  in Haiti 176
Smyth, John 74
social being and social
  consciousness 115–17
socialism
  developing new ISAs 47
  Hirst on 109
  mainstream resurgence of 8
  schools reproducing 48
  in struggle internal to ISAs 51
Socialist Register 91, 92, 107
Socialist Worker's Party 111
social reproduction 3*t*, 6
  Apple's critiques of 79–82, 87–8
  Arnot on 163–4
  Barrett on gender divisions and 160–2
  Baudelot and Establet on 141–2
  Carnoy on 138
  critical education distinguished
    from 77–8
  defined 17–18
  divisions of labor and 28–30
  Erben and Gleeson's critiques of 101–3
  Giroux's critiques of 78–9
  Hall on 133
  Hirst on 107–8
  Johnson on struggle and 131
  Poulantzas on 136
  Rancière on 97–8
  resistance vs. 4, 5, 74, 82–3, 86–7,
    124–5, 137, 163, 179
  rule of keys and 2, 17–19, 67
  schools and 19, 24, 31, 47–8, 56, 133,
    136, 137
  struggle rule and 49–50
  of submission to ideology 29–31
  Thompson's critiques of 113
  through state apparatuses 37, 41
  trade unions and 37
  Willis's critiques of 84, 121–2
  See also interpellation
social structures
  Apple on 80–1
  in base-superstructure models 34

culture in dichotomy with 129–30
  DiTomaso on 104
  Erben and Gleeson on 101–2
  Hall on 132–3, 169–71
  Hirst on 108
  immanent vs. transcendent 22–4, 28,
    62, 68, 129
  ISAs as site of class struggle in 50
  misinterpellation in 178
  Poulantzas on 134
  racial differences within 144–9
  theory of interpellation in 63–5
  Thompson on 117–20
  Willis on 121–2
society. *See* base-superstructure models;
  social structures
Sorbonne campus student protests
  (1968) 13–14
South Africa
  Bantu Education Act 7, 159
  Hall on race in 144–5
  Wolpe on education in 155–9
Soviet Union
  Kolakowski on 91–2
  misinterpellation and 177
  relations of production in 108–9
Sowetan uprising (1976, South Africa) 158
Spain, union resistance in 49–50
special thirds. *See* rule of special thirds
specular relations 61, 62
Stalinism and Stalin, Joseph
  Callinicos on Althusser and 111–12
  Dialectical and Historical Materialism 43
  idealism of 45, 47, 68, 74, 112, 130
  Johnson on 130
  Kolakowski and 91–2
  Thompson on Althusser and 114
state of nature 100, 102, 182
structural determination 129, 134–5
structural education 6
  Althusser's theory advanced in 6, 8,
    78, 125, 127–8, 131–2, 157–8, 178,
    180, 182
  Carnoy and Levin on
    reproduction in 137
  Hall's foundation for 129, 133
  interpellation concepts extended
    in 178
  pedagogy and 184–5

promiscuity critique and 183
Wolpe's foundation for 157–8
structuralism 1, 7
  in concepts of causality 4
  culture in dichotomy with 129–30, 184
  gender in 155–68
  immanent vs. transcendent 22–4
  race in 143–53
  in *Reading Capital* 22–3
  Thompson on 117–20, 123, 182
  See also social structures
struggle
  Carnoy and Levin on 137
  concepts of causality and 3*t*, 46–7
  content before form in 96–7
  differentia specifica in 145
  Ereben and Gleeson on 101–2
  ideology in 169–71
  interpellation and ideology 65–6, 170–3
  ISAs realizing 3*t*, 4, 6, 49–52, 61, 69, 134
  knowledge in 26, 97
  Marxist educational theory and 181–2
  practices of 134
  primary and secondary ideologies 44–6
  relations of production and 17, 23–4, 129, 133, 135, 163
  reproduction vs. 74, 82–3, 86–7, 124–5, 137, 163, 179
  schools as mediators of 137–40, 157–8
  schools impacted by 4, 28, 44, 134–7, 140, 156
  state apparatuses and 33, 37, 38
  theorizing political practice and 39
  See also resistance
struggle rule 49–52
  autonomy of schools in 73, 86, 133
  social structures changed under 104
  Thompson and 120
students 1
  agency of 5, 57, 68, 79, 101–2, 158–9
  Althusser's theory as framework for 78
  Baudelot and Establet on 141
  Erben and Gleeson on 101–2
  forced attendance and 160–1, 164
  Leonardo on 149, 150
  May 1968 rebellion of 13–14, 36, 44–6, 57, 96–7
  Rancière on 99
  submission of 29

  taking, drumming, and ejecting of 55–7, 69
  youth culture and 139
subjectivity and subject positions
  counter-interpellation and 172
  disinterpellation and 174
  domestic 165–6
  go rule on 65
  interpellations complicating 170–2
  misinterpellation and 177
  submission to ideology 28–31, 40, 67
subsumption
  absorption vs. 161
  of experience 116
  of ideology and culture by reproduction 81–2
  pattern variables and 104
  of race and ethnicity 144–6, 149, 152
superstructures. *See* base-superstructure models
supervisors 25–7, 30
  See also workers
system rule 3–4, 3*t*, 40–2, 68, 180*t*
Szwaja, Joe 173–5

teachers 1
  agency of 5, 50
  Althusser's pardon to 57–9, 78–9, 99
  Connell on 122
  Erben and Gleeson on 101–2
  gender divisions among 162
  ideological resistance of 50, 57, 68, 79, 97
  Rancière on 99
  submission and 29–30
Theoretical Practice 107
Therborn, G. 21
Thompson, Dorothy 114
Thompson, E. P. 5
  Anderson and 91, 113, 119
  Apple and 113, 114
  Barrett on 160
  Callinicos and 120, 122
  critiques of Althusser 113–21, 124, 179, 182
  critiques of structuralism 84, 85, 115
  Giroux and 85
  Hall and 117, 129–31
  Hirst and 108

influence of 121
Johnson and 129–30
Kolakowski and 92
The Making of the English Working Class 91, 113
The Poverty of Theory 75, 113–17, 129–30
Rancière and 114, 122
Willis and 84, 121, 122
toe rule 3–4, 3t, 41–2, 61–2, 68, 73, 180t
Torres, Carlos Alberto 4, 5, 75, 125
Torres, Rodolfo D. 143
totalitarianism 111, 112
  See also Stalinism
tragedy 5, 74, 179
  Apples's critique from 82, 87
  Erben and Gleeson's critique from 102
  Giroux's critique from 86
training 26, 28
  See also competencies
transmission view of social reproduction 18
Trotskyites and Trotskyism 111–12

Uljens, M. 74
unions
  as associative ISA 40
  effectivity of 51–3
  ideological resistance and 49–50
  May 1968 student protests and 14
  as schools 37
  social reproduction through 15
universities. *See* education; schools
urbanization 134–5

Valli, Linda 7, 127
  Becoming Clerical Workers 166–8
  on gender divisions in labor 166–8, 181
Vasconi, Tomás Amadeo 6
Vietnam Solidarity Committee 13–14
violence
  in abstraction 130, 184
  of repressive state apparatus 3, 36, 37, 68
Vogel, Lise 18
voluntarism 118–20, 182

Walker, Stephen 77
Weber, Max 19, 135

Westhill Conferences (England) 77, 84, 88
whiteness 148–9, 151–3
William Lewis, S. 9
Willis, Paul 75, 77
  critique of Althusser 121–2
  "Cultural Production is Different from Cultural Reproduction is Different from Social Reproduction is Different from Reproduction" 121
  Kolakowski and 92
  Learning to Labour 75, 121
  on social reproduction frameworks 79
  Thompson and 84, 113, 114, 121, 122, 124
  on youth culture 139
Wilson, Woodrow, "Fourteen Points" speech (1918) 8, 176–7
Winship, Janice 161
Wolpe, AnnMarie
  activism of 155, 167, 182
  Barrett and 160
  Carnoy and 137
  on causality 136
  in *Feminism and Materialism: Women and Modes of Production* 135, 155
  on gendered education 129, 135–6, 142, 155–61, 181
  interpellation and 168
  Poulantzas and 129
Wolpe, Harold 155
workers and laborers
  competencies and knowledge of 25–31
  in critiques of Althusser 85, 87
  ISAs as site of struggle for 49–52
  labor distinct from 23, 25
  Paris student protests (1968) and 14, 51–2
  preservation-nourishment of 18, 19
  relations of production and 22–4
  rule of hands and 24
  subject position of 61
World Trade Organization protests (1996) 173–4

Ylimaki, R. M. 74

www.ingramcontent.com/pod-product-compliance
Lightning Source LLC
Chambersburg PA
CBHW062222300426
44115CB00012BA/2184